The Victorian
GARDEN

The Victorian Garden

ALLISON KYLE LEOPOLD

PHOTOGRAPHS BY EDWARD ADDEO

CLARKSON POTTER/PUBLISHERS
NEW YORK

To D. M.

There's rosemary for you; that's for remembrance

WILLIAM SHAKESPEARE, 1601

Copyright © 1995 by Allison Kyle Leopold
Photographs copyright © 1995 by Edward Addeo

All rights reserved. No part of this book may be reproduced or transmitted in any form or by any means, electronic or mechanical, including photocopying, recording, or by any information storage and retrieval system, without permission in writing from the publisher.

Published by Clarkson N. Potter/Publishers, 201 East 50th Street, New York, New York 10022. Member of the Crown Publishing Group.

Random House, Inc. New York, Toronto, London, Sydney, Auckland

CLARKSON N. POTTER, POTTER, and colophon are trademarks of Clarkson N. Potter, Inc.

Manufactured in China

Design by Victoria Stamm, Platinum Design, Inc. N.Y.C.

Library of Congress Cataloging-in-Publication Data
Leopold, Allison Kyle.
The Victorian garden / by Allison Kyle Leopold.
Includes bibliographical references and index.
1. Gardens, Victorian—United States. 2. Gardening—United States. 3. Gardens, Victorian—United States—Pictorial works. 4. Gardening—United States—Pictorial works. I. Title.
SB458.7.L46   1995
712'.2'09034—dc20   94-37318

ISBN 0-517-58660-6

10 9 8 7 6 5 4 3 2 1

First Edition

ACKNOWLEDGMENTS

My grateful thanks to those who helped make this book possible by sharing their time, expertise, enthusiasm, homes, and gardens: my agent, Deborah Geltman; Edward Addeo, whose talents as a photographer rise to any occasion; Marie Proeller for unrelenting research, organization work on the directory, and all-around backup; Joanne Leonhardt Cassullo, for her styling, research, encouragement—and especially everything else; landscape designer Ellen McClellend Lesser for her careful reading and vetting of the manuscript in various stages and many helpful suggestions; Vickie Peslak, Victoria Stamm and Pernilla Nilsson of Platinum Design for their inspired design; and Clarkson Potter's team—Howard Klein, Jane Treuhaft, and Diane Frieden.

—

Also, thanks to Janet and Dr. Robert Cole; Wandz Costanzo and Richard Tuff; Itzhak and Toby Perlman; Faith Golding; Beth Rudin DeWoody; Robert Fuoco, Director of Horticulture, The Stowe Foundation, Harriet Beecher Stowe House, Hartford, Connecticut; Cindy Boyer, Education Coordinator, Ellen Manyon, Curator of Museums, and Beverly Gibson, Horticulturist/Gardener, Ellwanger Gardens, Rochester, New York, and The Landmark Society of Western New York; Sarah C. Donald, Landscape Architect, Chesterwood, Stockbridge, Massachusetts; Christie White, Program Supervisor for Horticulture, Old Sturbridge Village, Sturbridge, Massachusetts; Virginia S. Richmond, Horticulturist, Sonnenberg Gardens, Canandaigua, New York; Ruth Totten and the Home Garden Club of Morristown, who planned the restorations of the gardens of Acorn Hall, Morristown, New Jersey; Chet Davis, former Head Groundskeeper, Mohonk Mountain House, New Paltz, New York; Marilyn Rattner, Public Relations Coordinator, New York Botanical Garden, Bronx, New York; Lawrence Hollander, former Director, Berkshire Botanical Garden, Stockbridge, Massachusetts; and Joan and Dane Wells, The Queen Victoria Inn, Cape May, New Jersey.

—

And thanks especially to my husband, Thomas Cohen, and my editor, Lauren Shakely, whose care, perseverance, thoughtful editing, and diplomacy made this a better book.

Contents

Introduction 1

—1—

A Social History of
Victorian Gardens 19

—2—

Beds, Borders, and Romanticism 47

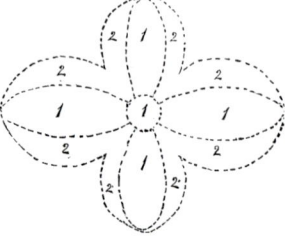

—3—

Rockeries, Rooteries,
and the Picturesque Ideal 71

—4—
The Furnished Garden 83

—5—
Small Gardens 101

—6—
The Kitchen Garden 137

—7—
City Gardens 157

Select Bibliography 170

Glossary 171

Guide to Historic Gardens 177

Sources for Historic Seeds and Plants 181

Index 183

Introduction

From recreational activities to the decorative arts to the language of love and courtship, the fascination for all things green and flowering influenced myriad aspects of 19th-century American life. More than any other motif, the emblems of the garden—foliage, flowers, fruits, and vines—were portrayed on wallpapers, textiles, and floor coverings, as well as on household objects such as lamps, vases, platters, teacups, and spoons. Delicate, tiny blooms were enthusiastically if incongruously carved into

Quaint, handcrafted items like a frame made from pine cones, beechnut hulls, and acorns, above, represented the 19th century's desire to glory in nature, not only outdoors, but indoors as well. Floral images proliferated during the 19th century— adorning albums, silver, china, lace, right, embroidery, beadwork, and other domestic decorative arts, below right— eventually turning the house into a veritable "garden" of its own.

massive walnut dining tables, over-sized sideboards, and capricious lady's chairs.

Wildly infatuated with the romantic possibilities offered by the natural world as well as by the only recent accessibility of exotic plant varieties and new hybrids, Victorian Americans enthusiastically crammed nature's rural bounty into the nooks and crannies of their urban homes. They encased lithographs with soothing pastoral themes in rustic frames made from branches, pinecones, and acorns; they encircled windows, doorways, and even family portraits with loopy twisted vines. They deposited Wardian cases—

portable terrariums initially used to transport fragile, exotic plants—in parlor windows. Hallway niches boasted vases filled with showy tiger lilies or larkspur, heavy majolica pots brimmed over with nasturtiums and roses. Every home, of course, had its requisite parlor palm.

Flowers bloomed, not only in the dark soil of the garden and in stenciled, stitched, or carved designs on walls, ceilings, and chairs but everywhere. Fresh violets adorned the lady's dressing table and breakfast tray. Preparing for balls and dances, young women carefully adorned the rippling waves of their hair with tender blooms of iris or milky camellias, and clutched small, top-heavy bouquets—tussie-mussies—in dainty gilt holders. Small bouquets of camellias also made pretty table decorations, massed into pyramids as centerpieces, then distributed to the ladies once the dinner was over. Elaborate floral centerpieces rested on heavy walnut sideboards; on the dining table itself stood fanciful fruit and flower assemblages, sometimes with shooting jets of water!

The Victorians truly loved flowers and attributed special meanings and lavish symbolism to them. Tall foxglove, elegantly mottled, with its huge, deep maroon and spotted white flower spikes, was treasured for its rich and dramatic coloring. Larkspur, the old-time name for delphiniums, whose

As depicted in the soothing 1871 lithograph, A Home on the Mississippi *by Currier & Ives, left, the ideal home had a semirural setting—and neatly manicured gardens. Below, lily of the valley was the true "home flower."*

shades of blue were said to surpass that of any other flower, was also much admired. The passion for red Oriental poppies reflected the Victorian interest in the exotic. Tiny purple-blue Johnny-jump-ups, very like miniature pansies that grew in shady nooks where no other flower could bloom, were considered ideal for ladies' nosegays, as was feverfew, a white daisylike flower.

Lily of the valley, a favorite from colonial times, was admired for its pearly bells and sweetness. It was considered by many to be a true "home flower," which meant it put in an appearance on all domestic occasions, both festive and funereal. No cutting garden was considered complete without them. Tuberose was also a frequently requested home flower—for celebratory parties and 19th-century funeral wreaths alike.

In addition, garden-inspired handicrafts filled feminine hours: women labored over conework brackets pinioned with spongy moss and plumes of swamp grass, fern shades on ornamental stands, boudoir tables enwrapped with leatherwork roses, and endless pressed flower and plant specimens. The phenomenon of "parlor gardening" and all its accompanying arts and crafts extended the mystique of the garden into the house and flourished for decades.

The social and cultural forces that propelled the garden mania of the 19th century were peculiar to their times. The passion for gardening itself, unlikely as it may seem, was a by-product of the Industrial Revolution, which brought affluence and increased leisure time to the American middle class. Although initially unaccustomed to gardening for

pleasure rather than sustenance, the Victorians quickly caught on, although those who could employed gardeners for the heavier, more labor-intensive work of the garden.

Even though gardening was at first regarded as a countrified activity by the self-conscious Victorian nouveau riche, soon the tables were turned: gardening became viewed as healthful, wholesome, and refined. "A beautiful garden, tastefully laid out and well-kept, is a certain evidence of taste, refinement and culture," began one garden guide in 1871. "A little garden, all one's own, is a real Eden! Earth possesses no greater charm; and there is no cosmetic equal to the fresh, sweet morning air, and the cheerful sunshine."

With sentiments such as these, and with its educational, aristocratic, and "improving" qualities endlessly extolled, Victorian Americans were soon convinced to devote much of their free time, and a good deal of their free income, to the rustic charms of horticulture.

In recent years, homeowners have begun to think about re-creating period gardens as they have the interiors of their period homes. But there is now no less than a wave of interest in the gardens of the 19th century, the lush and lovely landscapes of Victorian America, one of the richest and most varied periods in our garden heritage.

American Victorian gardens relied on a variety of elements to carry off their overall design, many of which will be explored here. They avoided foundation plantings. They adored roses. They reveled in broad expanses of crisp, green lawn on which they held picnics and parties and played outdoor games. Many of the features typical of Victorian gardens are so beguiling that even those who have no intention of creating a purely Victorian garden are often tempted to try them, adding historical flourish to an otherwise contemporary landscape. Indeed, the general appeal of romantic "outdoor rooms" in the garden, the taste for arbors, cast-iron and wicker furniture, rich flower beds, fountains, and statuary, crosses all period boundaries.

Because of the ephemeral nature of gardens, pure restoration—discovering the original positions of garden paths, flower beds, or the sites where trees once stood—can sometimes present insurmountable challenges. In most privately owned gardens, as opposed to those that are historical, little if anything of the shape of the original

As garden mania progressed, cast-iron fences sprouted dainty leaves, opposite. Houses like the one left, and its surrounding landscape, both designed by Andrew Jackson Downing in 1873, were models for homeowners as they sought to replicate the look in homes and gardens of their own.

Following pages: Historic Ellwanger Gardens, Rochester, New York, originally planted in 1867, where over 30 beds of perennials and bulbs are cultivated, as well as an old-fashioned lavender walk. Foreground, white single peonies and pink double peonies; center, the lush boxwood-lined path and double white, red, and deep pink peonies; background, peonies, pear trees, and fragrant, old-fashioned Harrison's yellow roses.

*A little garden,
all one's own, is a real Eden.
Earth possesses
no greater charm.*

1871

This color garden at the Day House, right, part of the Harriet Beecher Stowe Center in Hartford, Connecticut, features antique roses, pink poppies, lady's mantle, pink and red zinnias, dahlias, coral bells, bleeding hearts, and other 19th-century flowers. Nineteenth-century garden journals included detailed illustrations, like gladiolus, below.

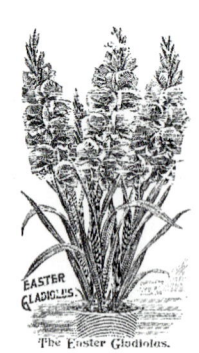

garden will be evident and documentation is rare.

As to the actual flowers planted, this can be near impossible to determine. In some cases, the location of the garden itself may have shifted, due to the preferences of generations of successive gardeners. As surrounding trees have thrived and grown, gardens that were sunny forty or fifty years ago may now be in shade. Conversely, once-shady conditions may become sunny, as trees and buildings have been removed.

Thus, gardeners who wish to landscape a private Victorian home or plant a Victorian-inspired garden with authentic reference are often stymied. Unlike an old house, where signs of past domestic life lurk under every peeling corner of wallpaper, the garden offers few clues to what might have been.

But while it may not be possible or feasible to truly restore an old garden, there are many satisfying approaches to re-creating one. A concentration on purely historically correct plantings, for example, is one route. Consulting vintage seed catalogs or old-time horticultural guides or newspapers—the more local the better—may tell you exactly what would have been planted in fashionable gardens in your particular region or even township at one time. Authentic construction methods and techniques can even be pursued by those who have the means and the time. For example, some garden restorationists prefer to use old tools solely in maintaining period gardens, avoiding power mowers, which can sometimes destroy grass and damage carefully reconstructed brick paths, borders, or walls. For purists and connoisseurs, a restoration such as this may benefit from advice from a licensed garden professional—a landscape architect, horticulturist, sometimes even an archivist—to help obtain only authentic plantings suitable for the site. A visit to a historic botanical garden or arboretum can be an ideal way to begin. Here, plantings may have been replicated over decades and the garden structure minimally disturbed. Even where a public garden has been completely

Copious plant lists in vintage horticultural guides (left, from 1892) that advised Victorian gardeners on proper plant selection are an invaluable resource to gardeners today. Below, a journal excerpt features asters, a popular plant for Victorian cutting gardens.

Following pages, left: Color printing made the possibilities for gardens come to life. Right, clockwise from top left: Columbine, laburnum, cosmos, and angel's trumpet are still as vivid in the garden as they were 100 years ago.

revamped, photographs and records may remain in its library that provide insight into its past. Old engravings and diagrams from 19th-century garden texts can also provide inspiration for the layout of proper period gardens, and you will find an abundance of these in the pages that follow.

A less literal approach is to re-create a period garden by allusion, evoking the spirit and style by selecting its most identifiable garden elements, taking into consideration available garden space, horticultural and climate information—including the now-standard zone climate system—time, and gardening skills. For example, an arboretum of exotic trees was one of the key features of the great gardens of the past; such tree collections denoted wealth and status. But despite such authenticity, a full-scale, bona fide Victorian arboretum would be impossible to reproduce on a typical city or suburban plot.

Plants in interpretive gardens often skillfully blend past and present, and in most cases, effective substitutions for many obsolete antique plants can be obtained from specialized nurseries. For example, though no authentic varieties exist, it would be a shame for a Victorian garden re-creation not to include at least a modern version of the China aster, which was one of the most typically Victorian of flowers and was extensively used in 19th-century beds and cutting gardens. As one noted landscape designer recently observed, it could take a trained horticulturist to tell the difference between a period petunia and a 20th-century hybrid.

Modern-day gardeners should also remember that the Victorians considered the garden an extension of the home: landscape design was an integral part of the architectural plans of the day. It was the perspective from the dwelling place—the view from the windows of the house—that often

The presence of garden ornaments, like this weathered urn suggesting the picturesque, above, as well as statuary, fountains, benches, and other furnishings, goes a long way to re-create the charm of the 19th century in a garden today.

determined the layout of the grounds. The most fragrant flowers would have been planted directly below the windows so that the homeowners might enjoy their scent every time they drew back the curtains and lifted the shades. Similarly, the most colorful flowers were frequently planted well within eyeshot of the drawing room windows so that their beauty could be appreciated by those indoors.

▪ Some types of Victorian gardens are easier to re-create than others. Duplicating the simple dooryard gardens so typical of an early Victorian farmhouse, for example, might present a fairly easy task. Perennials, herbs, and fragrant annuals and, for good measure, a picket fence enclosure to prevent animals from wandering in were all that a farmhouse required. For a later Victorian garden on a grander scale, practical adaptations are often necessary. For instance, most 20th-century homeowners could not afford the yearly nursery bill—or the labor—to replant the many hundreds of annuals needed for the intricate carpet-bedding schemes that characterized the gardens of the 1860s, '70s and '80s. And sometimes plant substitutions may be called for not only by economics but also in response to personal taste or gardening skill. One gardener, for example, replaced hollyhocks, an acknowledged Victorian favorite but one she had difficulty growing, with sunflowers, another popular 19th-century plant. Gardeners who find biennials like Canterbury bells—which the Victorians loved for their romantic-looking, heavy, bell-shaped flowers—too fussy to maintain can substitute great bellflower and still get a similar effect.

▪ Today's gardeners should also consider using plants from earlier centuries, as well as those that are strictly Victorian. Although the Victorians were enamored of the new, brightly colored annuals like petunias and verbenas that grew so easily in their gardens, they retained their fondness for the sweetly scented flowers of their grandmothers' gardens and often nostalgically set aside a plot of earth for what they called an "old-fashioned garden," which they filled with flowers like milky-white snowdrops, precious violets and pansies, forget-me-nots and gillyflower (the old-fashioned name for stock). In fact, in the later years of the 19th century the vogue of nostalgia for the 18th century made such retrospective gardening all the rage. Many once-forgotten 18th-century flowers also found their way into the borders of the late 19th century because of their softer colors.

▣ In addition, because 19th-century Americans were entranced with anything English—from English wallpapers and English manners to English titles for their daughters—the English influence on American domestic life—and gardens—was manifold. Consequently, gardeners today may find it helpful to refer not only to popular American garden guides of the time but also to English ones that might have influenced American Victorian taste. English author Shirley Hibberd, for example, wrote of a pirated American version of his popular (and wonderful) *Rustic Adornments for Homes of Taste*, first published to great acclaim in 1856 and reprinted again in 1870. Just keep in mind that there are some trees and shrubs which thrive in England but do poorly in the United States. Only a strip of the East Coast and parts of the Pacific Northwest have a temperate climate similar to that of England. In the northernmost parts of the United States, frigid winters turn perennials into annuals; during the hot, sultry summers of the South, narcissus bulbs must

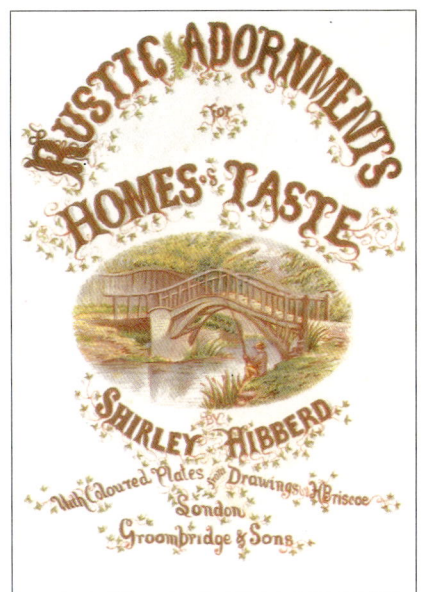

be prechilled in the refrigerator. Throughout this text whenever possible, it will be indicated if a plant variety was either exclusively English, or particular to southern climes.

▣ In practical terms, there are many specific references which gardeners can adopt that suggest the charms of Victorian gardens. A bower of roses may be planted to represent the century's infatuation with its most beloved flower, while beds of lobelias, petunias, verbenas, geraniums, and honey-scented sweet alyssum would clearly be a bow to the era's passion for ornament, vivid color, and bedding out. A vine-covered rockery can stand for the mania for the picturesque; dramatic-looking elephant ears and pampas grass suggest the new and exotic plantings that were being brought to this country for the very first time. Even "antique" fountains,

The frontispiece to Rustic Adornments for Homes of Taste, *top, was one of the many English gardening books that Americans took to heart. Of all the flowers in the garden, the Victorians adored the rose most of all. 'Beauté Inconstanté', above, offered by one nursery in 1895, was said to produce many differently colored flowers on the same bush.*

sculptures, rustic garden houses, and gazebos can have meaning—whimsical salutes to the garden furnished as an outdoor parlor.

In truth, there were as many different types of Victorian gardens as there were different architectural and furniture styles. Although roses were certainly the 19th century's favorite flower, the era's typical garden was far more than a sentimental rose bower. Late-era gardens, for instance, were paeans to the new and exotic. Frequently, they embraced flowers that were unusual then, like African violets, which were hothouse flowers, or red Oriental poppies, and included plants with variegated and bizarrely shaped leaves, as well as flowers in brilliant, robust colors not generally considered in fashion today.

It is also important to understand the form and spirit of the Victorian garden, as seen within the context of its times. Nineteenth-century Americans turned to gardening with passion and fervor, and as with all of their passions and pastimes, gardening played an important social role in their lives. Every activity, from cultivating a rose garden to creating a rockery to filling one's parlor with ornamental grasses and potted palms, had symbolic associations. Theme gardens like moonlight gardens, pansy gardens, or blue gardens all became popular. Conservatories, whether freestanding

on a great estate or merely a sunny adjunct to a more modest parlor, were de rigueur—although these are more a form of interior decoration and parlor gardening than outdoor gardening, and will not be covered to any great extent here.

One also has to attune the eye—and the taste—to the reality of the Victorian garden, which is often the visual antithesis of all that 20th-century gardeners have been taught to value. As it was in interior decoration, many 19th-century garden concepts were discarded as "garish" and "tasteless" by early 20th-century gardeners, whose prejudices still influence garden tastes today. As recently as the 1980s, even experts who specialized in historic landscape design were reluctant to accept the bold colors and profusion of sculptures and other ornamentation that crowded the Victorian landscape. Just as we have

Fuchsias, opposite, *with their graceful pendant flowers, were considered an ideal bedding-out plant, and particularly desirable in small gardens.* Left, *as with decor, flowers and plants had strong symbolic connotations. The undeniably exotic botanical arrangement—complete with waving cattails—complements this family's worldly collectibles and clearly marks the sophistication of their taste. Equally symbolic,* below, *a graceful lady arranges parlor flowers.*

Gardening for Pleasure *(about 1887) guided the novice gardener*, above.

learned to adjust to the riot of colors flaunted by "painted ladies" and to Victorian interior design—its colors, its textures, its sometimes overwhelming array of objects and distinct patterns of furniture placement—so we have to reexamine our concept of Victorian gardens.

▣ It is said that the 19th century saw a revolution—in industry, certainly, but in gardening as well. From the onset of the era in the 1830s to the final years of the century, the concept of domestic gardening underwent profound changes. From the 1840s onward, densely planted bedding schemes became the dominant style of the century. In 1842, Robert Fortune, a Scotsman who had never before left British shores, became the first botanist to travel with a Wardian case, journeying to China and bringing back scores of splendid specimens. It was during the 19th century that orchids first bloomed in American parlors. It was in the second half of the century that American gardens first saw such now common plants as chrysanthemums, baby's breath, bleeding heart, petunias, geraniums, and hosta. The passion for rockeries came . . . and went. Serious rose breeding began, giving rise to hundreds of dazzling new hybrids and, in 1867, the first hybridized tea rose. During the 1870s, cheap, mass-produced lawn mowers made it possible for everyone to have a lawn. By the 1880s, such was the fascination with gardens and gardening that a young Oscar Wilde glamorized the humble sunflower and the beauteous lily, turning them into recognized emblems of the budding Aesthetic Movement.

▣ Throughout the century the great garden experts heralded these landmarks, urging and encouraging a new appreciation of the delights of the garden. From John Loudon, who in 1822 published the first of many editions of his landmark *The Gardener's Encyclopedia*, to Andrew Jackson Downing, perhaps the first great American landscape designer, there were many notables. Horticulturist Frank Jesup Scott, nurserymen Peter Henderson, Robert Buist, and Joseph Breck—all of whom are quoted and referred to in the pages ahead—were household names in their time and among the most respected garden authorities of their day. Then there were the lady garden writers who were so active during this era, such as Anna Warmer, who wrote *Gardening by Myself* in 1872, and Mrs. S. O. Johnson, who charmingly styled herself "Daisy Eyebright." After her husband's death, Jane Loudon supported herself and her daughter nicely if not luxuriously by penning several garden books specifically dedicated to the women's market. Along with many others, these pioneers prolifically championed the cause of the garden in an endless flow of garden books and articles in horticultural journals, leaving us fascinating documentation—a literary legacy showing how ordinary people first thought about the gardens and gardening during the 19th century.

▨ Wherever possible, lists of the flowers, foliage plants, trees, and shrubbery that appeared in the different types of Victorian gardens have been incorporated in this book. These lists are not all-inclusive and contain only those plants mentioned most frequently in garden guides and horticultural magazines. This means that although every plant and flower listed is indeed Victorian, not all Victorian plants are mentioned. Keep in mind that in addition to their favorites, 19th-century Americans enjoyed an enormous array of blooms and that literally hundreds of new strains were introduced or discovered during the century. Consult one of the vintage reference books listed in the bibliography before you conclude that one of your favorites isn't "Victorian."

▨ Also note that the names of the plants mentioned have been taken from vintage reference sources. Because not only common names change—the pansy has been known by dozens of different names in the course of its history—but sometimes even scientific ones, some may not be familiar to modern-day gardeners, or found in typical garden centers. A reasonable number of them will, however—enough to fill your beds and borders in a manner suitable to the most abundant standards of high Victorian taste. The glossary at the back of the book identifies most of the plants by common and Latin names; the sources list nurseries and garden centers that specialize in heirloom seeds and sometimes plants themselves, many of them by mail.

The Victorians enjoyed an enormous array of flowers, providing tremendous choice to gardeners today. The glorious assortment above was highly touted in 1894.

A Social History of Victorian Gardens

Being a Look at the Victorian Garden as a Symbol of Social Worth, Moral Rectitude, and Aristocratic Taste

It was during the second half of the 19th century that Americans first fell in love with the garden. With the same earnestness and diligence that they applied to all other areas of their lives, and the same ardor for artifice and excess, they managed to arrive at an unusual variety of exuberant garden styles. Before the 19th century though, only the well-to-do had the land and the leisure to garden. Humbler families, feverishly engaged in the business of economic survival, had

The verdant joys of country life were celebrated in an 1855 print by Nathaniel Currier, right, helping to create a nostalgia for the simple pleasures of the land the Victorians had left behind only a generation or two earlier. Below, a small plot is set aside for flowers and lawn.

little time for such purely decorative pursuits as flower growing. If a family yearned for flowers, that urge had to be satisfied by wildflowers, or by thrifty commonplace blooms, like pink bouncing Bet, purple honesty, or weedlike mallow, that camped by their side doors and thrived scrappily on their own.

During the 1830s and '40s, as survival became less labor intensive, the desire to better oneself and beautify one's surroundings began to take root. In addition to the corn, beans, and prosaic potatoes that grew so persistently, country folk began to consider the merits of setting aside a small plot for flowers and lawn. City dwellers contemplated the pleasant prospect of a small but charmingly landscaped yard and colorful window boxes filled to overflowing. "To have no garden is to take the poetry, and nearly all the charms away from country life," said one English writer visiting our country. "To have a garden is to have many friends continually near."

In the coming decades, the idea of the middle-class garden was heavily promoted and popularized. During the 1870s one influential gardening guide, *The Art of Beautifying Suburban Home Grounds of Small Extent* by Frank Jesup Scott, a disciple of noted American landscape gardener Andrew Jackson Downing, went so far as to address homeowners of moderate income with little knowledge of decorative gardening, as opposed to the aristocrat. By linking garden design with the more familiar world of interior design, he cleverly touched on themes near and dear to upwardly striving Victorians.

▣ Rather than praising the inaccessible vistas of rambling country estates, Scott encouraged gardening on a more intimate scale, making shrewd reference to well-known terms of tasteful home decoration. This was not a new idea with Scott but one also mentioned by Downing, who in turn learned it from the writings of Humphrey Repton and the 18th-century landscape designers. For example, he pointedly referred to "the art of picture-making and picture framing," using flowers and greenery, and urged that gardeners cultivate "harmonious home pictures" in their gardens. This language touched a chord with themes that, not coincidentally, applied to house and garden alike.

▣ After 1850, adding further to the appeal of gardening was the social and moral cloaking it assumed. Associations of purity, refinement of character, and even virtue and moral worth were cleverly intertwined with the keeping and cultivation of gardens. Joseph Breck, a nursery owner and author of *The Flower Garden* (also known as *Breck's Book of Flowers*), published in 1851, pointedly wrote of the "moral lesson" that could be obtained from flowers: "Flowers not only please the eye and gratify the passing observer, but contain a beauty in their structure, in the most minute parts and coloring, that conveys a pleasing and natural lesson to the most accurate and intelligent observer." As late as 1898, the moral litany persisted. Particularly since flower seeds and bulbs were so cheap—a sum as small as a dollar was enough to fill a respectably sized garden with enough seeds to produce a magnificent array of blooms—there was no excuse for the homeowner who neglected to make his garden bright and attractive for the benefit of his family. "We pity the person who has acres of land but finds no room for flowers, seeing no beauty except in dollars and cents, and rearing their children in the same sordid manner," scoffed a garden advocate in Vermont.

▣ Far be it, the Victorians felt, for the art of pleasure gardening, a radically new idea to many, to risk acceptance on its own merits. Instead, horticulture was assigned uplifting benefits. The taste for trees, plants, and flowers was extolled as the love an enlightened mind and a tender heart paid to nature. One ladies' magazine proclaimed that flowers teach lessons of patient submission, meek endurance, and innocent cheerfulness under adverse circumstances. Another pronounced that "the most desirable qualities would automatically be instilled in a personality when put in contact with fresh air and nature's endless beauty, and when given the responsibility for the care of nature's gifts."

An enlightened mind and a pure and tender heart came to be associated with garden cultivation, as the beatific expressions and flowing white garments of the Madonna-like mother and child suggest, above.

Following pages:
A "charming abundance of vines" typified the garden ideal.

Flowers sweeten the air, rejoice the eye, link you with nature and innocence, and are something to love. If they cannot love you in return, they cannot hate you; cannot utter hateful words even if neglected; for though they are all beauty, they possess no vanity; and living, as they do, to do you good, and afford you pleasure, how can you neglect them!

LEIGH HUNT

Children and flowers were used to advertise Bell's Spices in 1895, above. Victorian children, below, were thought to have a special relationship with nature and were encouraged to garden to improve and strengthen their character.

Throughout the late 1860s and '70s, men and women, young and old, were persuaded to take to the garden. "You can make no investment which will give you such interest; health, happiness, and pure enjoyment will be the coin in which it is paid; and the returns are not paid semi-annually, but daily," declared Mrs. S.O. Johnson in *Every Woman Her Own Flower Gardener* (1873). To display an interest in gardening became a mark of cultivated good taste. Especially for the newly middle-class family, anxious to exhibit their culture and gentility, a well-kept garden became, like a tidy home, a signal to one's neighbors of refinement and worth. It was said that travelers passing by could distinguish pure-minded and intelligent people by the very appearance of their house—and garden. Homes of the more intelligent would have had a "charming abundance" of vines and window boxes filled with flowers, while in the sluggard's garden, weeds and disorder prevailed.

In the most up-to-date educational theories of the day, children were encouraged to prune, tend, and plant small garden plots in hopes they would learn the virtues of industry and perseverance and the rewards of hard work. "Children are born naturalists, and if taught to study the beautiful things in the bright world around them, they will always have a source of pleasure," pointed out *The Ladies' Home Journal* in August 1899. Gardening prompted a host of other useful habits for the young. Catharine Beecher and her sister Harriet Beecher Stowe believed that gardening would promote early rising from bed. In addition, if children were called upon to keep garden walks and borders free from weeds and rubbish, good habits of order and neatness would be nurtured.

Qualities of benevolence and charity could also be cultivated by influencing the young to share homegrown fruits and flowers with friends and neighbors, as well as to distribute roots and seeds to the poor. In Louisa May Alcott's classic *Little Men*, each of the twelve children at the school under Jo and Professor Bhaer's tutelage was given a small garden plot in which they toiled. Symbolically, the crops they chose to raise represented their characters. The lazier children inevitably chose vegetables that required little tending; the less imaginative boys, destined for supposedly dull mercantile careers, chose humdrum crops, foreshadowing the humdrum and prosaic business world they would later enter. Gentle, feminine Daisy, true to her namesake, grew flowers rather than anything "useful." Practical Nan, who later became one of the first women physicians and an early feminist, had a garden that flourished with herbs and medicinals. Scientifically minded Demi experimented with new strains of corn. In truth, the children's gardens became a moral metaphor for their lives. During one memorable, moralistic storytelling hour, God was described as the Great Gardener and the children were the little garden plots in which either weeds (bad habits) or flowers and fruits (virtues) thrived.

WHAT LADIES SHOULD WEAR TO GARDEN

Of course, flounces, puffs and furbelows, with their accompanying upper skirts, are not suitable for such occupations. A dark chintz skirt is the best, for it can go into the wash-tub when it is in need of cleansing. A woolen bathing dress makes an excellent garden costume—for skirts are always in the way. If it is admissible on the beach, where wealth and fashion do congregate, why not in the garden, surrounding one's house? A large shade hat, and a pair of kid gloves are indispensable. Rubber gloves are often recommended, but are far too clumsy for the fingers.

1873

Even as gardening wrapped itself in this banner of morality, gentility, and refinement, it was also extolled as a healthful activity. In an era when mother and infant mortality and epidemics plagued nearly every household, health was both a constant concern and a mystery, one that every Victorian strove to unlock every day. The Beecher sisters, for instance, were powerful advocates of the wholesome and invigorating benefits of gardening, specifically for young ladies. "No father who wishes to have his daughters grow up to be healthful women can take a surer method to secure this end," they believed. Many people, in fact, decried the sedentary habits of women and the preponderance of early female invalidism. American women were said to live indoors too much, at severe disadvantage to their health and spirits. "They cultivate neuralgia, dyspepsia, and all their attendant ills—rather than the beautiful and glorious flowers which God has scattered so abundantly all over the world," prodded Mrs. Johnson.

Promises of good health, though, were not enough. In order to convince women that the delights of a garden involved more than a feminine gossip fest while arranging tabletop bouquets, further justification was called for. One strong stumbling block was the physical labor involved in gardening—preparing the ground, laying out the beds, hardening the walks. Were these daunting tasks suitable for delicate ladies? Quickly, the importance of these very necessary garden chores was dismissed, consigned to a hired man or gardener. It was only after such masculine garden drudgery had been accomplished that women's gentler, smaller hands took over, quite capable of handling the purportedly more creative planting of seeds, weeding, staking, watering, and pruning. From that point on, no man's hand or foot was permitted to enter the "sacred precinct" of the garden, except as a guest—to admire its beauty and receive a posy or buttonhole of flowers.

Lest some ladies hold up their hands in horror at the idea of soiling their hands with garden work, it was also pointedly noted how much harder ladies already "worked" during the course of the social season, particularly at a crowded party or ball. To dance the popular dance known as "the German," considered by some critics as almost dangerously vigorous in fact, certainly required as much or more strength than planting a flower garden and pulling weeds. But in recognition of their fragility, beef tea and other "stimulants" were recommended to sustain women's "feeble knees" and uplift and strengthen their "nerveless fingers." "Women *can* find strength to cultivate a garden

The love of the garden translated into new outdoor pastimes, from frequent basket picnics to country fairs. Above, tickets to some of these popular excursions. Opposite: Dahlias, in their many hot colors, were special favorites.

successfully if they will commence by degrees," encouraged Mrs. Johnson. "Garden by degrees, my friends, and cultivate your muscles with your plants!" was her cry.

Surprisingly, more and more women heard her call. By the 1870s, even the most languid and delicately feminine of Victorian women, already partial by nature and education to the perfume, color, and ornamental possibilities of flowers, could see that a little light work in the garden, with a pretty spade and a becoming rose-bedecked hat, might prove a most graceful, attractive, not to mention socially profitable, pose to adopt.

Perhaps it was the scores of sumptuously color-illustrated seed catalogs from such noted seed houses and nurseries as Henderson & Company in New York City, Vick's Seeds in Rochester, Joseph Breck and Son in Boston, Burpee Seeds in Philadelphia, and D. M. Ferry and Company in Detroit, along with dozens of new garden magazines dispensing horticultural know-how, that proved the most invaluable inducement in coaxing reluctant women out of doors. All were simply bursting with improbably flawless specimens of Victorian fruits, flowers, and vegetables, and many were cannily designed to appeal specifically to the new audience of female gardeners. Chatty letters and correspondence from readers—gardening "sisters"—punctuated each issue. Some publications even sponsored exciting gardening competitions with awards for the largest fruits and vegetables or the most beautiful flowers—grown, of course, from their own seeds.

Simple nursery catalogs existed, of course, during the 18th century. George Washington was known to have purchased seeds for his estate from John Bartram's catalog, which was issued in 1783. The Bartrams, father William and son John, both self-trained botanists based near Philadelphia, were known for their passion for discovering unusual native plants. Their efforts in fact were frequently privately financed by wealthy plant enthusiasts in England who eagerly awaited shipments of their latest finds. But although Bartram's list offered a selection of over two hundred native plants—impressive for the time—this "catalog" was really little more than a list of densely set type on a single sheet of heavy paper, utilitarian and unadorned. Efforts from other early nurseries were similar. During the 1830s, the Rochester Seed Store and Horticultural Society (later the vast Mount Hope Garden and Nurseries) issued a modest seed catalog. In 1840, horticulturist, author, and garden journal editor Joseph

In addition to moral considerations, gardening developed social cachet: The marriage-minded realized that gardens provided a flattering and effective showcase for feminine charms, below.

Breck, of Boston, published what could be called the first real American seed catalog—an impressive 84 pages, with black-and-white illustrations. Including illustrations was quite a bold move for that time and other catalogs quickly followed suit. Soon, hand-colored plates (either lithographs or stencils with details added by hand) brightened the pages of many of these early garden catalogs of the 1850s.

It was not until after the Civil War, however, that the genre truly flourished, thanks to the vastly improved printing procedures that finally allowed for inexpensive and vivid color reproduction. In 1864, a year before the war ended, Rochester-based nurseryman James Vick, who wrote frequently for *The Genesee Farmer* and *The Horticulturist*, first made news when his catalog featured a picture of a double zinnia in full glorious color—zinnias, of Mexican origin, were enjoying a special burst of popularity at that time, especially in English gardens. Vick, by 1866, owned one of the largest seed houses in the world. By the late 1860s, glossy, brightly colored chromolithographs had transformed garden catalogs into enticing tomes thick with information, beautiful illustrations, and helpful hints. In 1869, Washburn & Company of Boston issued a highly successful hardcover catalog entitled the *Amateur Cultivator's Guide to the Flower and Kitchen*

The Shaker community pioneered selling seed by mail in the early years of the 19th century. By 1850, dozens of entrepreneurial mail-order companies were thriving, with images of flawless fruits and vegetables and rare, colorful blooms illustrating packets, above. A collection of 64 packets was advertised in one magazine for $2.30.

*Poppies are in favor again.
And it is well, for any one who has once grown them
will tell you what delightful things they are,
with petals that seem cut from shimmering silk of the richest
most delicate colors... They are charming
for use in vases, if cut before the buds expand much.*

THE MAYFLOWER, FEBRUARY 1899

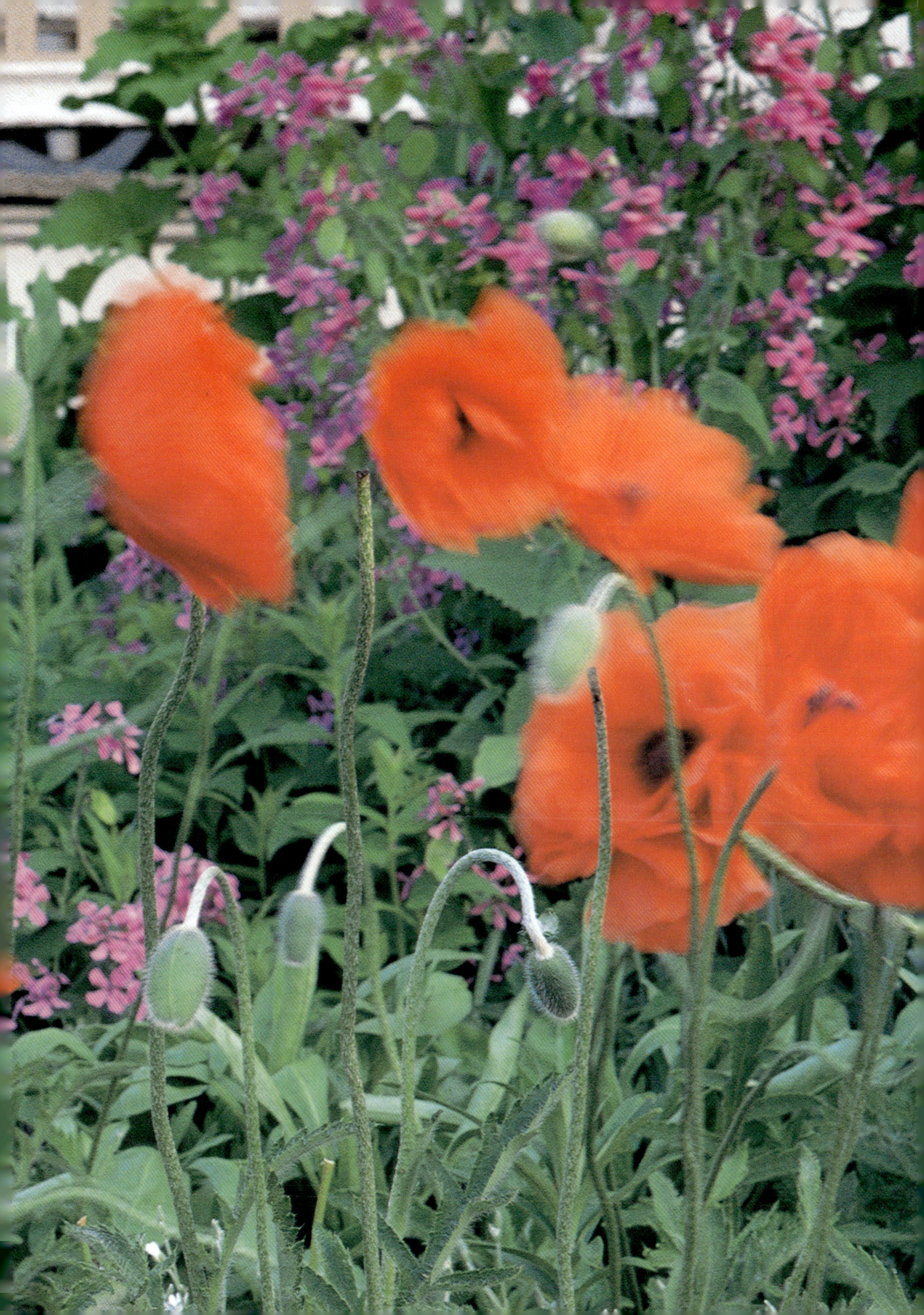

The Mayflower magazine observed that Mr. Childs, the well-known seedsman, had made a radical departure from usual custom in making up his fall catalog. "Fall catalogues are small and insignificant compared with those issued in spring," commented *The Mayflower*. "It is therefore refreshing to note a change for the better. The Catalog which Mr. Childs is sending out this month is composed of 64 pages bound in beautiful colored covers and is divided into three parts."

The commercial nurseries and seed houses that put out these catalogs, many of which developed directly outside of major urban centers, profited by the increased industrialization of the era, and during the 19th century became substantial businesses, with literally thousands of people in their collective employ. During the late 1870s, in addition to the acreage one would normally expect a nursery to allot for the growth of seeds and plants, and a store that sold garden tools and furnishings as well as plants and seeds, Vick's maintained its own printing office, a stable of on-staff artists and engravers to render the brilliantly colored art, a bindery and box-making facilities, as well as an impressively equipped, full-scale mail room and fulfillment house for processing, packing, and posting seed orders. "Tons of seeds are thus dispatched every day during the busy

Preceding pages: With brilliant red color, graceful stems, and exotic associations, poppies were a Victorian favorite.

Above: Full-color printing techniques made seed catalogs more beautiful, useful, and collectible.

Garden that ran to 150 jam-packed pages. The Burpee catalog, perhaps the best known, was first issued as a 48-page "pamphlet" in 1874. By 1915, it was well over 200 pages. Some garden catalogs eventually became so elaborate and expensive to produce—and so coveted by nongardeners who collected them for their colorful illustrations—that Burpee exacted a purchase price, previously unheard of for mail-order catalogs, to help offset production costs.

Enthusiastically involved with gardening, Victorians noted and remarked on even the smallest changes in each catalog's inventory and style. In 1896, season," according to one contemporary account. Selling seeds in small paper packets, a practice originated by the Shakers during the first quarter of the 19th century, proved a profitable business for enterprising Victorians in general. By 1877, Vick's employed 50 people just to weigh, measure, and dispense its seeds. And that same year, their modern, steam-propelled machinery was turning out more than 10,000 garden catalogs per day. Nor was Vick's alone. Other large nurseries and seed houses ran similarly impressive operations.

❋ George Ellwanger, the young German horticulturist who ran the Rochester Seed Store and Horticultural Repository during the 1830s, eventually bought the company. As Mount Hope Gardens and Nurseries, it became one of the largest nurseries in the world at that time, expanding from the original seven acres to over 600. In 1844, it opened a branch in Toronto; in 1854, one in Ohio. At its peak, it employed 400 to 500 people during the summer. Of course, as now, in addition to selling seeds the nurseries also shipped young plants and cut flowers, often by railroad express.

❋ Thanks to the fertile growth of the nursery business, other industries also prospered. Reams of paper and tons of pasteboard, for example, were used by the burgeoning nurserymen/entrepreneurs, who in addition to catalogs and magazines produced colorful posters and amusing trade cards for all manner of garden paraphernalia. More than 50 different types of fertilizer, both natural and chemical, were on the market by the 1880s; among the most highly thought of—and aggressively promoted—were Peruvian guano, a seafowl manure, and "Poudrette," a mixture of swamp muck and charcoal dust. Hapless Victorian gardeners often turned to these fertilizers after innocently dousing their garden soil with kerosene or coarse salt—home remedies for weed killing—which unfortunately rendered the soil temporarily barren.

❋ The era also saw the development of patented insecticides. While early in the century specially designed bellows were manufactured to dispense substances like tobacco smoke, which was used as an early insect repellent, by the 1850s and '60s all sorts of remedies like "Clarke's Preparation for Killing Mealy Bug etc."

Curious new plant foods, fertilizers, and all sorts of dubious garden novelties were developed to meet gardeners' growing needs, such as the paper flowerpot and rubberized plant atomizer, above.

Following pages, left: Intense colors from the summer garden; right, Montgomery Ward & Co.'s catalog was eagerly received.

FLOWERS HATING? WHAT A PARADOX! WITH THEIR FRESHNESS AND THEIR COLOR, AND THEIR PERFUME?

MONTGOMERY WARD & CO.'S CATALOGUE No. 56.

Spring Balance Brackets.
ron Brackets for hanging spring balances
t, 2 lbs. 9 oz. Each........................$0.45
z...4.85

Butchers' Scales.
42263 Market Scales with Marble Slab. To weigh 32 lbs. by ounces. Each.......$9.50
To weigh 64
2 ounces. Each...........................$10.50
, boxed for shipment,40 lbs.

Steelyards.
42267 Steelyards, with steel bars; weigh up to 300 lbs. These steelyards are for household use and for those having only a little weighing to do. They are not the best qualities and are not
teed.
0 to 200 lbs. Steelyards will not weigh a
y less than 6 pounds, the 250 and 300
l not weigh a less quantity than 10 lbs.
ty.....50 100 150 200 250 300 lbs
ach....27c. 37c. 47c. 53c. 60c. 65c.
eelyard with steel bars. These steelyards are
teed to weigh absolutely correct. They weigh up
50 lbs. size by ¼ lbs.; above this size by ½ lbs.
0 and 150 lbs. Steelyards do not start at zero
ot intended to weigh any quantity weighing
10 lbs. If you wish to weigh a smaller quan-
10 lbs. use a 50 lb. Steelyard, as all others
e 8 lb. point, and are accurate in weighing
lbs.
ty. 50   100   150   200   250   300 lbs.
...45c. 50c. 58c. 72c. 86c. $1.00

42269 Scale Beams with Poises. These beams are made heavy and capable of weighing to their full y without injury; they weigh by 1 lbs. only.
h. 250 400 1,000 1,200 lbs.
ach.$1.10 $1.50 $2.00 $3.50 $4.00
nish Poises for Scales Beams as follows:
0 lbs. Beam have each a 2 lb. and 8 lb. Poise.
0 lbs. Beam have each a 3 lb. and 12 lb. Poise.
0 lbs. Beam have each an 8 lb. and 16 lb. Poise.
00 lbs. Beam have each an 8 lb. and 32 lb. Poise.
00 lbs. Beam have each a 16 lb. and 32 lb. Poise.

e Standard Family Scales.
cales are warranted correct. Are very con-
and the best scales for family use made. There
ights to get lost, are light and easy to handle,
ot take up much room; are japanned and
ly ornamented in assorted colors.

he family Standard
o weigh 48 pounds by
es, with platform; no
eight, boxed for shipment,9 lbs. Each...$2.56
e Standard Family Scale, to weigh 12
y ounces, with tin scoop. Each.......... 2.25
e Standard Family Scale, to weigh 48
b 2 ounces, with tin scoop Each..... 2.75

42278 The Novelty Family Scale, no weights needed. Weighs 12 lbs. by 2 ozs. With platform; no scoop. Each ..$1.30

42279   42278-79
With platform and tin scoop

Scales—Continued.

42286—Platform Scale better than 42287; weight 240 lbs., by ounces all steel bearings, scales and wgts. officially scaled and each and every scale warranted—Weight, boxed for shipment, 35 lbs $4.00

M. W. & Co.'s Scales.
42287 The Montgomery Ward Co. Platform Counter Scales, steel bearings, tin scoop, brass beam; weighing ½ oz. to 240 lbs. Warranted reliable. (See cut.) Weight, boxed for shipment, 39 lbs. Price, each.....................$2.43

Weighs ¼ oz. to 25 lbs.

42288—The Housekeeper's Friend, price with platform, no scoop; shipping weight 15 lbs.; each.......$1.68
42289 With tin scoop 2.00
Our scales are all packed ready for shipment. We have some of these scales, which have been in constant use for several years, and they answer our purpose as well as those sold for $14.

Garden Trowels.
42292 Garden trowels; extra quality, cast steel; made in four sizes.

Length, inches........5   6   7   8
Price, each........$0.04 $0.05 $0.06 $0.07
Price per doz.......44   .54   .65   .75

Weeding Hooks.
42294 Weeding Hook wood handle, entire length, including handle, 10 in. This pattern is the most popular style of hand weeder; each............$0.07
Per dozen.. .75

Strawberry Forks.
42296 Strawberry Forks. Japanned iron fork. wood handle, length, including handle, 11 in. Made in two patterns, light and heavy.
Light pattern, each....$0.08 Per doz.....$0.87
Heavy pattern, each... .12 Per doz......1.30

Garden Line Reel.
42299 Garden Line Reel. Malleable iron, japanned; no line furnished with reel. Each........$0.37
Per dozen............................... 4.00

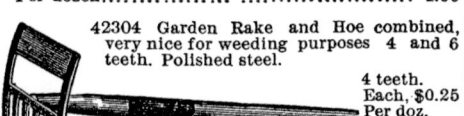

42304 Garden Rake and Hoe combined, very nice for weeding purposes 4 and 6 teeth. Polished steel.
4 teeth. Each, $0.25
Per doz. $2.70
6 teeth. Each, $0.35
Per doz. $3.85

42305 Garden Rake and Hoe combined, malleable iron, cast steel blade, 4 and 6 teeth.
4 teeth. Each.................................18
Per dozen................................... 1.95
6 teeth. Each..................................20
Per dozen................................... 2.16

Scuffle Hoe.
42307 Scuffle Hoe, malleable socket, steel blade, 6 foot handle. Each..$0.40
Per dozen.................................. 4.25

Onion Hoe
42310 Onion Hoe, polished, solid shank; a very convenient shape. Each. $0.25

Hoes.
42313 Garden Socket Hoes, blued.
Each..$0.30
Per dozen...................................... 3.40
42314 Garden Shank Hoes, blued. Each...........25
Per dozen...................................... 2.75
42315 Warren Garden Hoes, extra cast steel, polished. Garden size. Each..................40
Per dozen...................................... 4.55
Field sizes. Each..............................45
Per dozen...................................... 5 40

Garden Rakes.
42320 Garden Rake, malleable iron, polished, 12 teeth. Each............................$0.20
Per dozen...................................... 2.15
42321 Garden Rake, cast steel polished, 12 teeth. Each..35
Per dozen...................................... 3.55
42322 14 teeth Garden Rake, cast steel. Each....40
Per dozen...................................... 3.90

42323 The Gibbs Lawn Rake. Improved for 1891. The teeth are made of No. 9 coppered steel spring wire, and so formed as to comb the lawn, taking up the loose grass or leaves without tearing the sod; 24 inches wide, 30 teeth. Each..................$0.50
Per dozen...................................... 5.40

42324 The favorite Lawn Rake, strong and durable steel. Head 24 inch with 24 tinned No. 9 steel wire teeth. To unload rake simply push backward without raising it. Each....$0.38
Per dozen...................................... 4.10
42324½ Hay Rakes, wood, made of ash; mortised head. Each........$0.15   Per dozen...... 1.62

42325— Garden Tool Set, consisting of hoe rake and spade. The hoe is 3½ in. wide, rake 3 inches, spade 3x4½. Rake and hoe have 30 in. handle, spade 21 inch. Just the thing for ladies in making garden, and will furnish good healthy amusement for the children.
Per set, complete. $0.20 Per dozen sets.....$2.16
42326 Garden Tool Set, same number, kind and size tools as are in number 42325 set, but are a little better finished, and made of a little better material. Per set..$0.27   Per dozen sets...... 2.92

42327 Garden Tool Set, consisting of hoe, rake and spade. Spade measures 5¾x4. Rake is 6 in. wide with 7 teeth, hoe is 3½ in. wide. Rake and hose handles are 30 in. long, spade handles are 19 in. in length with T-head. Per set..$0.40 Dozen sets.$4.32

Garden Tools.
42328 Floral Set. Ladies' Favorite, for cultivating flowers, consisting of four pieces, a small rake with 7 teeth, hoe, fork used for weeding, and garden trowel, all with wood handles; entire length of rake and hoe, 13 inch, fork and trowel, 10½ inches. These floral sets are indispensable to the perfect cultivation of flowers and shrubs, and no lady who has a flower garden should be without one.
Per set complete............$0.22 Per doz. sets....$2.38
42329 Floral Set, Ladies' Favorive, same number

Child's Bug Scorcher, above, was but one of many creative ways the Victorians rid their gardens of pests. No item was more aggressively promoted than the lawn mower, suggestively hawked by a primly bonneted girl in an unusually short skirt, below.

and "Keating's Persian Insect-Destroying Powder" were heavily advertised and widely available. Some preparations were entirely bogus; others, while they lived up to their promise of killing insects, unfortunately destroyed the plants as well. By the 1880s, the most effective insect destroyer was a powdered compound that contained pyrethrum, which was sprayed onto plants with a dusting bellows. Interestingly, pyrethrum still counts as one of the "safer" insecticides available today.

Beginning in the 1840s, the growth of foundries allowed for the inexpensive mass production of garden tools. Just as dining implements became more specialized with each decade's passing—such specialization being considered evidence of middle-class gentility and increasing refinement—so the list of necessary gardening implements exploded after 1850. While gardeners of the early 19th century could get by with just a simple spade, a rake, a fork, a hoe, shears, a watering pot, and a wheelbarrow, the average gardener of the 1870s was advised to invest in more than 30 different tools—pruning knives and budding knives, seed sowers and hand-weeders, wooden rakes for the lawn and steel ones for beds. Cronk's pruning shears, made with a straight, solid steel blade and a malleable handle, were advertised as being much easier to use than the "old style" and at a very cheap price—just 40¢ by the mid-1890s. Small-sized, lightweight garden tools were marketed specifically for women and even smaller ones for children. A "floral set" of five garden tools promoted as "Ladies' Favorite" by Montgomery Ward, also during the 1890s, included a hoe, a dainty trowel, a five-prong weeder, and a strawberry fork, all with handsome polished wood handles. It, too, was just 40¢.

The most important Victorian development in the realm of garden tools, however, was the invention and popularization of the mechanical lawn mower, which not only changed the appearance of the garden but popularized new leisure activities such as lawn tennis, badminton, and croquet. Prior to the Victorian age, the grooming of lawns could keep gardeners busy for days on end. Lawns were trimmed—albeit shaggily—with sharp, polished steel scythes wielded by teams of hardworking gardeners on great estates. Although the lawn mower was first invented—by an Englishman—during the 1830s, it would be several decades after that, with many mechanical improvements, before its mass manufacture was even possible or practical. Brought to America during the 1850s, by the 1870s a variation with spiral rotary blades had become widely available. Marketed in many different sizes, some were small enough to be considered suitable for ladies.

Lawn mowers were aggressively advertised. The Excelsior mower, introduced in 1870, was one of the leaders. "So simple and safe a child can use it," lauded one of its advertisements, which depicted a nubile-looking girl child, skirts gathered up to reveal plump calves and trim ankles sheathed in tight high-button shoes. By the 1870s, thanks to the competitive nature of the Victorian marketplace, a mower for home use could be purchased for less than $15. Ladies' models, somewhat lighter and occasionally decorated, cost a little bit more. By 1895, $4 bought a quite serviceable mower from Montgomery Ward, more than equal, it was said, to a good substantial lawn. By then even an "Imperial," their top-of-the-line machine, cost only $7.92.

WHAT YOU NEED IN A GARDEN

A large, three-pronged iron fork, with a short handle to loosen the ground, removing plants and uprooting weeds
A rake and hoe on one handle • A trowel
A spade • A watering pot with a large nozzle and a fine sprinkler •
An old piece of carpeting to kneel upon while planting or weeding with a fork; and if your knees are not accustomed to that position, humor them by placing an empty raisin or soap box upon the carpet, and sit upon that—and if a cushion would also be agreeable, cover a small pillow with some dark chintz, and place that on the box. Now you will have a luxurious seat, and can garden without a sense of pain; yet don't stay too long, nor become too much heated.
The carpeting protects the skirts from the dampness of the soil, and should always be used. It can be kept conveniently at hand, with the box and the cushion.

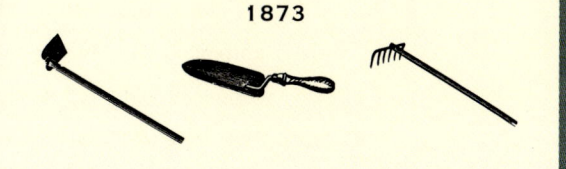

1873

Affordable lawn mowers, right, enabled the middle-class homeowner to achieve the status symbol of a lawn. New consumer products like lawn furniture were developed, as well as leisure activities like lawn tennis and croquet. Opposite: No plant was so popular as the geranium, the bedding-out favorite prized for its easy growth and bright, cheerful coloring.

Lawn Mowers.
The "New York."

This Mower is made to meet the demand for a good, substantial lawn Mower at a medium low price. It has several of our latest improvements in *ratchet, back roller hanger, handle, adjustment, etc.*, and has ready sale to the large class of trade who wish to buy a first-class mower at lower price than heretofore. It has steel shafts ⅝ inch in diameter, double ratchet. The knife is adjusted by one screw at each end of the knife bar, which is more simple and durable than the old plan. Its noiseless and light draft are very pleasant features with this mower, and there is more in it for the dollar than any other mower on the market. It is made in medium sizes only.

42424	12 inch, price, each	$3.60
42425	14 inch, price, each	3.85
42426	16 inch, price each	4.00

Without the lawn mower, the possession of a finely shaven emerald-green lawn on which one could play croquet and hold outdoor tea parties and luncheons would never have become the status symbol that it did. On a fine spring or summer day, families enjoyed nothing better than to be able to move tables and chairs out onto the lawn and relax in these "outdoor parlors" (later, of course, cast-iron and other types of furniture made specifically for the garden replaced this practice). Nor would the intricate and complex use of turf in bedding-out schemes ever been possible. Because the lawn mower had made maintenance so much easier—a staff of gardeners was no longer required—lawns finally became accessible to the middle-class homeowner.

At the same time that the Victorians embraced the lawn mower and other wonderful, patented gadgets that made their lives so much easier—and were signs of their progressive nature and modernity—they also took special delight in the exciting new plants they could now possess, thanks to the efforts of plant breeders and botanists who developed all sorts of new hybrids, particularly in the realm of vegetables and fruits. To have 60, 70, 100, or even 200 varieties of apples or strawberries or pears—regardless of how bland or inferior these new varieties might taste—was a sign of the scientific know-how of these exciting times, something of prime importance to progressively minded Victorians. In their efforts to produce superior plants, horticulturists bred for hardiness, for size, for richness of color, but all too often just for novelty. As for taste, unfortunately that was far down on the list of considerations!

New plants entered the Victorian garden not only through the attempts of the hybridizers, but also through explorations by professional plant collectors. Indeed, throughout the 19th century, not only did independent explorers undertake sorties, but horticultural societies, colleges, and various nursery owners sponsored dozens of botanical expeditions, mostly throughout the western regions of the United States, South and Central America, the Hawaiian Islands, the deserts and jungles of Africa, Australia, China, and Japan.

SEE OPPOSITE PAGE.

Pasteur, 14¢	Bertha De Pressily, 14¢	Mme Jaulin, 14¢	Marquise De Montmort, 14¢
Dagata, 14¢	Mme. Buchner, 9¢	Peter Henderson, 14¢	La Condole, 9¢
Leopold Bouville, 16¢	M. Anatole Roseleur, 16¢	Mme. Louise Abbenia, 14¢	Double Dryden, 16¢
Mrs. Lawrence, 16¢	Alphonse Ricard, 9¢	Mme. Recamier, 16¢	Jean Viaud, 9¢

Expeditions had begun of course prior to the Victorian explosion. Meriwether Lewis and William Clark, for example, brought back dozens of new seeds and specimens during their famous 1804–6 explorations, including Osage orange, which was later to become one of the most common trees in mid-century American gardens. The Bartrams, subsidized by the novelty-hungry British nobility, were also known for their early discoveries. As the gardener/explorers scoured the American West, California, and Oregon, many other wonderful early discoveries were made on the continent alone. Thomas Drummond, a Scotsman, explored Texas during the early 1830s, bringing back phlox, another plant that was especially popular in later Victorian gardens. And it was in 1862, on a venture through the Rocky Mountains, that Charles Christopher Parry discovered the Colorado blue spruce.

Flamboyant cannas, in fiery scarlets and orange, were one of the exotic floral finds that changed the character of the Victorian garden (above, McGregor's Brilliant Bedding Cannas).

As the years went on, thanks to transcontinental railroads, steamships, and other remarkable improvements in transportation—and the subsequent improved dissemination of information through the many dozens of new garden magazines and garden societies—the plants discovered on these journeys frequently reached American homes within a remarkably few years of their initial discovery. Traveling by steamship from the United States to Europe, for instance, now took only two weeks! This was fortunate because, due to the fickleness of Victorian taste, fashions changed fast. Elegant verbenas from Argentina and calceolarias from Chile and Peru were discovered during the 1820s, developed during the 1830s, and by the 1840s and '50s had become wildly fashionable in American gardens. Both appealed to the Victorian taste for flowers with strong, undiluted color. But by 1860, there were so many different varieties of calceolarias that some were already scorned as passé.

In their search for plants that were new, fascinating, and rare, the explorers brought back dramatic feathery palms, broad-leafed cannas, and ornamental banana plants. Water lilies, first found in the Amazon Valley in 1837, captured the Victorians' romantic fancy. Graceful bleeding heart, with its bright pink and white heart-shaped blossoms, was brought from the Orient into England in 1846 by Scottish botanist and plant collector nonpareil Robert Fortune, and first exhibited in the United States just five years later. Fortune, one of the leading plant collectors of his day—and one of the first to travel with a Wardian case to transport his precious finds—also introduced the forsythia to Americans, who called it "golden bells." It, too, became a beloved flower of the last quarter of the century. While in China and Shanghai, Fortune, who later wrote a best-selling book detailing his plant-hunting adventures, acquired other treasures, including new varieties of camellias and China rose.

▣ Verbenas, discovered in Buenos Aires in 1826 by one Mr. Tweedie, an Englishman (who also found pampas grass during his travels in Brazil), quickly gained a place as one of the most respected bedding plants. In the 19th-century "language of flowers," which accorded a special meaning or phrase for each plant, verbenas stood for church and family unity, making them a very proper mid-Victorian flower indeed. Among the exotics the Victorians enjoyed were tropical orchids as well as new peonies, different from those planted by the older generation, and said to be delightfully showy when planted alone but truly magnificent en masse.

▣ George Hall, an American doctor living in Shanghai, became known for sending all sorts of exotic plants back to America, including Japanese honeysuckle and Japanese wisteria. The taste for exotic plants such as these—and others—changed the character of the Victorian garden, making it more worldly and sophisticated but sometimes comically incongruous, as flamboyant, dark-leafed tropical cannas with scarlet-orange flowers sprang up against the unassuming, sweet-scented little blossoms of mignonette. But tropical beds, especially in the late 1890s, were all the rage and cannas were a big part of that trend, having made an extraordinary impact on public taste in 1893 at the World's Columbian Exposition. There, they were displayed in 76 beds extending more than 1,000 feet in length. In 1897, *The Delineator* suggested that gardeners even try planting entire beds with one single variety of exotic bloom, such as cannas, yucca, or exotic grasses like hardy Japanese dwarf bamboo or castor bean. Hall also brought back Japanese yew, an important addition to American gardens because of its hardiness (and form), but otherwise hard to distinguish from English and American yews.

▣ New glass greenhouses, which now could be heated by dependable cast-iron pipes, promised these exotic tropical blooms a warm and nurturing environment. The improved manufacture of

Forcing blooms indoors, as depicted by this handsome vase filled with pom-pom hyacinths, top, became common with the development of the greenhouse. Cold weather no longer caused interruption in the newfound pleasure of gardening. Tropical blooms could flower year-round, above.

glass, which subsequently made elaborate greenhouses and hothouses popular, also enabled people to garden all year round. Now, cold weather caused barely a pause in the newfound pleasure of gardening. The wealthy were able to raise their rare and costly strains of orchids, palms, and other exotics as well as to bring flowers into bloom out of season and to enjoy fresh fruit all year. Camellias, a symbol of chastity and a popular flower for Victorian weddings (along with sweet-scented orange blossoms), also made excellent pot plants for adorning a conservatory throughout the summer and, in a cool conservatory, could be made to flower at almost any time. For more modest dwellings, a tile-floored conservatory or "garden room" (sometimes called a fernery), usually just off the parlor, became essential.

Although the terms "greenhouse" and "conservatory" were sometimes used interchangeably during the 19th century, in actuality there were several important differences. While both were glass-enclosed, the conservatory, which adjoined the interior and was purely decorative, was intended primarily for the display of plants. "Greenhouse" and "hothouse," however, generally referred to a freestanding and functional structure, usually on a grand estate, used for propagation or as a plant shelter in winter. For example, if kept at a cool temperature, the greenhouse might have been used to grow delicate camellias and other plants that required a cool environment; the hothouse was kept warm and housed tender tropicals. Today, that distinction in temperature is stated rather than implied: a "cool greenhouse," a "warm greenhouse." As for hotbeds and forcing houses, which were used to grow fruit and vegetables out of season, these were utilitarian structures usually found in conjunction with the kitchen garden.

The Wardian case (also known as a Ward's case), which resembled a miniature greenhouse or covered terrarium, was originally intended as a means of safe transport for all sorts of plants, protecting them from such conditions as extreme cold or from

While not everyone could afford their own greenhouse or conservatory—especially one as grand as the Enid A. Haupt Conservatory at the New York Botanical Garden, Bronx, New York, opposite— Wardian cases, right, which resembled miniature greenhouses or enclosed terrariums, were the perfect substitute, and fancy ones soon became a fashionable status symbol.

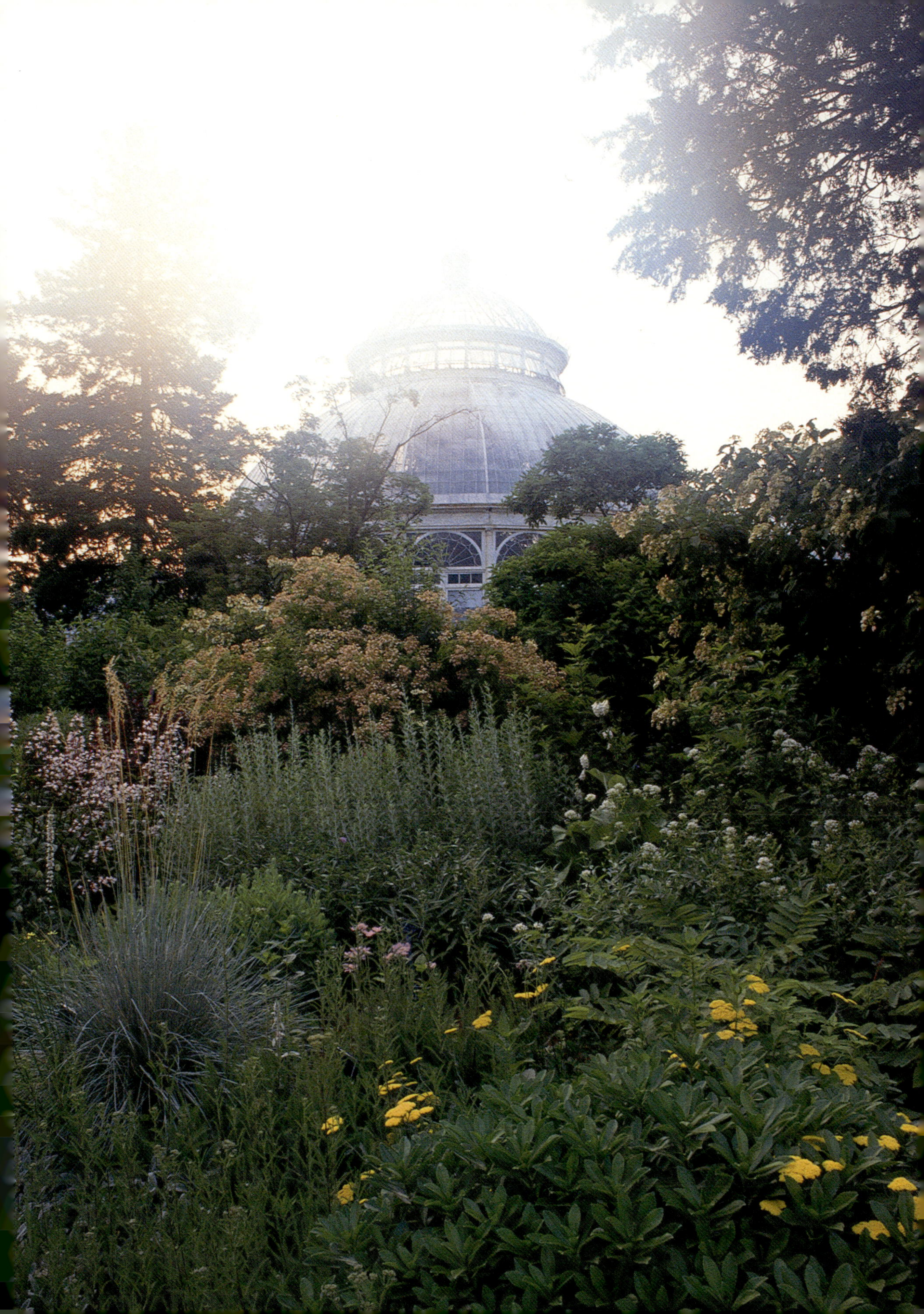

FLOWERS, VINES, PLANTS, AND TREES FOR THE WINDOW GARDEN OR CONSERVATORY

VINES: *Irish or German ivy, English ivy, cobaea, geranium, begonia, heliotrope, fuchsia, coleus, calla rose, rose*

HANGING BASKETS: *smilax, moneywort, saxifrage, Madeira vine, wandering Jew, trailing myrtle*

PLANTS FOR SMALL BRACKETS: *oxalis, Chinese primrose, musk plant, pocket flower*

WINTER BLOOMING: *ageratum, flowering begonias, geraniums, coleus, lantanas.*

GERANIUMS WITH FANCY FOLIAGE: *Happy Thought, Mrs. Pollack, Distinction, Cloth of Gold; in silver, Mountain of Snow, Italia Unita*

SUNNY WINDOWS: *geraniums, roses abutilon, lantanas, callas, fuchsias, begonias, ivies farfugium, Chinese primrose*

Wardian cases also were placed in an invalid's room to bring the joys of nature to the housebound. The slender Wardian case above houses a fern garden.

salt air and spray on ocean voyages. Invented in 1851 by Dr. Henry Chase Ward, it soon became a status indoor garden accessory like the attached conservatory, and one which helped promote the whole trend of parlor gardening by dispelling the widely believed theory that plants indoors emitted harmful gases. Mainly used for ferns and other nonflowering plants, the Wardian case was a special boon for city gardeners, protecting delicate plants from polluted urban air. It was particularly recommended for flower lovers who lived in smoky cities, and for helping to maintain a constant moisture level indoors.

Wardian cases were praised by many tastemakers, including the advice-giving Beecher sisters, who called them "the greatest and cheapest and most delightful fountain of beauty" imaginable and especially recommended them for housebound young mothers with small children. "The glass defends the plant from the inexpedient intermeddling of little fingers; while the little eyes, just on a level with the panes of glass, can look through and learn to enjoy the beautiful, silent miracles of nature," they said.

※ In 1869, Wardian cases could cost anywhere from $18 to $50, which meant they were primarily a luxury for the wealthy. This was especially true of those constructed on ornate black walnut stands and filled with expensive hothouse plants. But homemade versions could be constructed from common window glass mounted on a simple frame. The Beechers suggested such a home project, claiming that their version was not only large, cheap, and roomy but, when properly filled, could be even handsomer than the most elaborate store-bought variety. And, since common window sash and glass were no longer that expensive, any man with moderate ingenuity should to be able to construct such a glass closet for his wife—or a woman not having such a husband could even do it herself!

※ So widespread was the fad for Wardian cases that by 1882, mass-audience household guides like *The Household* offered pared-down instructions for making one's own: "A simple one may be made by taking five panes of glass of any size pleased; four to form the sides, one for the top; fasten the glass together with a light wooden frame; then take any tin dish, like a baking pan, or if round a tin plate or jelly cake pan, or a tin dish can be made to fit for a trifling sum of money; paint the tin green on the outside."

※ A Wardian case was the ideal receptacle for an indoor fern garden, one of the most important elements of parlor gardening. The Victorians adored ferns for their exotic and delicate beauty and, since they included them in nearly all their flower arrangements, it made economic sense to try to grow them at home. Women embellished their fern collections with shells, minerals, rocks, and fragments of broken mirror for the floors ("the effect of them will be magical," assured *The American Woman's Home*). In addition to ferns, Wardian cases everywhere were filled with mosses, tufts of a plant described as eye bright (not easily identifiable today), as well as violets, ground pine, princess pine, and wild anemones, all of which thrive in moist, shady places. Considered a necessity in the proper parlor, they were also regarded as a special comfort in an invalid's bedroom.

※ Thus, the passion for gardening which began in the late 1830s and '40s and took hold during the 1850s and '60s, virtually exploded during the last quarter of the century. The garden had become a room of its own, a well-loved place where husband and wife could sit in serenity and discuss the many burgeoning issues of their 19th-century lives. In barely the span of a generation, America had become a nation of eager gardeners.

By the end of the century, the garden had become a well-cherished "room of its own"—a place where husband and wife, above, *could bask in the serenity of nature, contemplating the issues of the day.*

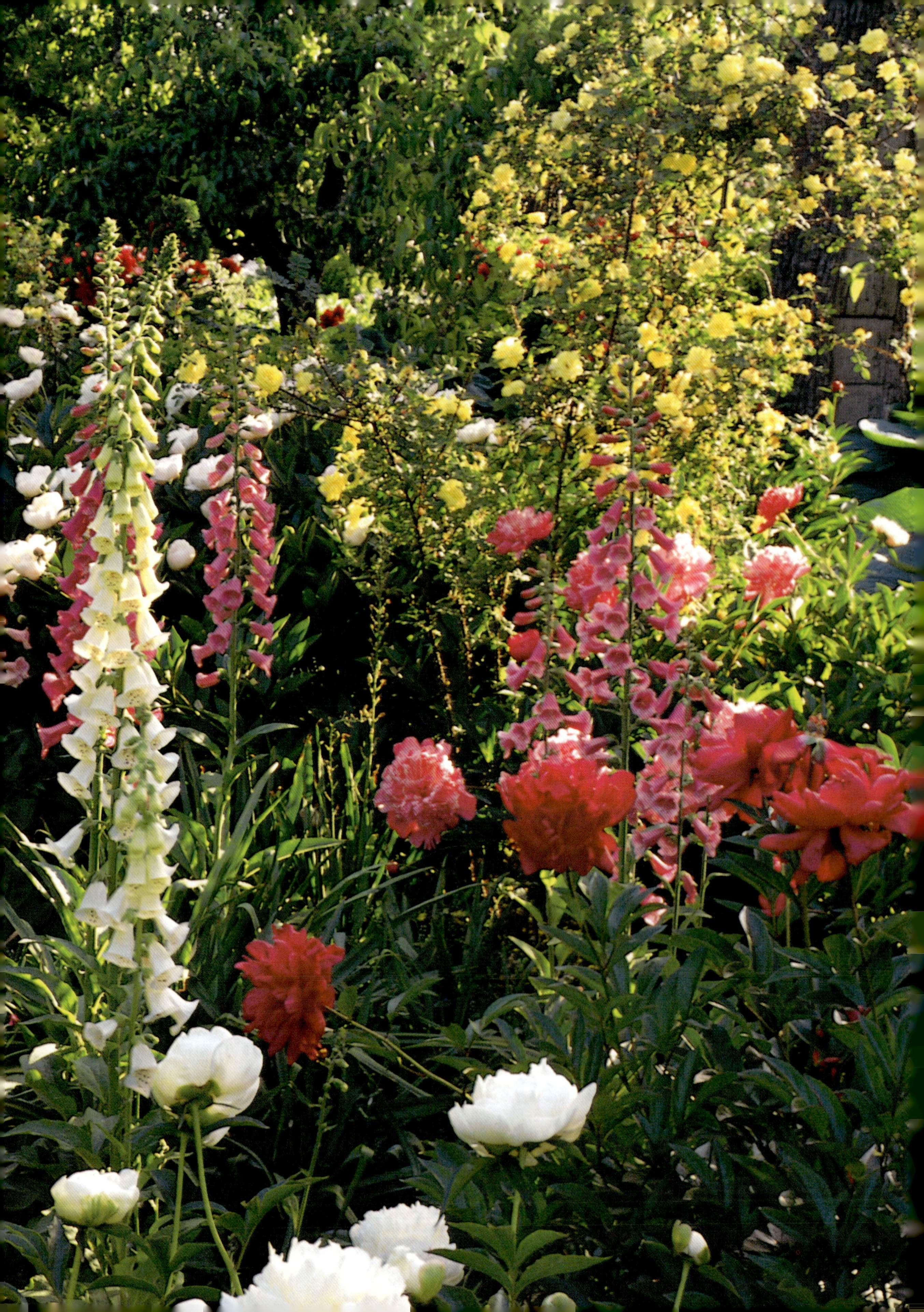

Beds, Borders, and Romanticism

BEING THE INFATUATION WITH THE CARPET BED, DEVELOPMENT OF THE BORDER, FLOWER FAVORITES, COLOR HARMONIES, ROSARIES, AND OTHER IMPORTANT THINGS

Two major gardening themes, beds and borders, defined the form and shape of Victorian gardens. Bedding was the keynote at the era's onset and during the high Victorian heyday; borders were a harbinger of its closing years. In the early Victorian decades, the typical garden retained many of the characteristics of its 18th-century precedent, particularly the European tradition of formal, geometrically shaped parterres separated by walkways or boxwood hedges and often

Geraniums, above, and petunias, below, planted in close, colorful masses, were key bedding-out flowers, dominating Victorian gardens from the 1840s onward.

enclosed by walls. Traditionally, these parterres, later called beds, were planted with a single variety of flower, usually in high-contrast shades in order to achieve the strongest delineation of design.

From the 1840s onward, bedding out, the close massing of large quantities of colorful annuals (plants that grow, blossom, and die in one season), dominated the look and defined the style of gardens everywhere—the primary way that flowers were incorporated into the landscape. Owners of great houses with great gardens created beds with plants raised in their own private greenhouses, while middle-class gardeners purchased their bedding plants. These, due to the development of the commercial greenhouses in the 1870s, were now raised in great quantities by nurserymen, and were sold cheaply by the thousands each spring to be planted after the last frost. Consequently, anyone interested in re-creating a 19th-century garden should be prepared to tackle bedding in some form or another.

SINGLE-SPECIES BEDS

In general, Victorian beds consisted of one single type and color of flowering annual. Spring bulbs, like tulips and hyacinths, were usually followed by what became the traditional trio of bedding-out favorites: scarlet geraniums, easily the most popular bedding plant, esteemed for its brilliant color but also because it grew so luxuriantly and with so little care; white, purple, and scarlet verbenas; and bright, almost electric-blue lobelias, a South African species which was often used for edgings. Other plants that went on to become bedding-out clichés were red salvia, actually an herb with rather fragrant, aromatic foliage, first available to gardeners in the 1840s; yellow-orange calceolarias; and pink, white, or purple petunias, which were introduced only in the later half of the century. Alyssum, white and yellow, is also frequently mentioned as a Victorian bedding favorite, when a low-growing edging plant was called for. Since so many common names for plants have changed, this is but one of the many instances that is confusing to modern gardeners. When white flowers were desired, the Victorians were probably referring to what we know as sweet alyssum or lobularia (also known as madwort). This is *Alyssum maritimum*, usually grown as an annual and a key bedding plant. The golden-yellow flowers the Victorians were most likely referring to are rock or golden alyssum, sometimes called basket-of-gold, a perennial that blooms in spring and early summer. Most garden dictionaries refer to this as *Alyssum saxatile* or *Aurinia saxatile*.

The key to understanding Victorian bedding out, particularly in early and mid-19th-century gardens, was the obsession with color. A show of fiery reds, glowing oranges, and brilliant yellows and blues was actually the garden's reason for being. In fact, the individual qualities of the plants themselves were considered insignificant compared to satisfying the Victorian appetite for color, so much so that any other planting possibilities were hardly considered. Instead, the merits of different color harmonies—what colors to plant next to what—were a subject for endless debate. For this reason, the plants used for bedding out were eventually limited to a handful of tried-and-true favorites capable of providing a rich and varied show of rainbow colorings.

The new and exciting fashion for bedding out caught on quickly, even though the enormous quantity of flowers necessary to achieve such tightly massed beds was a bit daunting. A smallish single bed could require as many as 30 plants; a large one—and this could be one of many such beds on a country estate—several hundred. When considering this prospect, even experienced gardeners should remember that many garden lovers of the 19th century, especially those who favored elaborate bedding-out schemes, employed a full-time gardening staff.

Above, *fuchsias and geraniums "drawn from nature" helped satisfy the Victorian appetite for rich, glowing color.*

Following pages: *Geraniums*, left, *made attractive beds for intricate designs*, right.

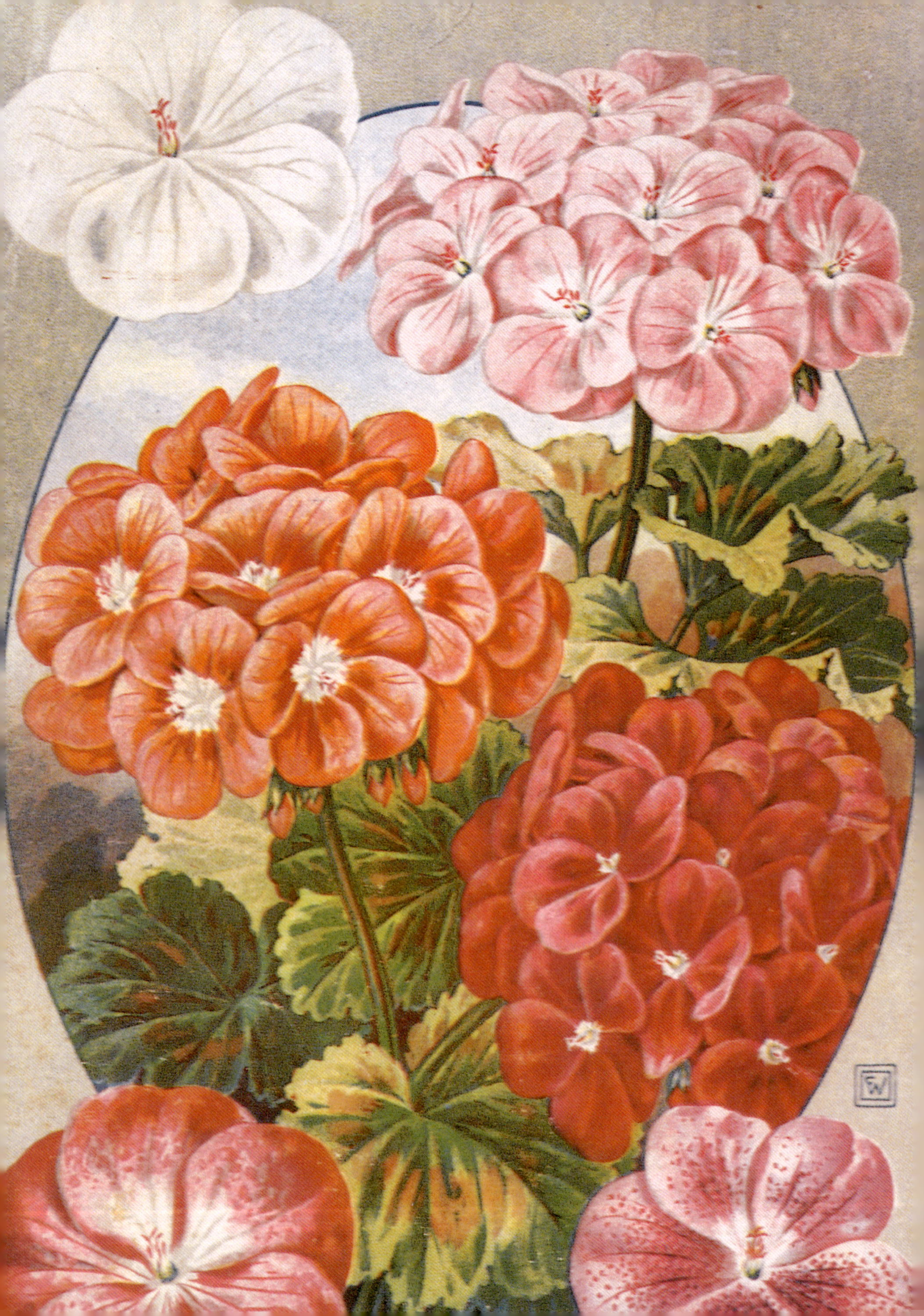

FLOWERS FOR 19TH-CENTURY BEDS

Geraniums   Verbenas   Calceolarias   Petunias   Salvia
Zinnias   Lobelias   Alyssum   Echeverias   Lantanas   Heliotrope   Coleus
Dahlias   Perilla   Ageratum   Cannas   Caladium

DESIGNS FOR FLOWER BEDS

1. Verbenas
2. Feverfew
3. Geraniums or Coleus
4. Strobilanthes
1 and 2. Echeverias
3. Alternanthera
4. Amaranthus Henderi

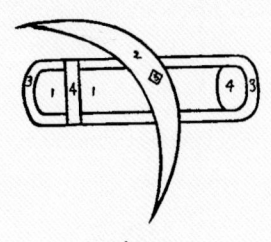

1. Lantana
2. Salvia
3. Centaurea
4. Heliotrope

1. Coleus
2. Achyranthus
3. Alternanthera
4. Heliotrope

1. Geraniums
2. Coleus
3. Centaurea
4. Alternanthera

TWO-COLOR SCHEMES FOR RIBBON BEDDING

DESIGN FOR A GEOMETRIC GARDEN, 1870

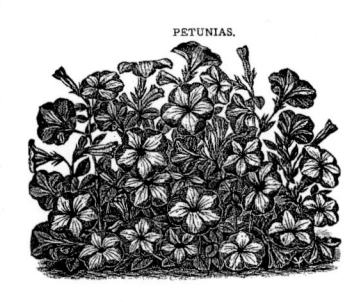

Bedding favorites included petunias like Howard's Star, about 1906, above. A petal-shaped bedding scheme offered blazing color, below.

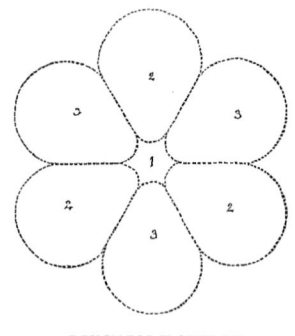

DESIGN FOR FLOWER BED
1. Coleus Verschaffeltii, Crimson
2. Geranium General Grant, or other Scarlet
3. Geranium Queen Olga, Pink

Single-species beds, which were always situated in bright sunlight, were generally shaped like chaste circles, ovals, or irregular forms, rarely squares or rectangles. They created vivid pockets of color when cut into the rolling lawns that were now possible because of the new mechanical mowing machines. Unlike the gardens of the first half of the century, these flower beds were not confined to any one area, and often were scattered around the property. It was considered particularly desirable, for example, to locate at least a few of them where they could be enjoyed from the windows of the house, particularly from the parlor and sitting room.

Some Victorian gardeners resisted the idea of planting a single species in a single color and compromised by growing a single variety in different shades. Other people clung to the tradition of the mixed or mingled flower beds of the past, which included perennials and biennials as well as annuals. But, acknowledging "more modern" tastes, they generally kept the mixture to just two or three different flowers. A. J. Downing was one tastemaker who straddled the line. He preferred single-species beds, arguing that mixed beds often became unsightly by midsummer; but in *Cottage Residences* (1842) he also admitted that an excellent effect could still be achieved with a mixed bed of ragged robin, Chinese pinks, larkspur, white hosta, Johnny-jump-ups, summer phlox, peonies, violets, and Madonna lily. Most arbiters of the new, dramatic single-species beds would have avoided such a look, which was scorned as "promiscuous" plantings, quite a damning judgment at the time.

Gardeners today can accommodate historic precedent by placing a tall, flower-filled urn or vase in the center of the bed and surrounding it with brightly colored bedding flowers. Such an effect was considered quite unusual and stimulating in the 1850s. In fact, the entire bedding style offered such advantages. Not only did the fashion for bedding present the opportunity to display one's innate taste in arranging colors, but the fact that such "attractive effects" as the use of a central fountain or urn could be produced without a great outlay of time or money was a tremendous inducement to middle-class gardeners.

In arranging their fashionable single-species beds, gardeners demanded not only maximum color but maximum color contrast. If, for example, one decided to plant verbenas, one of the most desirable flowers for bedding, bright golden coleus could be placed in an adjoining bed. Coleus, native to Africa, was introduced to the United States during the

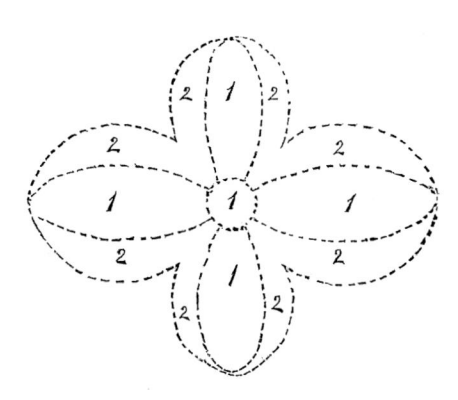

DESIGN FOR FLOWER BED
1. Crimson Coleus   2. Golden Coleus

second half of the 19th century. It was duly admired for its colorful, patterned leaves in shades somewhat more varied than those commonly seen today—greens, gold, bronze, pink, red, purple, yellow, and ivory. Today it is indispensable in a Victorian-style garden.

A bed of blue and white flowers was also considered attractive—not surprising in a society that revered the artistic quality of blue-and-white porcelain above all others. This could have been carried out with such low-growing plants as blue lobelia, surrounded by white sweet alyssum. Double forms of alyssum are now available, but the old-fashioned single is considered more beautiful—and is certainly more authentic.

By the 1870s, beds shaped like simple circles and pinwheels no longer sufficed, and those who wanted to keep up with fashion began to favor ovals, eggs, hearts, circles, four-leaf clovers, and triangles. Three feet square was the size recommended for a small bed of choice bulbs and small annuals, but large oblong beds that were four or five feet broad and 10 or 15 feet long were also planted. These had the merit of affording considerable border room for long, unbroken lines of petunias, pinks, and other small plants that the Victorians liked.

Leaf-shaped beds—common ivy leaf, oak leaf, heart-shaped ivy, horseshoe geranium—are yet another intriguing and traditional variation to consider. "Some of the prettiest beds for lawns may be made by cutting them out into the natural form of trees, shrubs and plants," explained *Beeton's New All About Gardening*. These beds purportedly had the advantage that they could be called by the name of the different trees, shrubs, and plants from which their shape was taken.

RIBBON BEDDING

During the 1870s, yet another variation, that of ribbon bedding, evolved. This practice involved the usual bedding flowers, now planted in strips or "ribbons" of contrasting color. Ribbons of flowers were divided by ribbons of foliage plants. Especially traditional would have been any of the varieties of coleus previously mentioned, or succulents like carpet echeveria or lavender-cotton, which were clipped low and used as an edging.

A single-species flower bed offered variety through color contrast, above left. Salvia splendens was another key bedding flower, notable for its deep, rich scarlet blossoms, above. "Give salvias a trial this year and if they do not surprise and satisfy you, write us and we will take back all the good things we say about them," a seed catalog promised.

Flowering 'New Century' caladium, about 1900, above, with its huge leaves and impressive coloration, was a summer bedding plant. Victorian carpet bedding blooms in a giant fleur-de-lis tapestry, opposite, at the Sonnenberg Gardens in Canandaigua, New York.

As with simple single-species beds, special care should be taken by today's gardeners to arrange colors in the ribbon bed for the most vivid contrast: orange and purple or scarlet and white, for instance, were both combinations the Victorians preferred—never blue and purple, a far too subtle effect. Rows of red alternating with rows of white were also popular. One vintage plant guide suggests planting a circular ribbon bed with a central white foliage plant (gardeners today might try artemisia, whose leaves have a silvery-white hue). This was followed by the familiar circles of yellow, red, then blue flowers. For gardeners who admire dahlias, which were among the most fashionable flowers in England in the first quarter of the 19th century, a traditional and attractive scheme is to plant dahlias at the back of the bed, then a line of perilla (a dark-foliage plant at least 18 inches high; it often grows much taller than that), next a row of scarlet geraniums, followed by a line of yellow-foliage plants, a row of white geraniums, and an outside edging of verbenas. The dahlia gained the reputation among some Victorian garden writers as strictly a florist's flower because of its "coarse foliage, gaudy flower and lack of perfume." Although it boasted perfect symmetry and geometrically arranged petals, it was said to be a queen in the garden but of little use elsewhere.

Easy to lay out and keep orderly, circular ribbon bedding became immensely popular, particularly for smallish gardens. As 19th-century gardeners became more adept at the style, the merits of each color variation were discussed in gardening journals of the day. Of all the patterns put forth, again and again, simple combinations of red, yellow, and blue, often with white accents, appealed most strongly to contemporary tastes and soon became the standard. Red salvia, for example, surrounded by a ribbon of porcelain-blue ageratum and then white sweet alyssum, giving the effect of a colorful—and patriotic—bull's-eye, is one simple and authentic treatment to duplicate today. For gardeners who prefer a more dramatic look, the combination of broad-leafed yellow cannas, surrounded by tall red cockscomb, then chartreuse coleus, is also authentic. A colonial-era flower, cockscomb, with its thick, crimped velvety texture and rich coloring, appealed strongly to high Victorian taste. Intricately fashioned, it seemed to resemble the overstuffed, tufted Turkish upholstery so popular in the parlors of the time.

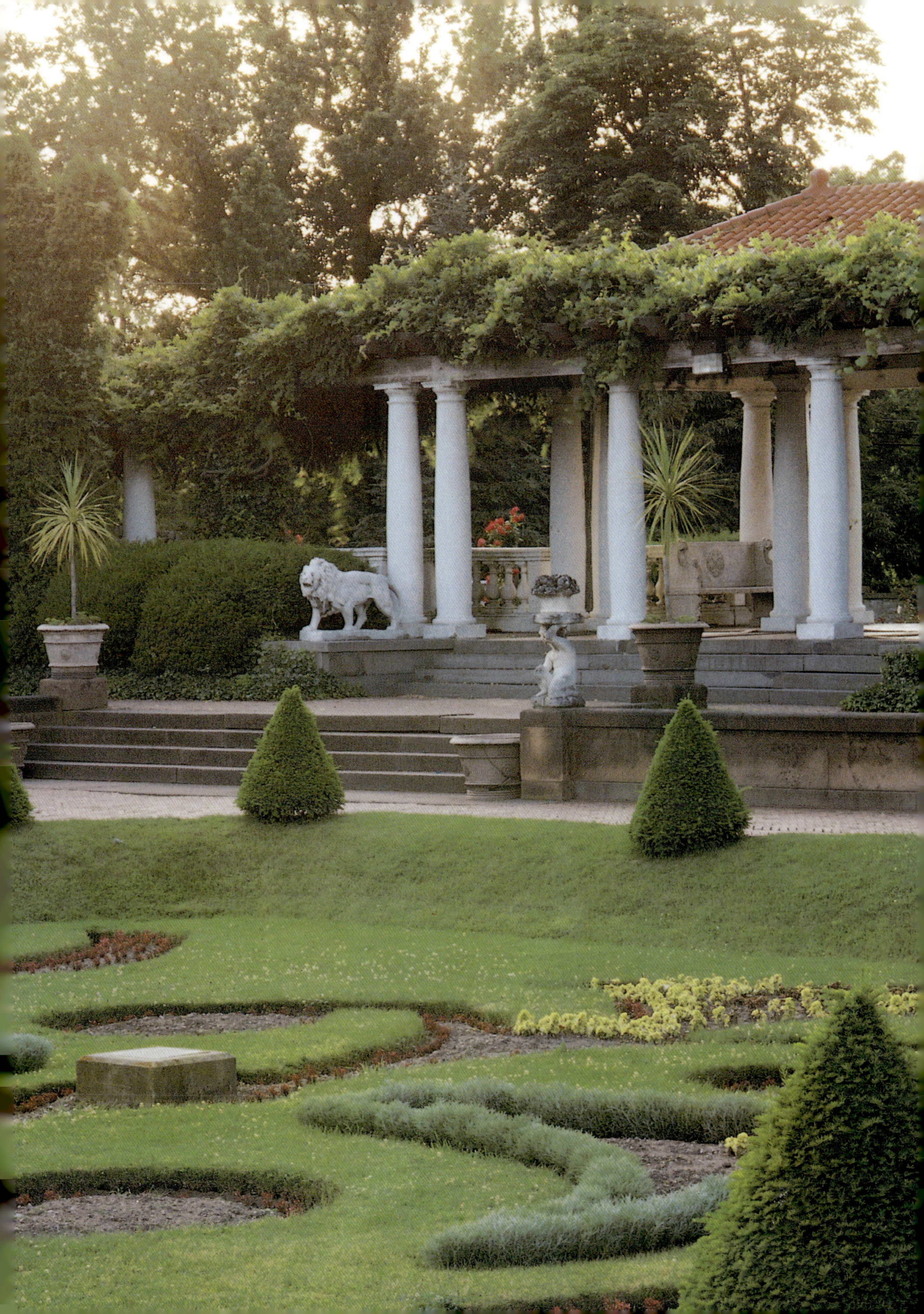

The modern example of a classic bed, above, shows the Victorian love of majestic expanses of color. Another bed design, below, plays cool colors against hot ones.

DESIGN FOR FLOWER BED
1. Alternanthera paronychioides major (Rainbow Plant)
2. Alternanthera aurea nana
3. Dwarf Scarlet Tropæolum
4. Blue Lobelia

Another exotic variation for a circular bed that gardeners can try was suggested by *Vick's Illustrated Monthly* in 1878. This bed began with towering castor-bean plants, an exotic African plant with coppery green leaves that frequently formed the massive centerpiece in display beds of annuals. It was ringed by cannas, caladium (elephant ears), coleus, and finally with the lacy, silver-gray foliage of dusty miller. Caladium, a tropical plant popular during the later 19th century, was admired by the Victorians for its spectacular, richly variegated leaves of white, green, red, and pink, though not for its blossoms, which tended to be small and rather insignificant.

Evolving Color Harmonies

Not coincidentally, the taste for strong colors in mid-century Victorian gardens evolved at the same time that bold, almost eye-shatteringly violent tones suddenly became available in upholstery and drapery textiles, the result of the development of aniline dyes in 1856. The Victorians found these new shocking colors absolutely enchanting in their homes and, not surprisingly, chose to replicate their impact in their gardens. With blissful complacency they carried out their mission, blithely positioning pink and purple petunias and ruby-red geraniums side by side, a habit that horrified later generations of gardeners.

This is not to say that there were no pastel gardens. Harriet Beecher Stowe was one early advocate of gentler shades; her Hartford, Connecticut, garden, filled with sweet peas, mignonette, and sunflowers, featured a rather painterly palette of blues, pale yellow, violet, and other pastel tones. Stowe, though, was the exception, not the rule.

In the later decades, although bright garden colors continued to prevail, some forward-looking gardeners began to find them harsh. Newer shades, such as cloudlike pinks, lavenders, and creamy roses, seemed softer and more harmonious. In 1901, Hildegarde Hawthorne was one garden expert who praised the "heavenly harmony of blue" in the garden as opposed to "screaming yellows."

Toward the end of the century, as gardeners began to reject these conceits in favor of traditional English garden styles, it became accepted to deride the love of crimson and scarlet as "vulgar"—perhaps the ultimate 19th-century smear. The tide had turned when even fairly traditional garden guides conceded that a sizable bed of vivid verbenas, rather than charm, would offend viewers by its "excessive glare." By 1911, gardener Alice Earle confessed that "it has been the custom of late to sneer at crimson in the garden, especially if its vivid color gets a dash of purple and becomes what Miss Jekyll [English garden authority Gertrude Jekyll] calls malignant magenta. It is really more vulgar than malignant, and has come to be in textile products a stamp and symbol of vulgarity, through the forceful brilliancy of our modern aniline dyes." Fifty years earlier, of course, no one had been the least horrified by the idea of "magenta" flowers. To the contrary—they were considered cheerful, modern, and bold.

The following tips on color and contrast in the garden, based on the advice and taste that guided gardeners in the last quarter of the 19th century, should help modern-day gardeners in their Victorian color plans.

— Cool colors, like gray, lilac, yellow, blue, or green, are best for gardens laid out on gravel—which is usually, though not always, itself a warm color. Warm colors, like pink, purple, scarlet, or orange, are best for gardens laid out on grass—which is usually a cold color. White is suitable for gardens of either description.

— The most intense colors should be placed in the center of beds, graduating to lesser tints for contrasting rings or edgings.

— The smaller the bed, the more freely intense colors, such as scarlet, may be used.

— Cool colors and neutrals—that is, mixed hues or plants whose colors are subdued—may be used to soften and tone down the influence of very brilliant tints.

Carpet Bedding

Carpet bedding, the third form of Victorian bedding and the culmination of the bedding-out craze, was something else again. Although today the term is often used to describe the fashion for bedding as a whole, originally it referred to a separate and specific style, far more elaborate and complex than the simple bedding-out schemes, ribbon or otherwise, to which the Victorians had become accustomed. Carpet bedding was the consummate horticultural expression of a society in love with flamboyant effects, at the same time that it cultivated a rigid decorum of etiquette and manners—points of view that may be difficult to

---

INDISCRIMINATE LIGHT AND DARK COLOR ARRANGEMENT

Dark blue, scarlet, green, buff, violet, green, pea green

❧

Black, dark green, scarlet, blue, scarlet, violet, orange

❧

Cool green, brown, salmon, pea green, blue, black

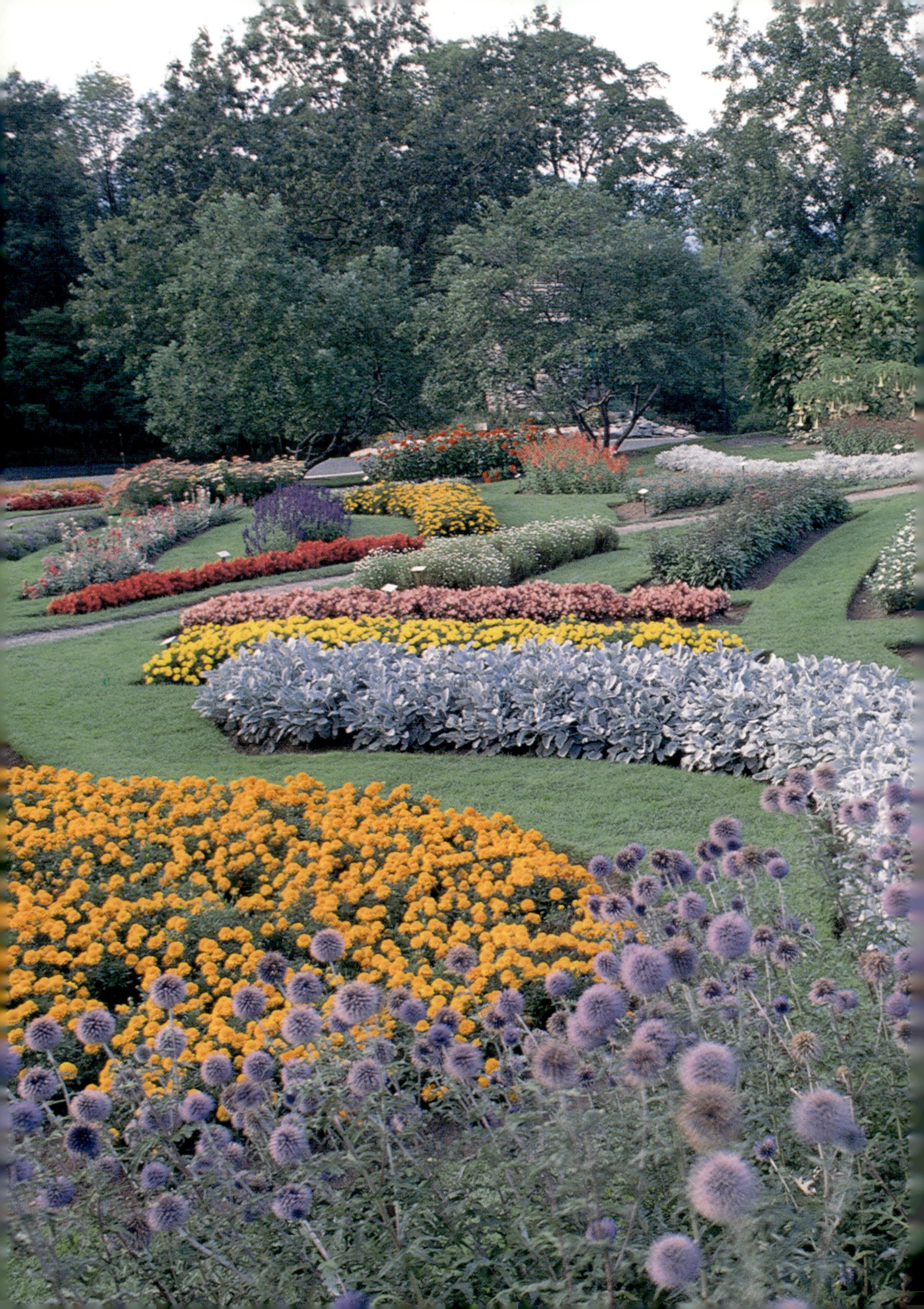

DARK AND BRILLIANT COLOR ARRANGEMENT WITH REGULAR INTERVALS, HARMONIOUS CONTRASTS

Dark blue, orange, sapphire blue, black, green, dark brown, scarlet

❧

Pea green, violet, salmon, black, pea green, scarlet, dark green

❧

Buff, violet, green, scarlet, dark blue

Below, *This intricate 1842 design specifies colors rather than specific flowers. The central beds (l, m, n, o, and p) were filled with masses of bright color; i indicates the placement of vases. The interlacing beds (d) called for contrasting colors such as yellow and purple or blue and white. The running guilloche beds (which form the boundary) required low-growing flowers, with the center circle (c) in white, then alternating white with brights—dark red, blue, yellow, and purple.*

Preceding pages: *Carpet bedding was styled to feature colorful patterns and designs.*

reconcile in the same character. As with the formal parterre, carpet bedding required separate beds filled with a single color of a single flower in order to achieve its desired effect.

As with single-species beds, the best carpet-bedding plants are low and have a long flowering season—from May through the end of the summer. Despite the fact that carpet-bed designs were originally meant to be executed only with subtly colored foliage plants in rich, contrasting shades of green and varied in texture (some of these, such as green-and-white variegated leaf plants, would be ideal today when creating a shady bed), invariably the most popular bedding flowers turned out to be vibrant ones. As with bedding out in general, the most admired color scheme eventually became primary bright red and blue, with golden yellow for the ribbon borders. Gardeners today can select from all the classic bedding flowers, varying them with nasturtiums, petunias, alyssum, dahlias, and assorted foliage plants.

Each immaculately manicured carpet bed was crammed with tightly planted annuals, all rigorously cultivated and trimmed to maintain the same general height and size. These were then shaped into calculatedly artificial patterns. Because the plants were kept low—dwarf varieties were preferred—and tended toward uniformity in texture and design, these stylized beds came to resemble the intricate designs of Victorian carpets, embroidery, and needlepoint—hence their name. A short-lived variation on carpet bedding was called "scrollwork," which referred to a bed in which the design resembled the scrollwork motifs common in Victorian wallpaper.

Unlike the parterre, which would have been surrounded by prim, graveled walkways, boxwood hedges, or walls, carpet beds were always surrounded by lawn, a feature the Victorians felt offered the best contrast, as well as being stylishly up-to-date and more soothing to the eye. To further define their shape, carpet beds were outlined by narrow, contrasting ribbon borders. Keep in mind that during the 1860s and '70s it was also common practice to plant charming little ribbon borders alongside walkways and paths and around shrubbery, as well as to provide a pretty fringe of color around small evergreen trees.

Gardeners today might try a thin border of marigolds—a historically correct accent to a carpet bed of geraniums or lobelias. Outlining carpet beds with a thick border of acorns, with hollies (which would have been raised on a seedbed and then transplanted), or with terra-cotta brick tiles were also traditional treatments. Clay tiles were popular in England and in the southern parts of the United States—one can still see them today in the gardens of Charleston and Galveston. Tiles such as these were used for decoration rather than retaining soil. Varying in size from about the size of a standard brick and going up to 8 inches by 8 inches and 1½ to 2 inches thick, they can still be purchased through many mail-order garden catalogs.

In positioning tiles, gardeners usually placed them upright, embedded four to six inches in the ground, with the earth and the beds then raised to the level of the visible part. A typical pattern would have consisted of brick borders placed between alternating rows of calceolarias, lobelias, and geraniums. Such a treatment had the advantage of remaining attractive even in winter because of the appealing contrast between the bright red tiles and the green grass.

Whatever was chosen, however, a border of some kind was key, not only for beds but also for walkways and paths. Otherwise, to Victorian eyes the garden appeared unfinished—as did drapery and upholstery indoors without their all-important braids, fringe, and trim. In fact, without its beds and walks precisely outlined by some kind of border, the garden was said to lack the finishing touch essential to any work of art. "Hang your picture, without its frame, against the wall and note how unfinished it appears," compared *The Mayflower*. "Then frame it and try the effect again. Compare the garden where each bed is bordered, with one in which no such rule is observed, and, at a glance, the effectiveness of the border will strike you."

While the original French parterre gardens were formal and geometric, carpet-bed designs were wildly idiosyncratic, richly curved, and emotionally frenzied. Ambitious gardeners manipulated their carpet beds into all sorts of strange serpentine forms and floral whimsies—birds, butterflies, animals, fish, and abstract embroidery-like patterns with complex curls and intricate scrolling. Then as now, the more involved the pattern and the greater the variety of the plantings used, the higher the risk of a blurred or muddled design.

Carpet bedding became most closely identified with 19th-century parks, railroad stations, cemeteries, and other public grounds as well as with large-scale stylish country estates. There, carpet beds cultivated in elaborate patterns like clocks, flags, medallions, monograms, and even such icons as the Liberty Bell teetered closely to the absurd. Today, similar extravaganzas can be seen in some public locations, such as Florida's Walt Disney World; New York's Mohonk Mountain House, a country resort

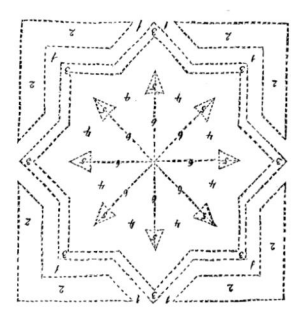

DESIGN FOR FLOWER BED
1. Grass
2. Blue Lobelia
3. Dwarf Scarlet Tropæolum
4. Grass
5. Alternanthera paronychioides (Rainbow Plant), Crimson
6. Alternanthera aurea nana, Yellow

The plants chosen for carpet-bed designs like the geometric square, above, and floral pattern, below, from Gardening for Pleasure *(1887) were said to be largely a matter of taste, though it was emphasized that the most sharply contrasting colors created the most striking effects.*

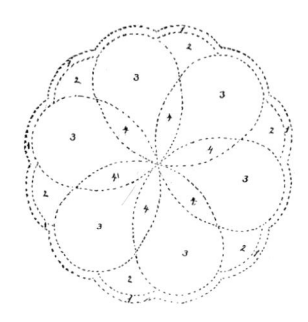

DESIGN FOR FLOWER BED
1. Coleus Golden Bedder
2. Geranium General Grant, or other Scarlet
3. Coleus Verschaffeltii, Crimson
4. Dracæna indivisa

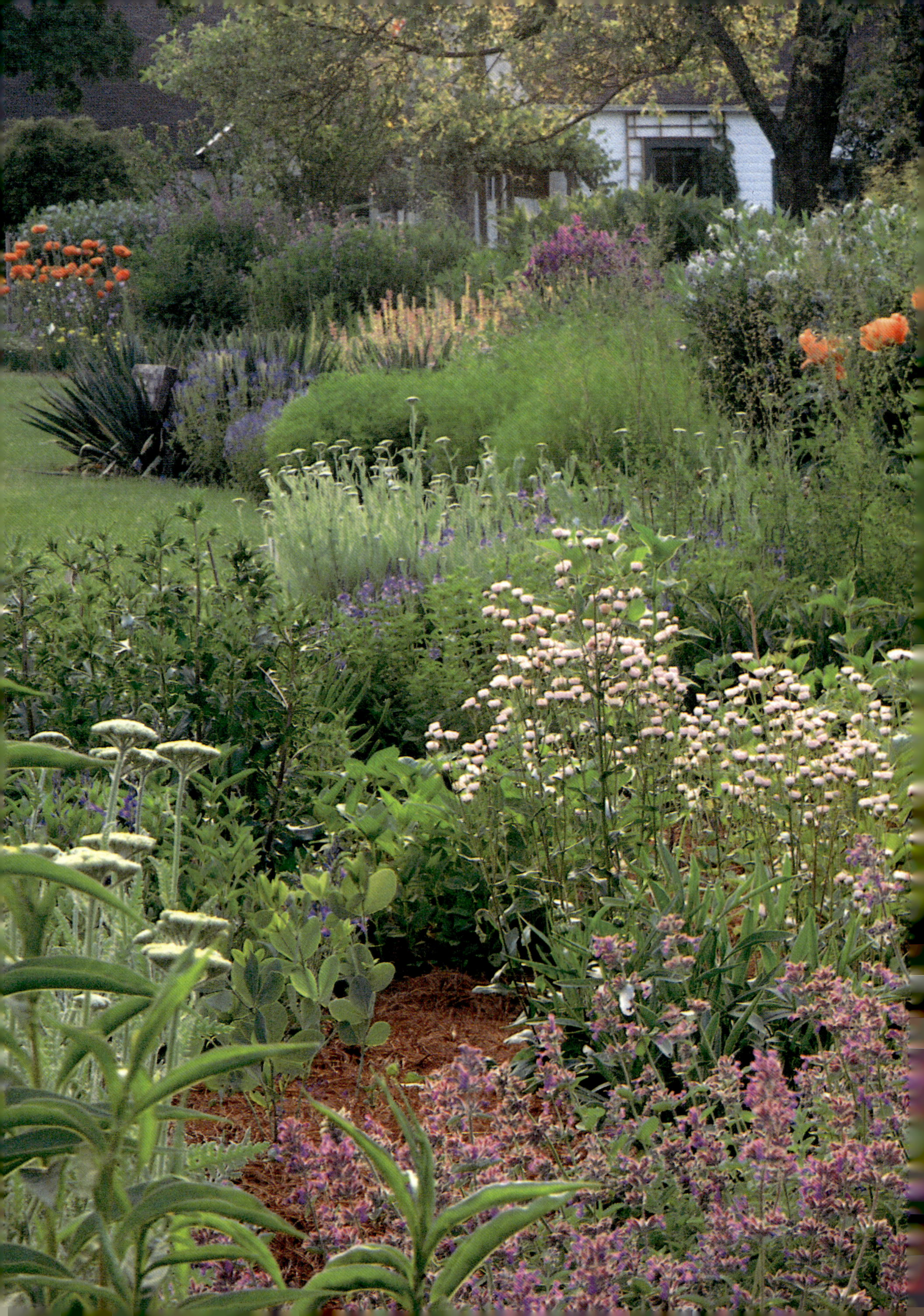

known for its 19th-century gardens; and the Sonnenberg Gardens. But middle-class Victorian homeowners and cottage dwellers fancied the challenge of the carpet bed also, and from instructions in their garden books created smaller, simplified carpet-bed designs, many of which can be reproduced today. Many a proper small Victorian lawn was spotted here and there with charming little flower beds that were shaped like stars, triangles, or fleurs-de-lis.

Bedding out in general and carpet bedding in particular had a quaint, unself-conscious charm that suited the Victorian age to a T. It became so highly regarded not only because it was undeniably ornamental but also because it required constant tending and clipping—and in a large garden, often hundreds of plants—making it time consuming, difficult to maintain and costly to achieve. Done successfully, therefore, it was a telling statement. Even as late as the 1890s, when the cachet of the style was clearly fading—and more sophisticated garden writers were scoffing at the preponderance of beds shaped like sausages, leeches, and commas—diehard supporters were still pondering the merits of effective schemes, and some of the most expansive schemes in the United States were done.

Various sorts of crosses, for example, were still regarded as "very ornamental"—which of course was highest praise at the time. A Maltese-cross bed, each arm filled in with different shades of verbenas, was suggested by one garden guide. In 1898 *The Mayflower* related the story of a man noted for the odd but creative designs of his gardens: "His place is large, and it is good for the nerves and digestion to study out his curious ideas. In one place he has the sun, moon and stars. Another shows a staircase, with the richest of Coleus carpets, and surmounted on the top landing by a giant Palm. On his grassplot is a watering pot, with sprinkler, and handle, made of Echevarias [sic]. And among the shrubbery is a floral cow, horns and all."

But styles moved on. Charming and aggressively new in the 1850s, immensely popular in the 1860s and '70s, and still prevalent in the '80s, bedding out soon became ubiquitous and conventional—clear signals of a shift in fashionable taste. The celebration of color, so novel and exhilarating in the early and mid-Victorian years, was now decried as garish and even overstimulating; there were elements in a garden other than mere color to consider, scolded the tastemakers.

Beds also languished because they were difficult and expensive to attend, particularly as inexpensive labor became scarcer. Soon they were further criticized as stiff and artificial,

A GEOMETRIC FLOWER GARDEN
A. Terrace of the house
B. Garden walk
C. (center) Fountain or statue
D. Surface beds of low, massed flowers
E. Fountains or statues
F. Vases, pedestals or orange trees in tubs

DESIGN FOR FLOWER BED
1. Vase
2. Coleus Bacon
3. Coleus South Park Gem
4. Achyranthes metallica
5. Coleus Mary Stewart
3. Geranium Wonderful
7. Geranium Madame Thebaud
8. Geranium Mountain of Snow
9. Gnaphalium lanatum
10. Coleus Verschaffeltii

Intricate and artificial bedding schemes like these, above, *eventually gave way to the fashion for borders,* opposite. *This long border in the studio garden of Daniel Chester French at Chesterwood in Stockbridge, Massachusetts, was laid out at the turn of the century and includes tall white hollyhock (back), low yellow coreopsis (center), and spiky red atilbe in the front.*

The challenge of creating borders (above, at Chesterwood) excited 19th-century gardeners who were bored with bedding-out schemes.

especially in light of the encroaching taste for more natural gardening. In addition, there was the undeniable fact that though they glowed with color for four months a year, for the remaining eight months they sat brown and fallow. Some gardeners, particularly in England, attempted to remedy this eyesore by creating winter gardens, filling in the beds with temporary evergreens, ivy, and other hardy shrubbery that could survive twice yearly replantings. Others crafted clever designs with colored earth, crushed bricks, gravel, shells, and pebbles. But for the most part, the bed was a three- to four-month phenomenon.

As the tyranny of bedding began to slip from its pedestal in the forefront of good taste, the scions of other upstart styles began to eye its crown. Taste was all—a tactic of social intimidation exercised by the tastemakers on the new, largely insecure aspiring society. Of course the fact that beds of red (geraniums) and blue (lobelias) bordered with golden yellow (*Alyssum saxatile*) had long since become a mid-Victorian cliché made no difference to the vast majority of middle-class growers. They liked this cheery combination and used it again and again. But as bedding-out schemes came under attack, it was supplanted by a revival of interest in perennial flowers planted in herbaceous borders.

Victorian Border Schemes

Largely forgotten in the rush of excitement over the dazzling color possibilities of the bedding system, the quiet grace of perennial borders, with their haze of softer, harmonious colors—not to mention their pleasant habit of reappearing for years on end—began to be extolled. Although the switch to borders took place in England as early as the 1870s, the style did not overtake American gardens until the turn of the century. Mixed borders of hardy perennials like delphinium and phlox, supplemented as needed by colorful annuals such as dahlias and gladiolus had, of course, coexisted with bedding out; they were simply eclipsed by the rage for beds. Other perennials had long been relegated to the confines of the cutting garden, where they supplied flowers for the house and table but were not required to put on a show of their own.

But suddenly borders seemed to offer the late Victorians rich diversity and a refreshing burst of informality—both welcome changes from the now stifling monotony of bedding. Unlike the inexhaustible annuals, perennials bloomed for just a few weeks each season, challenging the gardener to create a carefully planned scheme for successive bloom. And borders engaged the eye with their variety, whereas bedding out suited only a limited variety of plants. Now there could be many different kinds of flowers, in many fascinating shades: exciting new blooms as well as old-fashioned plantings long abandoned from Victorian garden schemes, and all in varying heights and sizes, could now be grown. Tall spires of hollyhock and foxglove, both of which had been grown in American gardens since the 1600s and then forgotten by the mid-19th century, now lined the back balconies of the border. Dahlias, a pet flower of the early 19th century, were often planted in front of them to camouflage their stalks, while successively smaller plantings of peonies, lavender, rosemary, and fuchsia might crowd the orchestra.

Unlike beds, borders did not abruptly interrupt the lawn, a practice that was losing favor as the popularity of lawn sports like croquet continued to grow. Instead, they drifted along the exterior walls of the home, silhouetted against stone walls, fences, hedges, or other property enclosures. Pathway borders were necessarily narrow, but when feasible, long, deep borders, often as deep as 12 feet on a grand estate or more commonly five to six feet on a smaller property, were admired.

Borders present different challenges to those creating period gardens today. Height and time of flowering have to be considered, instead of mere color. The object is to have an equal number of plants in flower in each of the "floral months" with colors in "agreeable contrast."

In a typical border, flowers should be arranged to bank from front to back. In England, small flowers like pansies, English daisies (Belis sp., not the Shasta daisy of American gardens), and aromatic primroses might line the front of the border; in America, coral bells and Carpathian harebell could be typical. Behind those, the Victorians

---

FLOWERS FOR LATE-CENTURY BORDERS

Pinks   Carnations   Stock

Gillyflowers   Wallflowers   Hyacinths

Heliotropes   Tulips   Peonies

Phloxes   Asters   Monardas   Delphiniums

Gentians   Aquilegias

Camassias   Lychnises   Gnaphaliums

Penstemons

Borders provided a refreshing burst of informality to the garden, right, where tall border plants in soft gentle shades waved in the breeze.

tended to favor spicy-scented pinks like sweet William, and carnations and veronicas. Next came phloxes in colors that ranged from snowy white to deep purple, where winters are mild—no frost till after Thanksgiving. (This would be Drummond phlox, an annual, not garden phlox, a tall perennial.) Phlox could also be used for ribbon borders and bedding around statues and fountains. Then chrysanthemums, an autumn flower and a special prize of the Victorian garden, would be planted. These were first brought to England from China in the 1840s but not introduced in the United States until the later part of the century.

Various sorts of campanulas, in particular romantic-looking Canterbury bells, were also welcome in borders. Indeed, their soft colors—pinks and blues—and romantic bell-like shape made them a Victorian favorite in annual beds and perennial borders alike. Still other border flowers included summer bulbs such as gladiolus and irises, which were both used in colonial gardens before the 1700s. Finally, at the back of the border, one planted the tallest flowers, like hollyhock, foxglove, purple coneflower (*Rudbeckia purpurea*), and especially stately delphinium, whose spikes of blue created a rich background for all the lower-growing flowers.

Despite all this floral richness, some Victorians were loath to give up their former bedding favorites. "The general revision of feelings against 'bedding out' has extended to the poor plants thus misused, which is unjust," defended a sympathetic Alice Morse Earle at the turn of the century. Although she too was bored with, and spoke spitefully against, ubiquitous coleus, lobelia, and calceolaria, she made exception for the humble geranium. "I love its clean color, in head and blossom; its clean fragrance; its clean beauty; its healthy growth. It is a plant I like to have near me."

Others also praised the mid-Victorian favorite. "I hope all readers of *The Mayflower* have not become so aristocratic in growing Roses and the more difficult plants as to leave Geraniums off their lists," wrote "Cousin Delight" of Massachusetts. "For the Geranium is a good, wholesome plant, honest and sensible; it has a well-to-do look one often misses in greenhouse pets, or that fad which every one runs after and praises—a novelty. Like a stiff north wind or a bracing day in winter we need geraniums among our plants. To bed out in summer and place in the window garden in winter what is better? How they brighten and cheer up the house plants toward spring with their strong and high-colored blooms!"

But gardens *had* begun to look alike. Where were the sweetly scented old-fashioned flowers that people remembered from grandmother's day? Such flowers, they had been told, could not be grown in "today's gardens." Whereas in borders they could.

THE COTTAGE STYLE

In the final decades of the 19th century, a major influence in the revival of perennial borders was the sentimental wave of nostalgia for gardens that suggested, in perception if not in reality, the early years of the century.

In their reaction against bedding out, some Victorians attempted romanticized colonial garden schemes, with clipped hedges of boxwood or yew and mixed beds of traditional flowers, whose formality now seemed quaint and charming. But many more turned to the informal aspects of the early English cottage garden. These rural gardens, whose traditional, seemingly untended, herbaceous blooms tumbled every which way, plants spilling over paths, climbers festooning the porch, picturesque tangles of roses and honeysuckle everywhere, seemed the very expression of natural gardening.

From the sooty vantage point of the Industrial Revolution, looking back to these idealized rural gardens of the preindustrial past was a revelation. In them, the Victorians, many of whom were now city dwellers or suburbanites, saw a lost innocence, a pastoral charm that they yearned to recapture. Cottage gardens seemed enchantingly simple, their colors soothing rather than stirring, their only structure a hedge, a picket fence, a tumbledown stone wall, along which randomly planted borders of blooms and vines grew in seductive confusion.

The dainty English cottage, above, designed by Andrew Jackson Downing (which cost $830 to build in 1842 and $1600 in 1873) exemplified the nostalgic style with ornamental vines and other climbing plants such as Virginia creeper, honeysuckle, and white climbing roses.

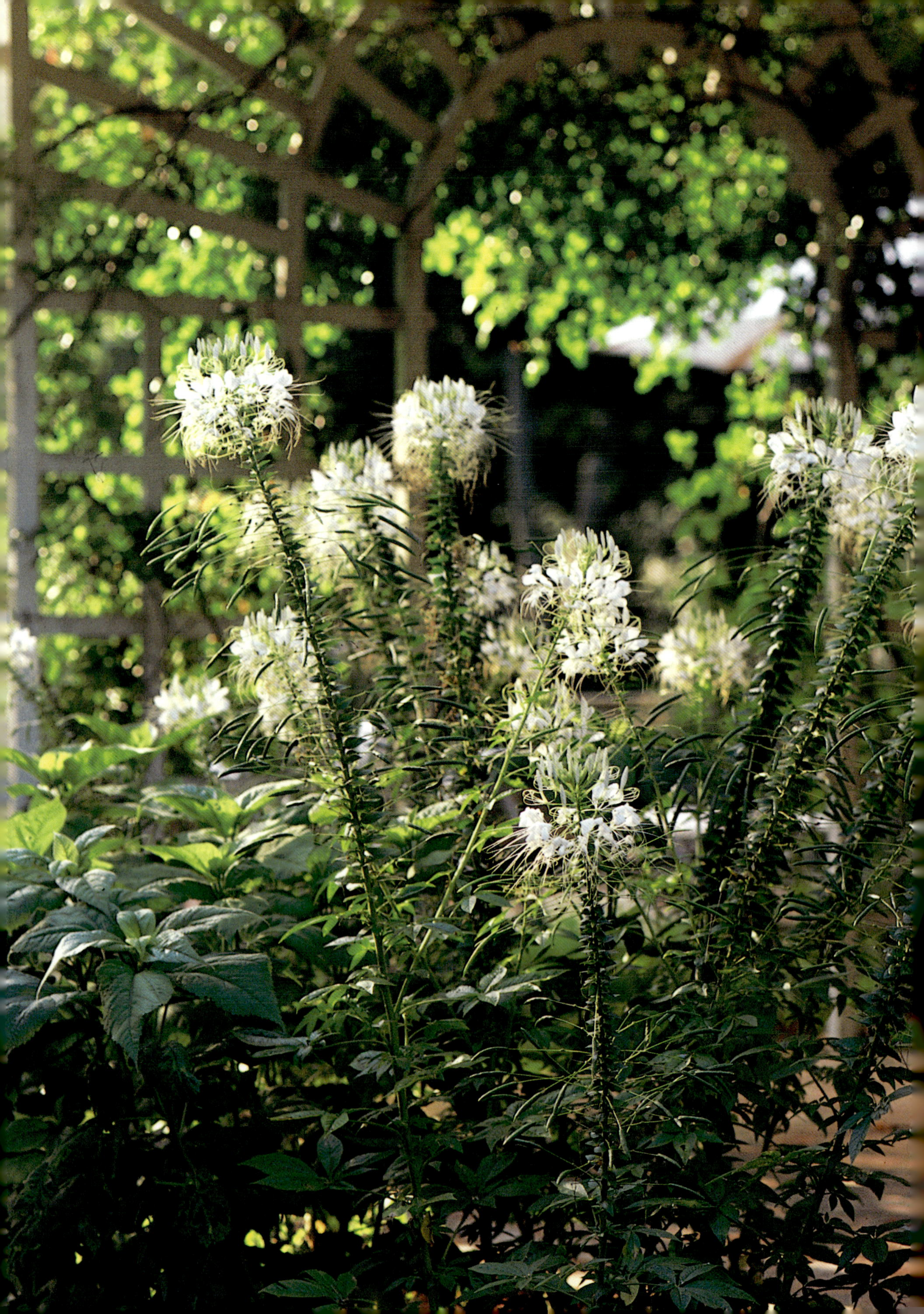

Of course the romantically untidy cottage gardens for which the 19th-century Americans longed, while popular in England, were little more than a fantasy. Actual cottage gardens of the past were far more prosaic, modestly planted with a practical mixture of vegetables, useful flowers, and herbs like lavender, sage, and foxglove. Beginning in the 1870s, however, nostalgia for sentimentalized cottage gardens that never really existed helped reintroduce late Victorians to the charms of the herbaceous border.

In principle, the flowers of the cottage garden were meant to be arranged informally and naturally, in the "sweet disorder" that was just starting to become pleasing to the eye. In actuality, such an achievement was due more to art than nature: it was hard to avoid plantings arranged in stiff and soldierly lines. And one had to take into consideration not just color harmonies but overlapping flowering seasons and the juxtaposition of differing heights, shapes, and even types of foliage. Soon the Victorians found that rural simplicity took more than dewy sentiment; to be done well, it required skill and a keen artistic eye.

But never ones to leave well enough alone, the Victorians just could not help embellishing the traditional cottage style. After all, they had been nurtured on the more conspicuous glories of bedding out. So they added new hybrids and even exotics to the genteel old-fashioned garden medley, further piling on "old" wooden garden benches and timeworn stone birdbaths and sundials—all allusions to bygone days. The resulting garden became a complex, more *Victorian* version of the traditional cottage style, often with orderly, boldly colored beds and uneven, gently shaded borders, old-fashioned flower favorites and exciting new varieties, all blossoming side by side.

Cleome, opposite, *held Victorian affections because it was easy to grow and filled the back of the cottage border with lacy color. Two pristine views of cottage charm: in an old engraving,* above, *and in Currier & Ives's* American Homestead Autumn *(c. 1869),* below.

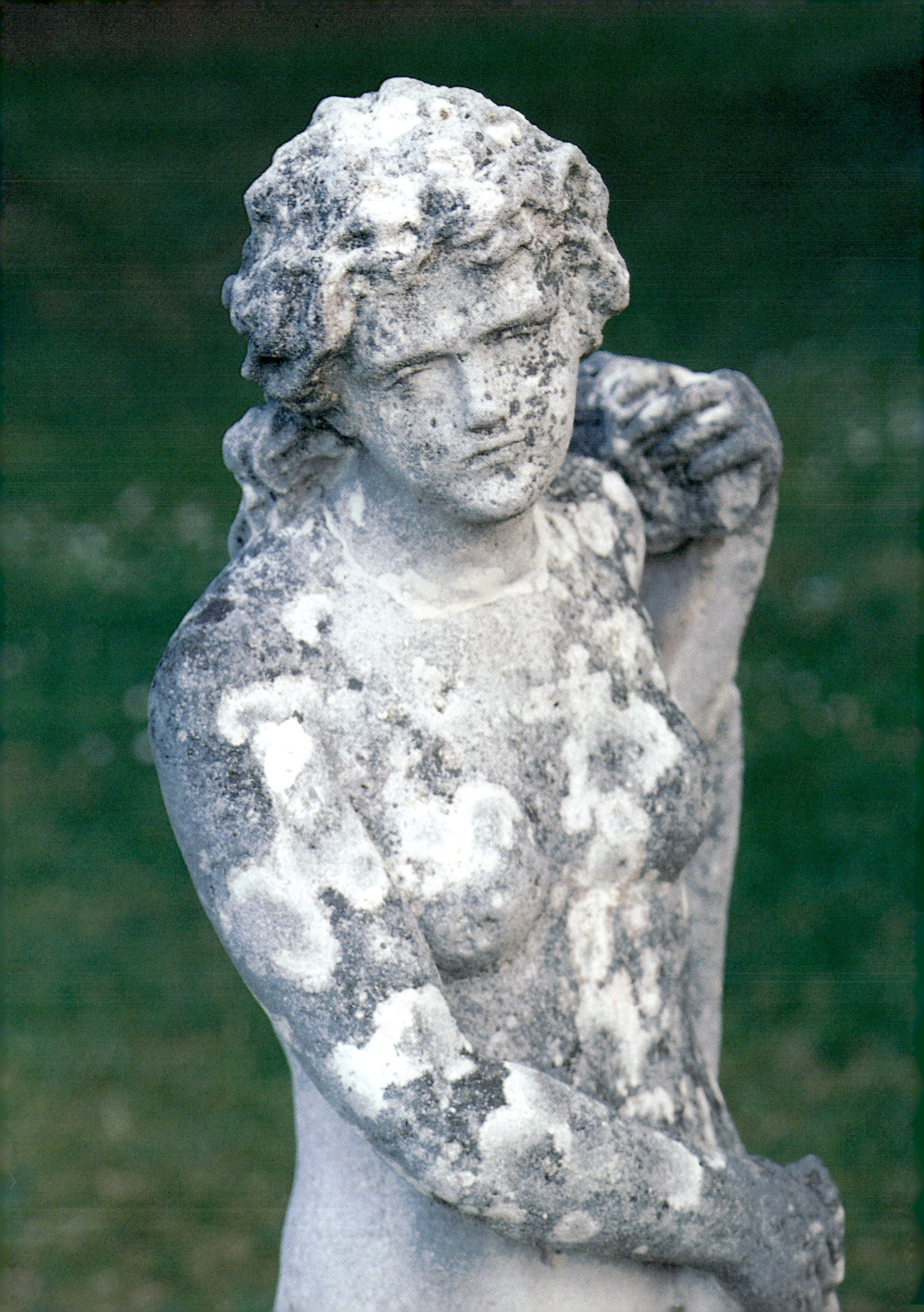

Rockeries, Rooteries, and the Picturesque Ideal

BEING THE RISE OF THE NATURALISTIC, PICTURESQUE IDEAL AND HOW THE VICTORIANS INCORPORATED IT INTO THEIR GARDENS; ALSO ROOTERIES

The Victorian garden was more than just the evolution of the various bedding styles and the waxing and waning in popularity of different types of flowers. Its appearance was also determined by provocative new ideological theories and a whole new set of garden elements—rockeries, arboretums, garden furniture—all of which were to become some of the most identifiable features of what we know today as the Victorian garden. During the last quarter of the 19th century, even as garden

Strolling along shady woodland walkways, above, *was one way that the Victorians paid tribute to the picturesque mystique. And what better garb for enjoying the charms of an "antique" garden than a Worth gown!* Below, *the residence of Elijah A. Morse in Canton, Massachusetts, was perfectly picturesque with its clumps of trees arranged randomly, as in nature, and its romantic outbuilding.*

bedding remained strong among the American middle class, one could almost hear the first rumblings of discontent among those who considered themselves in the forefront of educated, artistic taste. In response, the desire arose to embrace a more natural, wilder sort of garden, at least in theory if not in fact. This was the beginning of the picturesque ideal, a theme long advocated by tastemakers such as John Ruskin and by John Loudon, A. J. Downing, and others like them, who were at their peak of influence in the U.S. during the 1840s and '50s.

Granted, at first these gardening ideas were difficult for most people to implement; few had gardens vast enough to create the craggy, naturalistic landscapes, the thickets and glades of copper beeches (in England) and specimen trees, the winding walkways issuing into secluded glens, where one might pause to meditate, for which the style called. And then there were those all-important temples, emerging fortuitously from a mist! Nevertheless, the cult of the picturesque had a profound influence on 19th-century gardens.

In essence, the cult of the picturesque was a leaning toward a more naturalistic form of gardening. It found willing converts among those who were tired of formal beds, yet found the random plantings of the nostalgic cottage style untidy and countrified, rather than romantic. It was in the picturesque that world-weary inhabitants of the 19th century first paid tribute to the charms of the "antique," venerating age and decay over glaring industrial newness, lauding the untamed beauties of nature rather than the overformalized, overcivilized, and manmade. Rooted in philosophy and a quasi-religious spiritualism—the style had strong Gothic overtones—the picturesque embraced the wilder side of nature, but in a studiedly contrived way.

From about 1790 to 1820, the earliest romantic-style gardens were begun. But the first popularization of the picturesque style came in the 1840s, with Downing writing about these now-mature gardens that had been in existence for some time. The timing seemed right, coinciding with America's romantic era in the arts—with romantic literature, poetry, and painting and high Gothic romanticism in the worlds of architecture and interiors. That architectural styles and landscaping should complement each other, though now self-evident, was but one of the suggestions that seemed new and provocative at the time. Few could dispute that while classical Greek Revival homes (often in the South) were suitably served by formal gardens, more northern rural "Gothic cottages," their quaint gables and windows ornamented with tracery, required "informal" picturesque landscaping to complement their unsymmetrical effects, as did Italianate and, much later, Queen Anne, and other irregular architectural styles. But while debated in the 1840s, still these ideas did not gain true force in gardening until far later in the century, as Americans began to search for alternatives to bedding. Washington Irving's Sunnyside is an example of an earlier manifestation of the picturesque, while the wildflower gardens and woodland walks of Chesterwood are examples of the later. And even though the picturesque always remained more an influential theory than a gardening fact, its tenets present intriguing alternatives to those recreating Victorian gardens today.

Arboretums, Shrubbery, and Vines

▣ For example, one of the key characteristics of the picturesque landscape was the creation of an arboretum—a collection of specimen trees, including shrubbery, at least some of which were exotic or unusual or, if one was especially lucky and well-connected, planted by some notable like a visiting English lord. For Victorian homeowners, the possession of an arboretum was a sign of status and wealth; while collecting was rampant during the 19th century, only people of means, after all, could have enough land to collect trees.

▣ Long discourses were published on the proper planting of an arboretum, should one have the grounds, means, and inclination. "If well arranged, trees and shrubs could be the chief ornaments of the garden, giving the most pleasure and affording the greatest delight, though they give no nourishment, nor produce edible fruits," urged Robert Buist as early as 1854. For gardeners with enough acreage to attempt this today, "well arranged" basically meant avoiding planting in straight lines and parallel rows, which would seldom be found in a natural landscape, and grouping plants with similar characteristics.

▣ Although few homeowners were able to develop full-fledged arboretums, the planting of some trees in natural thickets and groves, as they appeared in nature, was an aspect of the picturesque ideal that people could cultivate, as they attempted to adapt 1840s ideals of romantic Gothic

Above, the pensive view from the rustic gazebo (from Frank J. Scott's Beautifying Home Grounds) *takes in scattered trees and a fine lawn.*

Climbing vines served to hide a house's architecture and contribute to its character, above. Demurely concealed by shadowy foliage, this serene gabled cottage (c. 1842), below, is richly decorated in a quaint Gothic style.

landscaping to 1880s and 1890s suburban plots. Embowering trees, providing shade in the summer and shelter against chilling winds in winter, were necessary to shade porches, accenting the architecture of the home and joining it to the surrounding circle of nature. A charmingly decorated house or gabled cottage, particularly one that reflected Gothic ideals in its ornamentation, would never have been erected on a bare plot of land. According to Downing, the bareness of such a landscape would have rendered its look absurd, wholly out of keeping with the picturesque ideal. A more appropriate treatment would be to partially conceal the home by clustering foliage, "assimilated, as it were, with nature, by the interlacing and entwining branches and bowers around it."

Accordingly, late Victorian gardeners dotted their properties with silver maple, American elm, weeping ash (not at all common today), and European beech trees—all varieties sanctioned by Downing in his works. Other popular trees from which gardeners today can choose include European larch, balsam fir, white pines, umbrella magnolia, and all varieties of willow.

Most engravings of typical Victorian dwelling places tell us that the use of foundation shrubbery, softening the boundaries of a house and marrying it to the landscape, did not come into widespread practice until after the turn of the century. Yet shrubbery, dotting the property, either in groups or singly, was still an integral part of the Victorian landscape. Sometimes shrubbery was used to form living fences for privacy, or to enclose a croquet field. A single shrub could be used as an accent or the centerpiece of a bed, while flowering shrubs like lilac, which burst into bloom in May, or hydrangea, which followed in summer, might be planted along the veranda's edge or under a window where one could enjoy their heady fragrance.

Vines like ivy or honeysuckle, which climbed the walls of the picturesque home, added that all-important "character" so essential to the picturesque ideal. But vines were considered a key element of the garden, picturesque or not. Whenever possible, people strove to veil the angular outlines of their house and hide unsightly fences with the delicate foliage and brilliant flowers of climbing vines, just as indoors they clothed the embarrassingly bare surfaces of tables and mantels with soothing drapery and textiles. "Your homes may lack the paint, gilding and tapestry that adorn those of your neighbors, but if vines are trained over the doors and windows, they will present a fresh beauty and glory every Summer's morn, which the products of art cannot surpass," advised Mrs. Johnson. Scarlet runner bean was suggested as a covering to the pantry windows; hop and grape vines to trail over a kitchen garden wall. Particularly in warmer climates, old-fashioned morning glory, with its trumpet-shaped blossoms and large heart-shaped leaves, was considered ideal for the dining room piazza, shielding its windows from the scorching noonday sun. The Victorians also loved to trellis these around benches and patios.

Another vine that gardeners can consider is the fast-growing Virginia creeper, a very hardy vine with dark green foliage, said to be able to withstand the coldest New England winter. Typically, it festooned the fronts of Victorian houses, covered patches in the ground, and turned brilliant scarlet every fall. Subtropical jasmine, on the other hand, a very fragrant and delicate vine, thrived in the South. Hardy English ivy, ideal for bordering flower beds, was perhaps the most admired of evergreen vines. It clung to the walls of town houses and balconies, adding elegance, dignity, and charm; on country cottages, it suggested the epitome of rustic coziness. English ivy was so popular that it was even considered desirable to cultivate it for its

Boston ivy adds a touch of the picturesque to a handsome stone urn, above.

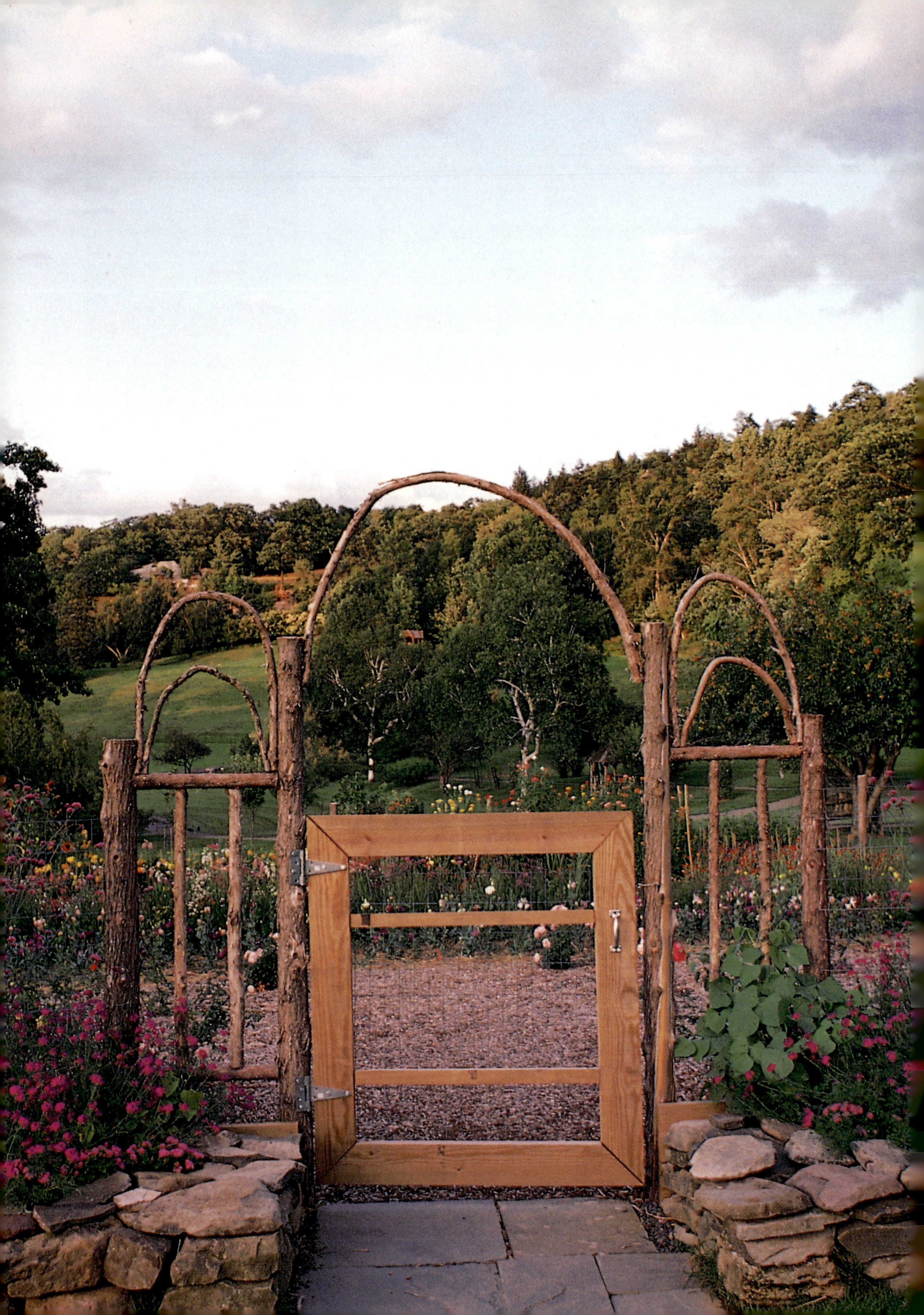

own worth: its lovely dark leaves were used to set off floral bouquets and flower vases, in hanging baskets, around picture frames, and on rustic benches, plant stands, and other garden accessories.

▣ Japanese honeysuckle, brought to America in the 1870s, was another Victorian favorite, as was clematis, sparkling with garlands of star-shaped little white flowers. One of the many cultivars first brought to England from China by the indefatigable Robert Fortune, nothing was considered prettier than clematis for Victorian piazzas and verandas.

▣ But many of the ideals of the picturesque were grandiose indeed. A picturesque landscape, for example, might have called for rushing streams and rugged bridges, ancient villas and temples, and especially meandering woodland paths, perhaps leading to a "natural" sunlit glade. Ideally, the main walks of a typical Victorian garden were supposed to be wide enough to allow two people to walk comfortably side by side—and if wide enough to allow for a child, too, so much the better. During the 1850s, a substantial five to six feet wide was considered a good average; later, walks of just three feet were more common. Internal walks, of course, were much narrower, their width determined by the size of the garden.

▣ The "best walks" were composed of oyster shells, coarse gravel, small stones, or broken bricks covered with five or six inches of fine gravel, the gravel color determined "by fancy and convenience." Ground oyster shells and granite chips were also used, but some people thought them too bright for the eyes on a sunny day. Today, walks can be covered with gravel, fine shale, or other locally available material.

Adapting the Picturesque to Smaller Gardens

A style that called for ancient and classical (European) outbuildings and sprawling glades of trees presented special challenges to the average American homeowner. For those with smaller gardens, there were many ways to pay homage to the picturesque. In designing a scaled-down scheme, however, the Victorians were warned not to err on the side of oversimplification. "There is a limit even to simplicity of design, and this should be carried only so far that it might not interfere

With its embowering shade trees, even this plain little house, above, *has proper Gothic overtones. The charm of the rustic is seen in an inviting handcrafted garden gate,* opposite, *and an 1870s garden bench,* below.

Quaint summerhouses, rustic gazebos, and other outbuildings allowed one to pause, rest, and meditate on a picturesque landscape. This unique stone "gazebo," right, is one such structure—just the sort of oddity that Victorian homeowners would have adored.

with as much diversity as possible," advised Beeton's. In true Victorian fashion, nothing was thought to add more to the pleasure derived from even a small garden than as many objects as possible.

In a small picturesque garden, walks were laid out in curves rather than at sharp angles; beds were circular, rather than pointed; and the irregularly shaped plantings of both annuals and perennials were as open as possible. Instead of formal beds, gardeners assembled a showy collection of flowers in the turf bordering the walkways near the home. In this way the flowers could be enjoyed without marring the natural beauty of the grounds. Where edging of the beds was concerned, they liked boxwood ("if obtainable—nothing is so handsome"), or if money was a concern, white sweet alyssum, ornamental grasses, or ornamental tiles ("both cheap and elegant"). Finally, surprisingly, nothing was said to enhance a small garden more than trees, specifically one or two smaller ornamental trees like a silver birch, or in English gardens, a pine or cypress.

Gardeners today who want to include an offhand allusion to the picturesque in a garden otherwise made up of bright little single-species beds, or shaped carpet schemes, might add an urn, a sundial (an Edwardian affectation), or the odd tree as a picturesque accent. Weeping birch, horse chestnut, beech, and other ornamental and certifiably picturesque trees could be planted, along with shrubs like lilac and althea (rose of Sharon). Or graceful willows could serve as focal points along a curving garden pathway. Weeping willows, popular since the beginning of the century for their romantic associations with mourning, still held an important place in American gardens by the century's end.

Yet another way to allude to the picturesque is by including some appreciation of rustic Victorian garden furniture—a twig garden bench or basket instead of a fancy urn or expensive cast-iron settee. Garden furniture that embodied the picturesque ideal had to look as homemade and handcrafted as possible. In fact, during the 1870s rustic plant stands made by ladies from gnarled twigs and broken branches became all the rage, not only for the garden but for the fashionable porch and parlor as well. But so conscious were the Victorians of their newly acquired gentility that a dilemma arose. What if these crude, if charmingly crafted, plant stands resulted in a social misunderstanding, implying that their rusticity was a necessity and not an affectation? As a precaution, one oracle of the home and garden advised that when "materials of little value" were employed in the plant stand, the "flowers grown in them should be of the highest possible state of cultivation." That way, it would be absolutely clear that any crudeness was intentional and not the result of carelessness or poverty. Inferior construction could always be covered by the indispensable ivy.

ROCKERIES, ROOTERIES, AND MOSSERIES

The most manageable picturesque device was the rockery. In fact, it was an immensely important part of the Victorian garden scene, whether one leaned toward the picturesque or not. During the 19th century it was the firm belief that no garden large or small, no suburban plot, no backyard however dark or miserable looking, could not be improved by the introduction of a rockery. Rockeries and ferneries were just the sort of amusing garden oddity that Victorian homeowners adored pointing out to visiting guests.

Partially surrounded by trees or shrubs, rockeries were collections of large stones of a single type, piled up in as natural a manner as possible, over which plants and vines were trained to grow. At the bottom, the niches and grottoes that formed were filled with ferns and vines that flourished in such moist situations, while plants that thrived in heat and sunshine were placed at the top. Occasionally, roots, mosses, a small fish pond, or even broken bits of pottery or shells were discreetly added to enhance the picturesque effect. Deliberate artifice was key.

Pausing to capture the moment with umbrella and staff in hand, this young girl and her companion, above, were indulging in a healthy (and most fashionable) nature walk. Below, ferns make an old stone wall into a verdant rockery.

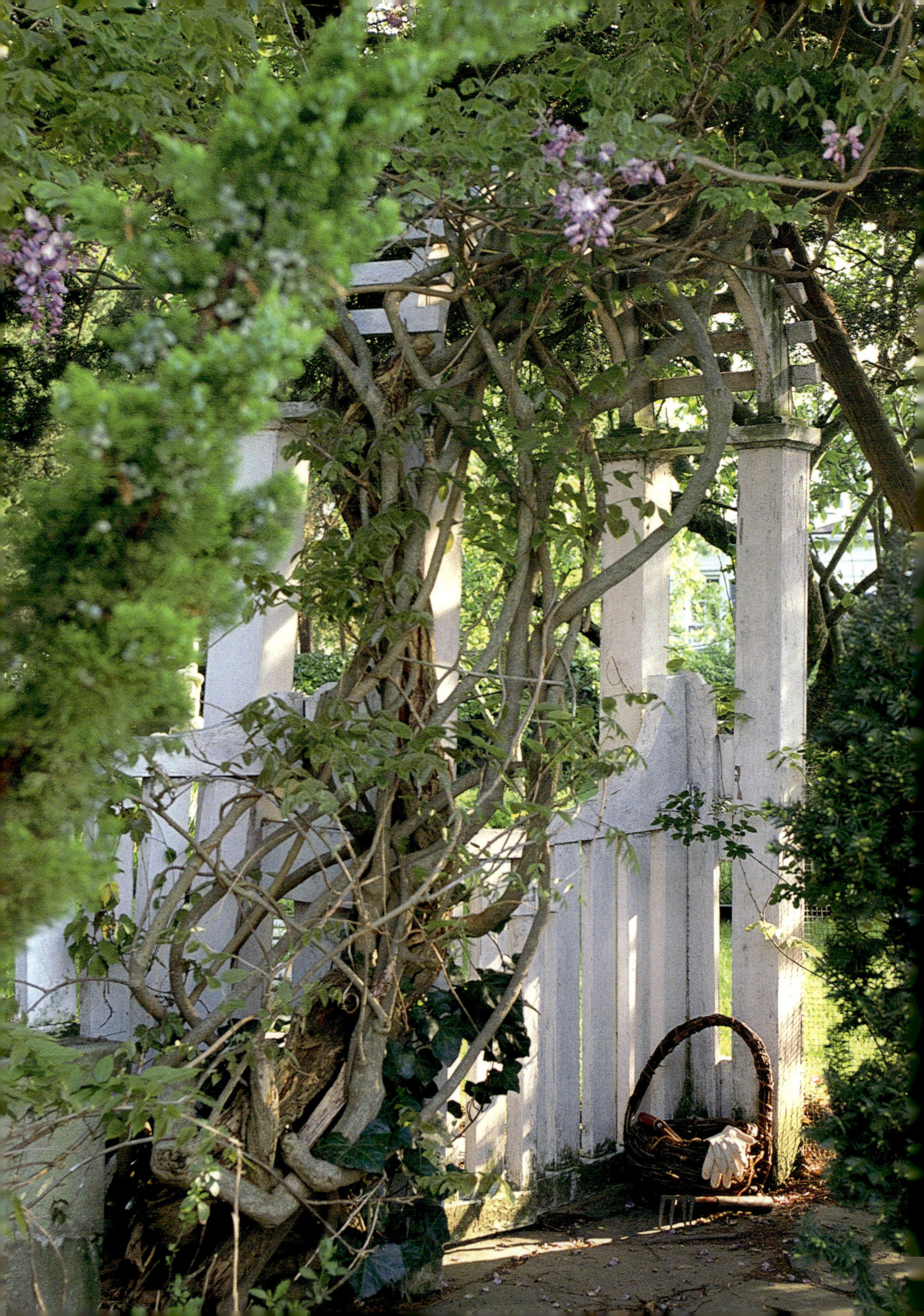

▣ No garden was too small for a rockery. In fact, it was considered the ideal way for homeowners with only modest garden space to pay homage to the picturesque ideal. But rock gardens, although simple in concept, were rampant with the usual pitfalls of Victorian taste. It was not enough, for example, to merely assemble a variety of rocks and lay them out on their broadest or flattest sides, as most garden guides suggested. Rockeries also required a tasteful eye to construct them and a loving hand to tend them.

▣ To create an authentic rockery today, select stones with jagged irregular shapes and pile or cement them together in pyramidal form, many feet across the base. The arrangement should allow ample room for the formation of nooks and pockets for soil for holding growing plants and vines.

▣ Anything that grows in shade or shallow soil can grow in a rockery, but alpine plants, which are habituated to rocky settings and do best in cool conditions, are often chosen. Typical and appropriate are the gnarled and knotty roots of trees, vines like moneywort (creeping Charlie) or Virginia creeper, mosses, lichens, dwarf evergreens, Dutchman's pipe, clematis, paniculata, jack-in-the-pulpit, wandering Jew, caladiums, coleus, and acheranthus. If the rockery is not entirely shaded and has an hour or two of sunshine, plants can also be placed on the sunny side. Species of cactus and succulents—like alpines, used to harsh conditions—can be planted in the dry areas of the rock garden.

▣ A touch of color was also considered appropriate in a Victorian rockery, and flowers such as mignonette, pansy, geraniums, and particularly wild columbine were often grown near the top. Brilliant yellow and scarlet nasturtiums and, where the winters are mild, chrysanthemums in purple, white, or yellow are other traditional floral choices.

▣ Somewhat similar to a rock garden was a rootery, structured around roots instead of rocks. After first piling up a heap of soil, one then carefully arranged the roots of old trees, branches, and tree stumps to form pockets, into which moss, ferns, plants, and trailing vines and climbers were inserted. Needless to say, the result was rarely pleasing to the eye, and rooteries never really caught on. Mosseries or moss houses were also a minor detour in the garden scheme, primarily during the 1840s and '50s. These were actually small huts, typically built on concrete foundations and with colored glass windows, whose interior walls and ceiling were covered with moss, often grown in decorative patterns. Rustic furniture—chairs, tables, a settee—were placed inside.

The charming tangle of wisteria, opposite, *is in the picturesque spirit, as is this rockery,* above. *Rockeries were often artistically arranged in a casually disordered way—a decided contrast to the orderly lines of flowers that surrounded it.*

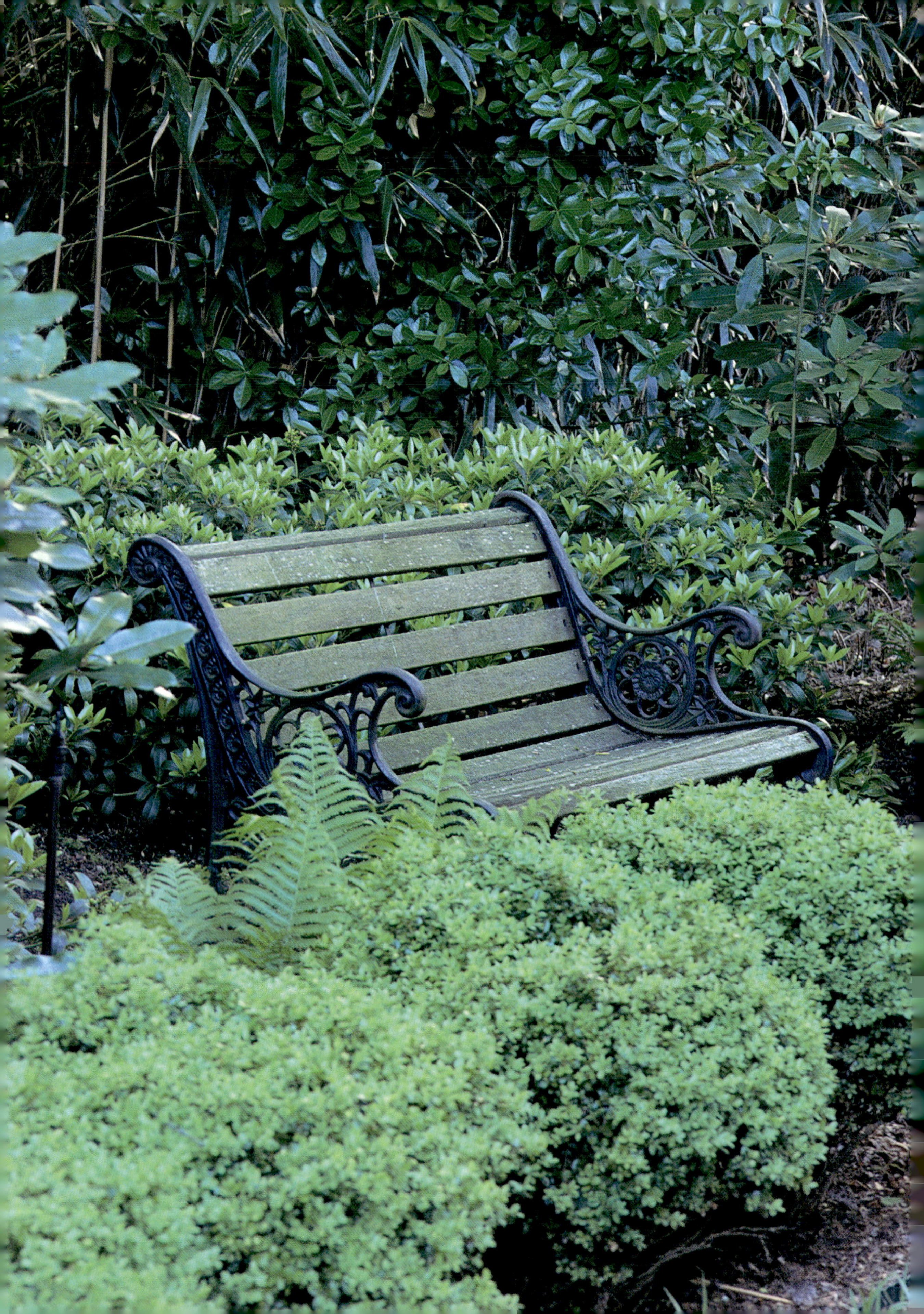

The Furnished Garden

BEING THE GARDEN BENCHES AND SETTEES, THE CAST-IRON ANIMALS, URNS, STATUES OF GODDESSES, SUNDIALS, FOUNTAINS, BIRDBATHS, AND OTHER ESSENTIAL ORNAMENTS WITH WHICH THE VICTORIANS CREATED COMFORT IN THE GARDEN; ALSO GAZEBOS

While for some rare 19th-century individuals the most appropriate garden ornament was nature itself, for most others the garden was merely another room, albeit outdoors, waiting to be furnished. During the second half of the 19th century the Victorian garden found itself positively crammed with an excess of furniture, statuary, and other types of embellishment. Wandering its walkways, one would have come across charming cast-iron benches, tables, and settees in intricate

Garden furnishings provided a touch of civilization to nature's wilderness, as with an elegant jardiniere, top, and an 1870s garden, bottom, which is enclosed by shrubbery and cozily furnished with a bentwood chair and gazebo.

grapevine patterns or other leafy designs. Fashionable, organic-looking rustic chairs crafted from gnarled twigs, roots, and twisted vines were tucked into little woodland corners, while sculptures of graceful nymphs, stone cherubs, classical goddesses, and grinning gargoyles peopled the grounds. Farther on, one might have enjoyed the sight of old-time sundials, overflowing urns, elegant fountains, birdbaths, vine-covered arbors, and outbuildings such as gazebos, pavilions, and teahouses.

Truly—and how had this happened?—the Victorians' penchant for material abundance had surpassed the home boundaries and was now straining the seams of its outdoor grounds. It is not surprising that even the garden terminology of the day—the popularity of "carpet" and "embroidery" gardens—reflected the unique relationship between house and garden.

The creeping encroachment of civilization into nature's world began with the front porch, that spacious veranda which wrapped itself so invitingly around the house, playing host to an engaging array of hammocks, porch swings, planters, and easygoing wicker furniture. Thus outfitted, the porch became the site of breakfasts in the early morning coolness or tea in the shaded comfort of the late afternoon. Here, with a sisal rug underfoot, a lap robe draped on a nearby cushioned chaise, a painterly sunset on the horizon, one could feel virtuously in touch with nature, surrounded by newly mown lawns and glowing flower beds, while still sheltered in an environment that was as welcoming and homey as one's own living room. Indeed, popular periodicals like *Godey's Lady's Book* and *The Horticulturist* christened the porch—and soon the garden—a "country parlor," an ideal place for civilized outdoor living.

Today, we tend to romanticize the lazy life of the Victorian porch, possibly because these were the years in which many of America's traditional summer pastimes had their roots. As science began to discover the healthful effects of fresh air and exercise, leisure began to move outdoors, with picnics in the garden, croquet or tennis on the lawn, archery teas and other gatherings significantly causing the light and portable wicker chairs to drift from their front-porch perch to the garden itself. As people began to feel in harmony with nature, the garden became a living space, a place in which to relax, to browse through a book, to sketch, to contemplate solitude and natural beauty. Since neither air conditioning nor electric fans had yet made their arrival, life in the garden was also a means of surviving the dog days of summer. A garden seat,

Left, *the detail on a delicate wire garden chair resembles a spun spider web, with dewdrops.*

carefully positioned, was now a gracious invitation, beckoning one to pause for a moment and enjoy a breeze and a view.

These attempts at furnishing the garden were not without precedent. The formal parks and pleasure gardens of the 18th-century well-to-do often included a solitary stone bench or an austere classical chair—no-frills spots in which to rest and meditate. Some gardens, grand indeed, boasted cool, elegant fountains and recreational adjuncts such as aviaries and pheasant grounds. But often these efforts tended to emphasize, rather than bridge, the distance between man and nature.

In contrast, the inhabitants of the 19th century strove to feel at home in the garden, at first dragging their carved walnut and mahogany upholstered-seat rocking chairs and side tables out from the sitting room under the trees, so they could take in the sights and sounds of nature while still sitting in solid comfort. Emboldened, they eventually created furniture expressly for the outdoors, filling the garden with familiar forms of cast iron, wicker, and other Victorian novelties, taming and domesticating any lingering wildness of the outdoors. "If the leading principles of garden taste are kept in view, the smallest plot may be so ornamented as to convey an impression of luxurious completeness and present at all seasons a wealthy fullness that shall prove its owner to be an artist in the work," encouraged English garden expert Shirley Hibberd. The more ornaments, he pointed out, the more there was to interest the eye and to occasion pleasurable emotions in the mind.

CAST-IRON GARDEN FURNITURE

Products of industry—the very world from which 19th-century gardeners were longing to escape—filled the garden. Weighty cast iron, the fortuitous building block of cookery pots and locomotives, became the primary

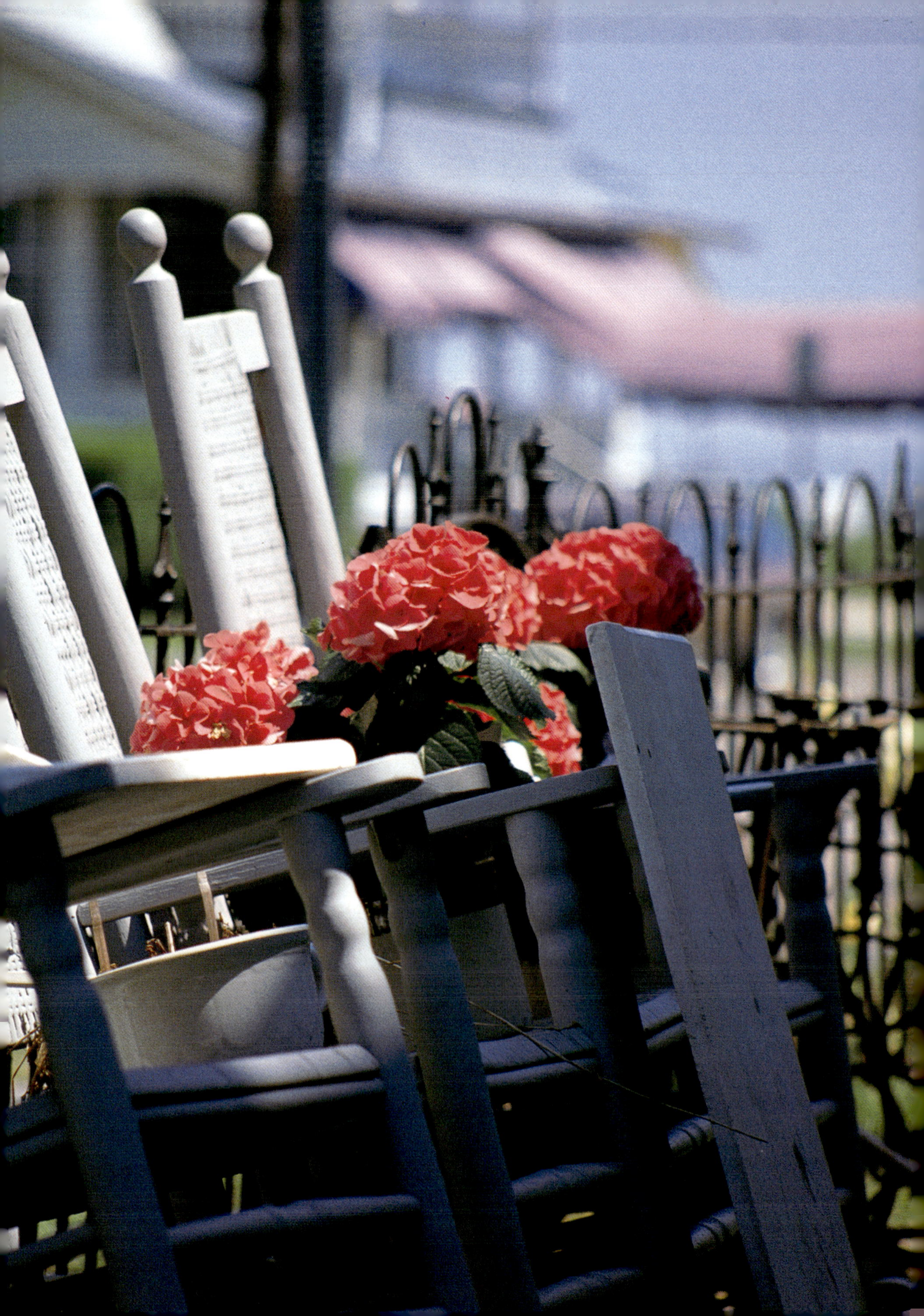

MAKE YOUR EARLIEST SCHOOLROOM THE GARDEN, AND YOU ARE NOT LIKELY TO REGRET IT.

A splendid cast-iron fountain, above, *would have been an important focal point.* Below, *an ideal place for sharing a confidence was in the garden-as-parlor.*

Preceding pages, left: Old-fashioned rocking chairs enhance the cozy charms of this front porch; right, *statuary, birdcages, and flowerpots were all part of the furnished garden.*

medium for stylish Victorian garden furniture. Gaining its first wave of popularity in the 1840s and '50s, cast iron had a heavy molded appearance that was a sharp contrast to the delicately made, hand-forged wrought iron of previous decades. But advertised as "cheap, beautiful, and imperishable," as it was by one foundry in 1860, it managed to imitate carved stone at a fraction of the cost, besides being perfectly suited for reproducing the intricate pierced ornamentation that the Victorians adored. Southern Victorians especially took to its graceful, feminine contours, and cast-iron settees, chairs, and tables immediately punctuated the manicured grounds of many an antebellum mansion.

▪ The cast-iron explosion embraced many patterns and forms. There were fern-patterned armchairs, holly-leaf seats with winged griffins adorning the legs, Eastlake-inspired benches and Gothic Revival loveseats, all of cast iron. Often, pieces took their stylistic cues from the garden itself and bloomed with metallic morning glory and lily patterns. Naturalistic Rococo Revival motifs, paralleling the intricate carving of mid-Victorian parlor suites, were the most popular and widely produced of all. Prim little garden chairs with curved legs and ornate medallion backs mimicked in iron their indoor antecedents.

▪ Everyone loved the grapevine motif, a true Victorian "best-seller"; after 1870, when fern gardens were elevated to a veritable passion, fern fronds became the favorite pattern for garden settees and chairs. A third variation was cast iron resembling naturalistic twigs and branches. Although most cast-iron pieces were painted dark green or black so they would blend and harmonize with their leafy surroundings, these "rustic" pieces were frequently painted brown.

In addition to providing mere seating, cast-iron garden furniture was a decorative accent; these accessories "finished" and improved the surrounding landscape. Set along garden walks or under the spreading shady branches of a tree, they provided civilized counterpoints to the more luxuriant and natural aspect of the garden, which was both comforting and appealing.

Although the mass production of cast-iron furniture in the second half of the 19th century—not to mention the entire troupe of cast-iron urns, pots, lawn animals, and the like—made its acquisition possible for many people, the fact remained that it was not as cheap as purported. In 1893, the beauteous grapevine-patterned settee that so many Victorians so urgently desired still cost about $18, a respectable week's wages and a hefty enough sum to outfit a family of five in new shoes from the 1893 Montgomery Ward catalog.

Rustic Garden Furniture

For middle-class gardening enthusiasts who longed for proper garden accoutrements but could not afford cast iron, rustic furniture proved an alternative that was both ideologically and aesthetically attractive. Made from gnarled and twisted branches and twigs, and held together by dried vines, it not only was inexpensive but was sanctioned by many tastemakers as a choice more in keeping with the gardens of a modest home. Even the well-to-do liked to amuse themselves with charming rustic pieces, peppering their gardens with strategically placed chairs made from knotty branches and gnarled twigs, or imaginative, crudely made (if structurally sound) benches in the fashionable Adirondack style which had emerged from old resorts of that region in the 1870s. If its quality was sometimes poor ("Rustic furniture is often badly made and of the worst materials," warned Hibberd, cautioning would-be purchasers against furniture with dry rot, made of cheap oak timber or with wormholes) and not as weather-impervious and durable as cast iron, it was nevertheless more easily replaceable.

With the new garden furnishings, and the realization that the porch was an outdoor room of its own, it became possible for the Victorians to enjoy tea, above, and the beauty of nature at the same time.

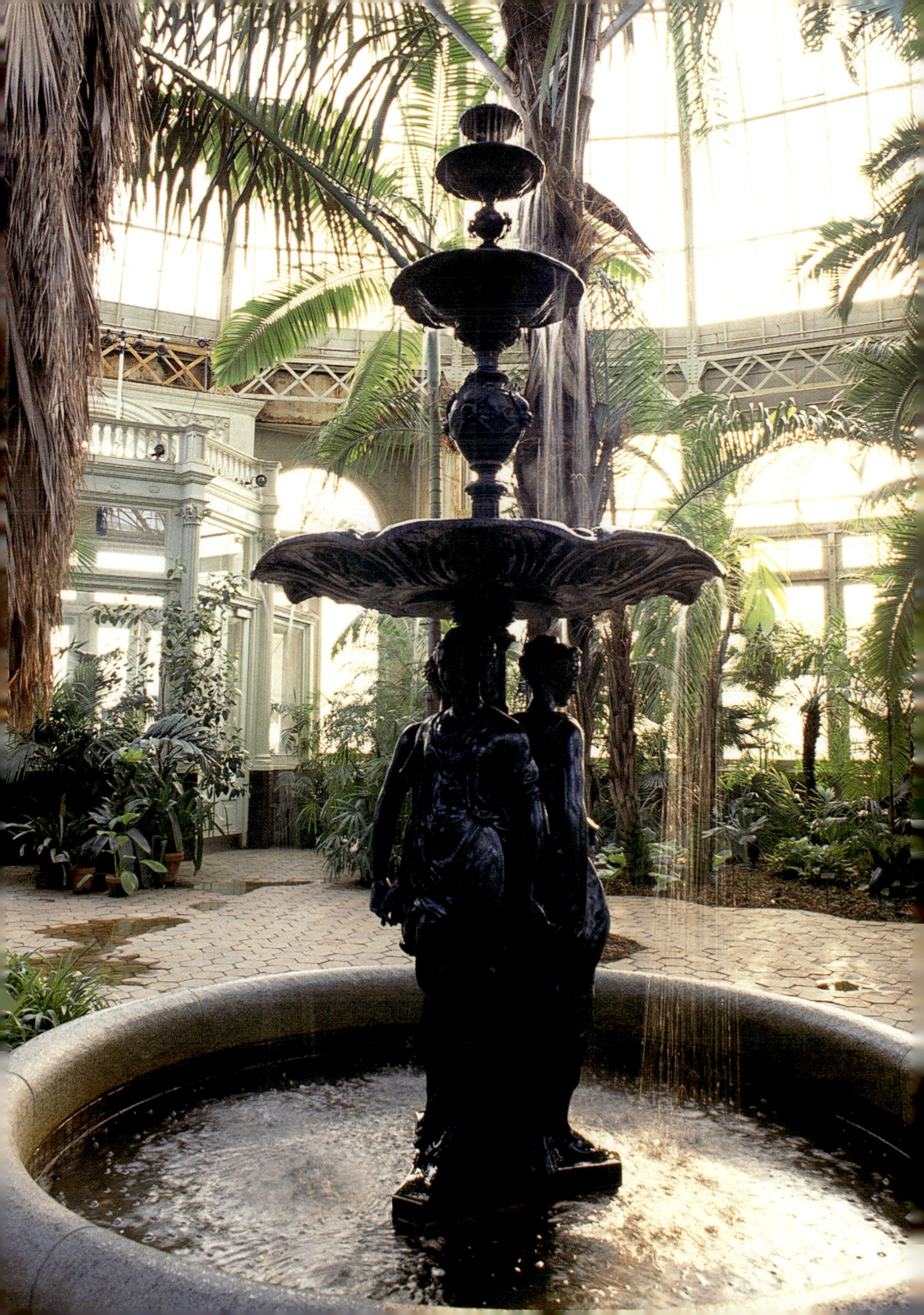

While rustic furniture could be purchased from catalogs, because its materials were so accessible it became the delight of do-it-yourselfers, and many home guides contained detailed instructions on how to build a rustic bench, a planter, a vase, or a chair. "The pretty articles in rustic work I had long admired, but those I saw at the stores were costly affairs, too much so at least to admit of my possessing one in the way of purchasing," wrote Reba L. Raymond, a subscriber to *The Household Magazine* in February 1880; she had compromised by making her own.

Other types of furniture filled the garden, too. There was airy, bendable wire furniture, a charming whimsy of the 1880s, most often seen in the popular ice-cream parlor chair. There was also wirework netting or mesh, which could be used to create baskets and flowerpots. The latter were advised to be coated with tar, buttressed with two strong crossed rods for extra strength, then filled with moss and plants. After the Civil War, folding canvas-back chairs, known today as director's chairs, and folding canvas stools moved easily from the porch to the garden as needed.

ORNAMENTS OF ALL KINDS

In addition to furniture, landscapes cried out for other types of decoration. After all, according to A. J. Downing, the desire for rural embellishment—the taste for ornament—was proof of the progress of refinement. Fortunately, never before had so much been manufactured to satisfy this newly emerging taste.

Lawn animals made of cast iron could be an important part of the natural setting, in particular handsome stags with majestic antlers, winsome deer, rabbits, and dogs—whippets and retrievers primarily, either crouching or standing at stiff attention.

Cast-iron garden urns, in classically inspired shapes, sometimes as large as three feet wide and four feet high, were another essential part of the Victorian landscape's ornamentation. These were considered most attractive when placed in remote places of the garden—at the edge of a secluded glen or end of a path, so one might come upon them by chance while exploring the garden's furthest boundaries. Always left empty, they were intended to suggest time-worn antiquities and call to mind ancient ruins.

After 1860, however, garden urns began to be more ornamented, often in the fashionable Rococo style. Now they were attractive focal points of a garden. Situated at the center of a carpet bed, placed in tan-

Urns, above, jardinieres, chairs, statues, and other ornaments, below, created a sense of urban comfort in the garden. Opposite, splendid fountains, both costly and showy, were always impressive, whether in the garden itself or in conservatories like this one at the New York Botanical Garden, Bronx, New York.

The gazebo in the Cole Garden, right, offers a pleasant view. It was said that the grander the garden, the greater the need for some sort of outbuilding, gazebo, or teahouse.

dem on a porch or terrace or majestically in the middle of a lawn, they would overflow with colorful annuals and spilling ivy. One garden writer found an "artistic effect" could be achieved by planting urns with lacy, grayish-white dusty miller, which was also considered an excellent plant for garden borders.

To fill out the empty corners of the garden—if there could possibly be any—the Victorians mounted statues of nymphs, goddesses, and classical busts. Sundials, which had been popular in both English and American gardens in the early years of the 19th century, were also revived. "In many of the formal gardens planned by our skilled architects, sun-dials are now springing afresh like mushroom growth of a single night, and some are objects of the greatest beauty and interest," one late Victorian writer put forth. Other types of ornamentation included elaborately constructed birdcages built in all the fashionable architectural styles, with gabled or mansard roofs, piazzas, and even miniature gingerbread trim.

A sure symbol of elegance—and expense—was a cast-iron lawn fountain, perhaps adorned with a statue of some sort, from whose mouth, be it man or beast, the spray of water might emerge (it was recommended that the interior of one basin be painted black to give the illusion of depth). These became popular only after 1870 with the development of improved plumbing systems, piping, and power-driven pumping stations which delivered water to Victorian homes, yet they were still prohibitively expensive for most people and were always an upper-class luxury item.

FANCIFUL OUTBUILDINGS

In addition to the plethora of furniture, planters, and statuary, no Victorian garden of any size could possibly be complete without some sort of picturesque outbuilding, collectively called summerhouses but further distinguished as gazebos, pergolas, belvederes, teahouses, temples, pavilions, and a host of other appellations. "Summer-houses of some sort are desirable, and indeed almost necessary features in gardens of all dimensions and styles," advised Shirley Hibberd. "Indeed, the grander the garden, the greater the need for places of retirement, for rest, shelter, conservation, and sometimes for that blessed change 'out of the house' which comes over every one of us at times, when the air is balmy, the trees leafy, and the routine of domestic life a little tame or wearisome."

The summerhouse was most inviting when it was shrouded in greenery, and prettiest when only partially hidden from view—how charming to catch a glimpse of one of these dollhouselike structures embowered in a woodland glen! When the structure was fashioned like a temple or a Japanese teahouse, both styles that flourished during the 1870s and '80s, its function as a sanctum for meditation was further enhanced. Situated at the side of a stream, in a grassy field, or in a spot shaded by a few glorious trees, the summerhouse was, as needed, a snug retreat for a nap or private conversation, a shelter for stargazing, a convivial gathering point for an outdoor luncheon, a peaceful observatory from which to match the habits of nature's wildlife. Hibberd, for example, loved to read in a summerhouse, recalling no greater pleasure than "to lounge in [its] cool, shady recess, with a favorite volume and a canister of that seductive, sedative weed [!], which wafts us on its thin blue wreaths of smoke to the highest region of the most dreamy Elysium." One can only speculate as to which weed he meant.

Built in every sort of design, many of the most typical summerhouse styles are reproduced quite effectively today. Some are fashioned like public-square bandstands; others resemble old-fashioned temples or teahouses. But the range was once vast. There were thatched-roof rustic creations, summerhouses decried as "sweet-meat stalls, destitute of elegance, use and propriety." In deciding on a style, tradition called for the summerhouse to harmonize in style with the main dwelling of the property, although many a home with a majestic "Greek" frontage boasted a summerhouse with gnarled wood supports and a moss or thatched roof. This was considered less of a faux pas if the summerhouse was on the outskirts of the garden property as opposed to being in close

Above, this summerhouse adorned with rustic latticework is a design from about 1870.

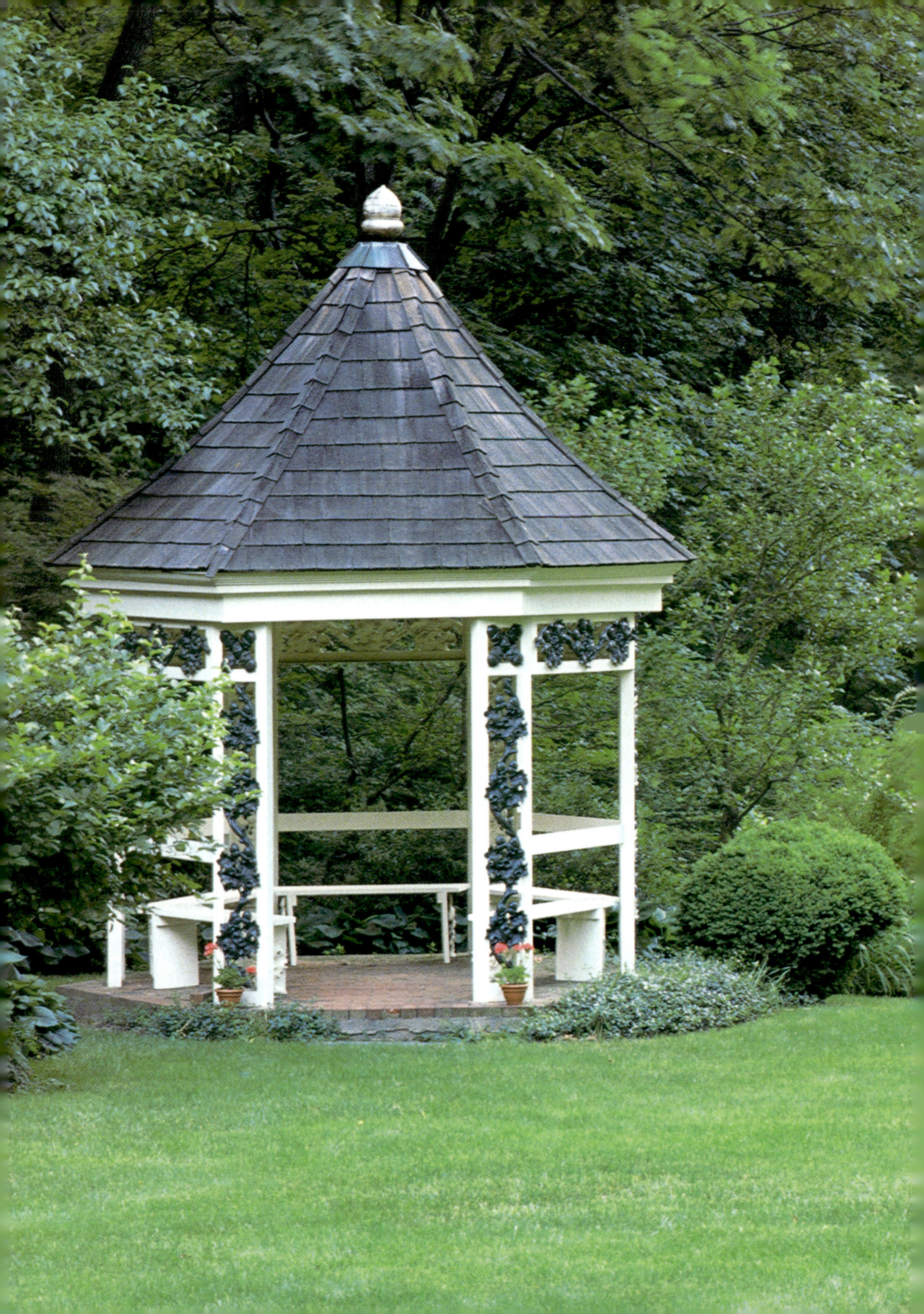

Where shady trees invite the wanderer to a seat, how pleasant is it to find the means of rest and shelter in a garden.

SHIRLEY HIBBERD, 1870

Preceding pages: The classic Victorian gazebo provides shade from the afternoon sun in a corner of the old-fashioned garden at Acorn Hall, Morristown, New Jersey.

No home was complete without a glass-enclosed conservatory or greenhouse. In 1898, this miniature greenhouse, below, *was annexed to the residence of Mrs. Fannie A. Crocket of Iowa, a* Mayflower *reader*

proximity to formal gardens and walkways. But unity of tone was desirable, and a rustic summerhouse was felt to be more appropriate in a garden connected to a rustic dwelling than to a severely classic mansion with terraces and formal, geometric gardens.

GREENHOUSES AND CONSERVATORIES

By the 1870s, nearly every proper Victorian lady, whether mistress of a grand Victorian estate or a small suburban "villa," possessed a well-furnished glass conservatory. Lush with palms, the conservatory was a decorative symbol of elegance and prosperity—part of the wonderful world of interior parlor gardening. In the later part of the 19th century, no proper upper-class home was considered complete without one.

It was in these glass-enclosed, tile-floored enclaves, usually adjoining the parlor or dining room (at Mark Twain's fashionable Hartford home, the library opens onto a small but stylish conservatory) that ladies indulged the fashionable obsession to tend greenery indoors. "This always affords the most satisfaction when it is so attached to the dwelling, that opening a door or window from the dining-room or parlor reveals the glories of the greenhouse," commented Peter Henderson in *Gardening for Pleasure* in 1887.

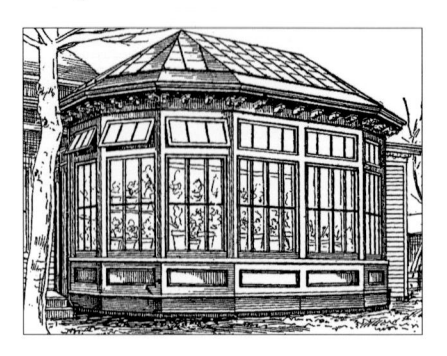

Horticultural structures designed to force fruit out of season go back as far as ancient Rome, while conservatories, which sheltered delicate and exotic plants from the cold, existed centuries prior to the 19th century, developing from early orangeries that protected precious citrus fruits from the chilling effects of winter frosts. As techniques of glassmaking advanced, conservatories became the prerogative of wealthy English aristocrats with a passion for collecting unusual plants. Foremost among the great English conservatories were Chatsworth, designed by Jos. Paxton and built from 1836 to 1840, belonging to the Duke of Devonshire, as well as the Royal Botanic Gardens at Kew, which were started in 1759, expanded in 1771, and by 1820 had become a botanical model known for their vast conservatories filled with literally thousands of species.

Key mid-century advancements of Victorian industry changed all that, bringing the elegance of conservatories within reach of American homeowners. That's when conservatories as we think of them today, horticultural structures attached to the house for the purpose of displaying tender tropicals, first came to the U.S. Landscape gardener and horticulturist J. C. Loudon invented the technique of curvilinear glazing (which was used at the great conservatory at Chatsworth, and later for the Crystal Palace in 1851), which created widespread enthusiasm for the glamour of plants under glass. Further new methods for the inexpensive production of plate glass (and the abolishment of the glass tax in 1851), as well as the production of cast iron (which provided a strong but light framework) all happily coincided with the accelerating interest in horticulture, as well as the accelerated arrival of all sorts of tender exotic plants from abroad.

The typical American conservatory was filled with jardinieres and cachepots of everblooming geraniums—bright crimson and so large they might take up an entire corner—as well as pedestals and shelves containing, in their seasons, begonias, jasmines, primroses, petunias, heliotropes, pinks, weeping fuchsias, and a wide assortment of exotic palms, all of which thrived indoors. Nasturtiums were considered magnificent in a window garden or a conservatory, as were trailing lobelias, verbenas, and other sun-loving plants. Aspidistras and hanging baskets of orchids filled the corners, along with cast-iron and wicker chairs, tipsy birdcages lined with flannel or felt and inhabited by singing canaries, an actual working fountain, and more. Sometimes the conservatory might even include a charming little artificial pond, with trickling water and swimming goldfish. Other times, a handsome Wardian case filled with ferns and rare plants was its focal point. Orange trees grown in square wooden boxes, exotics like feathery ferns and bougainvillea, and climbers like pink lapageria were all favorites.

Exotic, fragrant, and decoratively picturesque—no wonder the conservatory was considered a romantic spot, a place for a courting couple to exchange a private intimacy, an attractive vantage point in which a young lady might pause, surrounded by flowers, when sitting out a dance, the perfect room in which a society matron might write letters or

A typical conservatory, above, was the receptacle for all sorts of ferns and rare, tender exotic flowers. On occasion, it might even have housed a singing canary in a cage or a parrot or two, below.

IN OUR CAREFULLY THOUGHT-OUT GARDENS, STATUARY IS A THING OF BEAUTY AND OFTEN OF MEANING.

take tea. And not surprisingly, because of its glass enclosure it became a favorite picture-taking place for photographers, who appreciated the abundant light streaming through its panes. At times, though, frosted or whitewashed glass was employed to soften the light, which was considered better for ferns, palms, and general greenery.

So widespread was the popularity of the conservatory, whether a deep bay window or a full-sized room of its own, that many magazines, including *The Mayflower*, regularly ran a separate column solely devoted to its appropriate plantings. Carnations, geraniums, chrysanthemums, and violets, for example, all bloomed well indoors. "Sow now some Schizanthus, Marigold and Lobelia in pots,—they will give you no end of pleasure in winter time by their constant blooming," conservatory gardeners were advised by garden expert Adolf Jaenicke in the October 1899 *Mayflower*.

When building a conservatory, it was important to place it on the sunny side of the home, unshadowed by trees or other houses, especially if one wanted to grow flowering plants. In such a case, it would never do to have it facing north, although ferns, palms, and shade-loving foliage plants would still be able to thrive. A south-facing aspect was the warmest, but one facing slightly east or southeast would also be able to catch the morning sun. In addition, its architectural style and ornament should harmonize with the house.

WHEN EMBELLISHMENT RAN WILD

While there could be no denying the charm of a delicate iron tea table set with linen and cool lemonade beneath a shady arbor of roses, or an ivy-covered gazebo or cool white marble statue rising up from a green and glossy glade, too much of a good thing eventually spoiled the effect. Tastemakers pleaded vainly for restraint. By 1870, Frank Jesup Scott, for example, was already deploring the attempt to crowd "an ostentatious display" of sculptured figures, vases, seats, arbors, and the like in a less than ample garden.

But there was no turning back. By the 1890s, garden embellishment had descended inevitably into cliché. Revived today and used as intended—as an aesthetic accent, a signal to an inspiring vista, or an artistic counterpoint to the luxuriance of nature—no garden could be considered in the Victorian tradition without it. Faced with the new prospect of venturing into nature, even within safe view of the house, Victorians were comforted by signs of civilization.

Palms, above, thrived in the parlor and the conservatory and soon became a Victorian cliché. Opposite, Statuary appeared everywhere in the Victorian garden, on pedestals, walls, urns, and fountains.

"CLIMBING METEOR"

CRIMSON RAMBLER

WHITE RAMBLER

YELLOW RAMBLER

Small Gardens

BEING THE RICH AND VARIED TYPES OF SMALL, SPECIALTY GARDENS WITH WHICH THE VICTORIANS ENRICHED THEIR LIVES AND LANDSCAPE

The new burst of gardening mania gave rise to the creation of many types of "specialty" gardens, each small and self-contained. Walled, hedged, bordered, set off in a secluded place, or defined in some other way, they were meant to be experienced separately. Just as the Victorians developed idealized special rooms in their homes—a Chinese room, a Dutch kitchen, a "colonial" room, a Turkish corner—as marks of their worldliness, refinement, and artistic sensibilities, so they created

Color gardens were of manageable size—sometimes no larger than a bed or two. The south blue border garden, right, of the Stowe House contains Johnny-jump-ups, foxglove, blue echium, blue cranesbill, campanula, and yarrow, enough for a basket of blue flowers, below.

these small, uniquely themed gardens as evidence of their sophistication, artistic sensibility, and gardening skill.

To a certain degree, the growing influence of women as amateur gardeners led to the development of the specialty garden. As women embraced gardening as one skill in their battery of domestic accomplishments, they tended to eschew formidable landscaping plans, which required a throng of garden designers and other experts. Formal landscaping remained very much a male domain and the province of famous male gardeners and experts. In creating their own highly individualized specialty gardens of manageable size—and within their own powers of maintenance—women escaped into private fantasy worlds, no longer dependent upon elaborate layouts, extensive labor, or even didactic books with fussy rules and information. These gardens were their own turf, evidence of feminine cleverness and creativity. And they could be tended, managed capably, and pretty much arranged as freely as they pleased.

Color Gardens

Color gardens were one category in which Victorian women felt free to experiment. These rather contrived little gardens, some scarcely bigger than a bed or two, were, as their name suggests, devoted exclusively to different types of perennials all in the same general color family. To successfully plant a color garden, one had to be reasonably clever in one's plantings, yet one also had all the freedom possible within that particular color family. Color gardens differed from single-color bedding schemes in that single species beds were usually geometric shapes filled with annuals. A color garden was planted with a variety of perennials, all in the same color, such as the white or red gardens at Sissinghurst.

Yellow, pink, and white were typical of the color gardens planted at various times throughout the century, producing bold and beautiful effects. Mingled gardens with exclusively red flowers were frowned upon as inharmonious and in poor taste—"scarcely endurable" was how one garden authority put it. It was the blue garden, however that was said to be the greatest challenge, and consequently the most consistently and widely admired.

Victorian gardeners on the whole simply adored blue flowers. To their sensibility, nothing was quite as lovely as a garden whose flowers vied in hue with the pure blue color of a cloudless sky. As a result, since blue is somewhat rare in flowers—with of course some notable exceptions—19th-century hybridizers went all out to try to develop azure hues in plants that had never been that color before—with "blue" roses and "blue" phlox being the somewhat dubious results.

Fortunately, the Victorians were fairly indiscriminate in admiring all shades of blue—purplish blues might blossom next to green-blues and sapphires, and were never thought to clash. Even steely gray "blue" roses were tolerated. Often blue gardens even embraced tints of pale lilac and purple, and included flowers such as violets and pansies within their borders.

Planting a Victorian blue garden today is a fairly straightforward matter. Traditional flower choices include fringed gentians, forget-me-nots, bachelor's buttons, and of course delphinium, all of which were Victorian favorites and are certainly among the bluest of flowers. For blue borders, gardeners can consider Johnny-jump-ups, blue and white Canterbury bells, and campanula. Grape hyacinth, because of its deep blue color, was also thought to be especially effective bordering a bed of lighter blue flowers. Another low-growing blue flower, authentic to the time and suitable for edging, was dwarf ageratum. Just three to five inches tall, with delicate heart-shaped leaves and flowers in puffy bunches, it was a prime addition to a blue garden.

On occasion, the Victorians also found that their blue larkspur borders and mixed blue borders were improved when a few white flowers were allowed to bloom by their side. In those instances, white foxgloves, delphiniums, lupine, hollyhock, and bellflower were planted, technically creating a blue-and-white garden.

Pansy Gardens

Except for the rose, no flower appealed to Victorians more than the pansy, which they regarded as an emblem of love and sacred to Saint Valentine. "Long, long ago, it invaded the garden and border, holding up its bright face-like flowers before the last snowdrift had melted, and was caught yet in bloom by the first swirling snowflake of winter," wrote a turn-of-the century pansy fancier from Montana. She was not alone in her enthusiasm.

Pansies, below, were enthusiastically bred, and countless varieties were grown. Dark or light, mottled or blotched with all sorts of markings, they were the 19th century's most beloved flower next to the rose.

Through the centuries, there have been no less than twenty-five affectionate pet names for the pansy. "Heartsease" was one of the most common Victorian names, but every country gave the flower its own term of endearment.

It was during the 19th century that pansies first became the sweetly scalloped, exuberantly colored, velvety little blossoms we know today. The first major pansy show was held in 1841, and from that time onward pansy societies began to form and florists and nurserymen began to breed all sorts of pansy hybrids. Initially, about 400 different varieties were said to be exhibited. It is generally thought that *Viola cornuta* is the true viola of Victorian times and that "pansy" is the term representing the many variations on this theme.

It was during the 1860s, with so many different varieties of pansies being bred, that the bedding possibilities of pansies and idea of a separate pansy garden first began to be considered. By that date, there were countless types of pansies, some with large flowers, some with small, each with different "fancy" markings on their faces. In addition to classic pansies with dark amethyst faces marked with yellow and black, there were rainbow pansies, white pansies flushed with purple, an extraordinary black pansy, and even a bronze one. Sometimes the hybridizers went to extremes. When the classic black markings of the traditional pansy began to be considered "too busy" in a bed, new hybrid pansies without any markings at all were grown. Whichever one preferred, it was considered most effective to plant each separate variety by itself, rather than intermingled.

On the whole, a pansy garden was one that a Victorian woman could manage easily. Small and simple, it usually took a circular form. Of course, some were more elaborate, carrying through the pansy theme in other garden elements as well. The wealthy Mrs. Mary Clark Thompson of Canandaigua, New York, for instance, created a pansy garden on her vast estate, where even the six-foot-high birdbath/fountain reflected the pansy shape. Designed for meditation, the garden was tucked away in a secluded corner of the grounds.

One of the other advantages of a pansy garden was that this perennial bedding plant loved shade. The Victorians found that pansies could flourish beautifully in a garden with a northern exposure or on the northwest side of the house, shaded from the noonday sun. "Of course you will have

Sweet pansies adorned this late-century trade card, above. A garden of Johnny-jump-ups, opposite, flourishes in the shade.

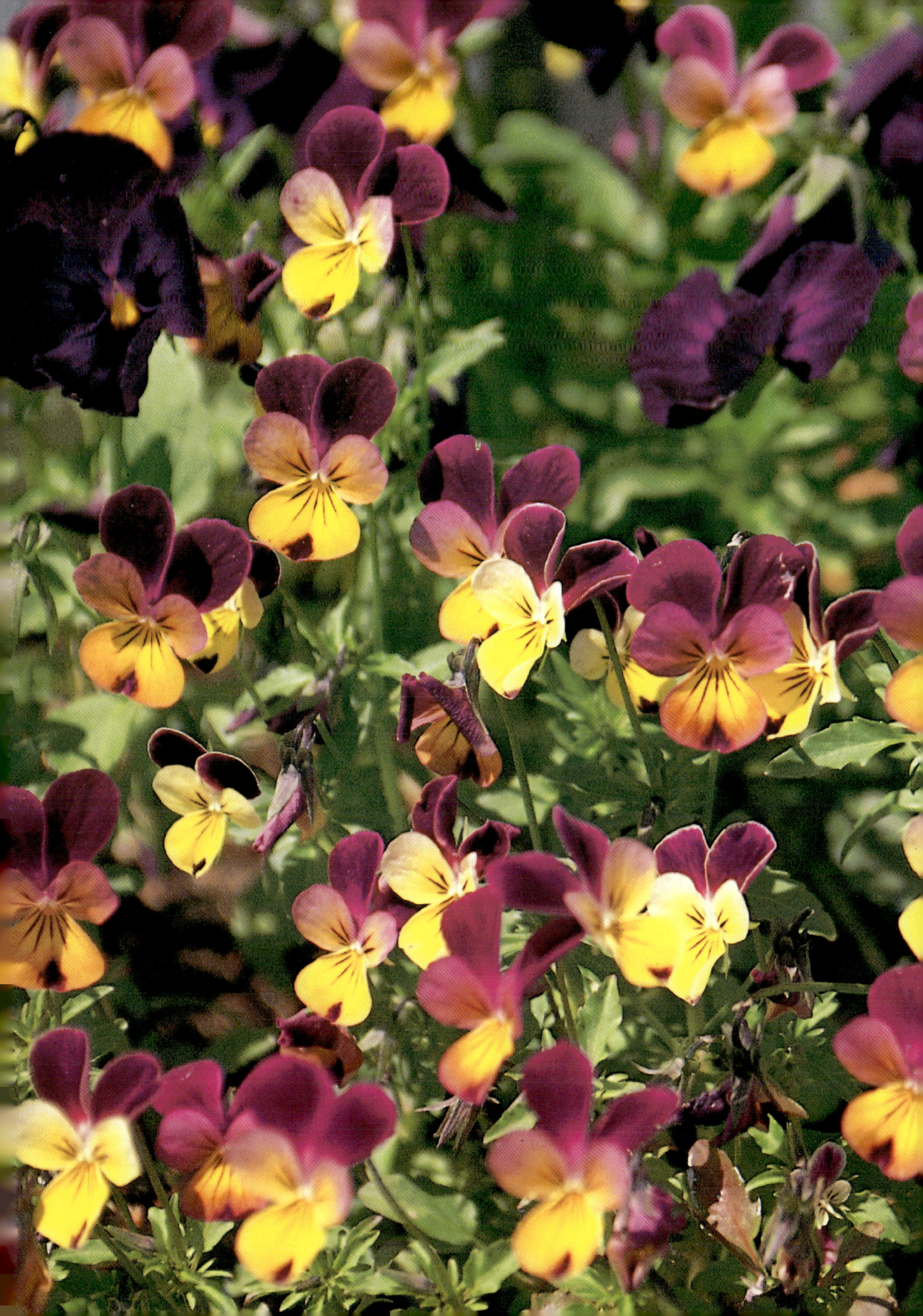

> **PANSY NICKNAMES**
>
> Heartsease   Kiss me   Love-in-idleness
> Jump-up-and-kiss-me-quick   Pull me   Pink-of-my-Joan
> Ladies delight   Garden gate   None-so-pretty
> Kit-run-about   Johnny-jump-up   The herb-trinity
> Three-pretty-faces-under-one-hood
> Kiss-me-behind-the-garden-gate   Cuddle-me-to-you
> Jove's flower   Pensée (French)
> Little stepmother (German)   Idle thoughts (Italian)

Pansies," wrote garden expert Eben E. Rexford in 1899. "No flower-lover can afford to be without them. Give them the coolest, airiest place in the garden, and, if possible, keep the afternoon sun from them."

Since pansies bloom from early spring to late autumn, a pansy garden also provided Victorian gardeners with a satisfying mass of brilliant color not only all summer long but through September as well. "There are few flowers grown in my garden that give the same satisfaction, and delight visitors, as do Pansies," wrote in one Vermont reader, also in 1899.

Occasionally, all-violet gardens were also planted—the violet was considered a sister flower to the pansy and was the Victorian symbol of modesty. Yet the pansy's various blotchings and veinings, diversity and brilliance of color, were preferred. Still, the pansy was scentless, while the sweet and heady fragrance of the violet was one the Victorians considered unsurpassed. Violet-scented toilet waters and eau de cologne were favorites of Victorian ladies, and cakes flavored with violet extract and decorated with candied violet petals, and even violet sherbet, colored a rich grape shade, all graced the Victorian table.

Today, pansies still appear in shades from violet to peach, with infinite markings. Their versatility as cut flowers, potted plants, and front-of-the-border regulars makes them valuable assets to almost every garden. Although they are said to love cooler weather and are among the first annuals to be set out in the spring, some hybrids now endure hotter, harsher conditions. An edible flower, now the pansy also features in salads, extending the dinnertime palette to include those shades of blue once reserved for exotic drinks.

The exquisite white-and-purple blooms, above, excited gardeners of the 1890s.

OLD-FASHIONED GARDENS

As they became more urban and began to view their rural past with increasingly misty eyes, the Victorians enjoyed two very different types of old-fashioned gardens. The first, suitable to grand estates, was modeled on the colonial "pleasure ground." These rather elegant schemes recalled the stately formal gardens of the genteel well-to-do in the closing years of the 18th century and early decades of the 19th. Filled with prim, low boxwood hedges, arbors draped with old roses, and elegant walkways bisecting geometrically patterned parterres of scented flowers, these gardens had a quaint and courtly aspect, especially as seen from the vantage point of the end of the 19th century. Compared to the more flamboyant glories of the typical Victorian gardens of the 1860s and '70s, they even seem rather chaste. And although they often were mixed with more modern elements—most Victorians just could not resist adding a rockery or perhaps a sundial of flowers—these gardens somehow seemed to suggest life as pictured in the gentle Arcadian scenes so admired in the paintings of artists like Fragonard.

▪ Because of their size and scope, the re-creation of these old-fashioned pleasure grounds was generally confined to the Victorian well-to-do. A more popular old-fashioned garden of the time, also a colonial remnant, was the "grandmother's garden," a version of the simple traditional gardens common to old New England villages, small towns, and well-kept New England farms. These were also sometimes known as front-yard or front-dooryard gardens.

▪ It was in these gardens that the Victorians sentimentally planted those once forgotten, sweetly scented flowers from their great-grandmothers' times, the flowers supposedly "best beloved" of the mistress of the house. For the most part, these were blossoms

Peonies, first brought to England in 1200, when they were considered an important healing herb, were one of the "old-fashioned" flowers that the Victorians enjoyed. These are seen in the gardens of the Day House, part of the Harriet Beecher Stowe Center in Hartford, Connecticut, above.

OLD-FASHIONED FLOWERS FOR "GRANDMOTHER'S GARDENS"

Sweet rocket   Violet   Columbine
Bachelor's button
Sweet William   Spiderwort
Fleur-de-lis   Daffodil
Gillyflower   Larkspur   Lychnis
Nasturtium   Marigold
Cottage pink   Tiger lily   Mignonette
Wallflower   Aster
Hollyhock   Foxglove   Snowball
Lily of the valley
Peony   Johnny-jump-up   Ambrosia
White lilac   Hyacinth
Phlox   Canterbury bells   Narcissus
Love-lies-bleeding
Snapdragon   Purple loosestrife
Guelder rose   Heartsease (Pansy)
Ladyslipper   Eglantine   Ivy
Honeysuckle

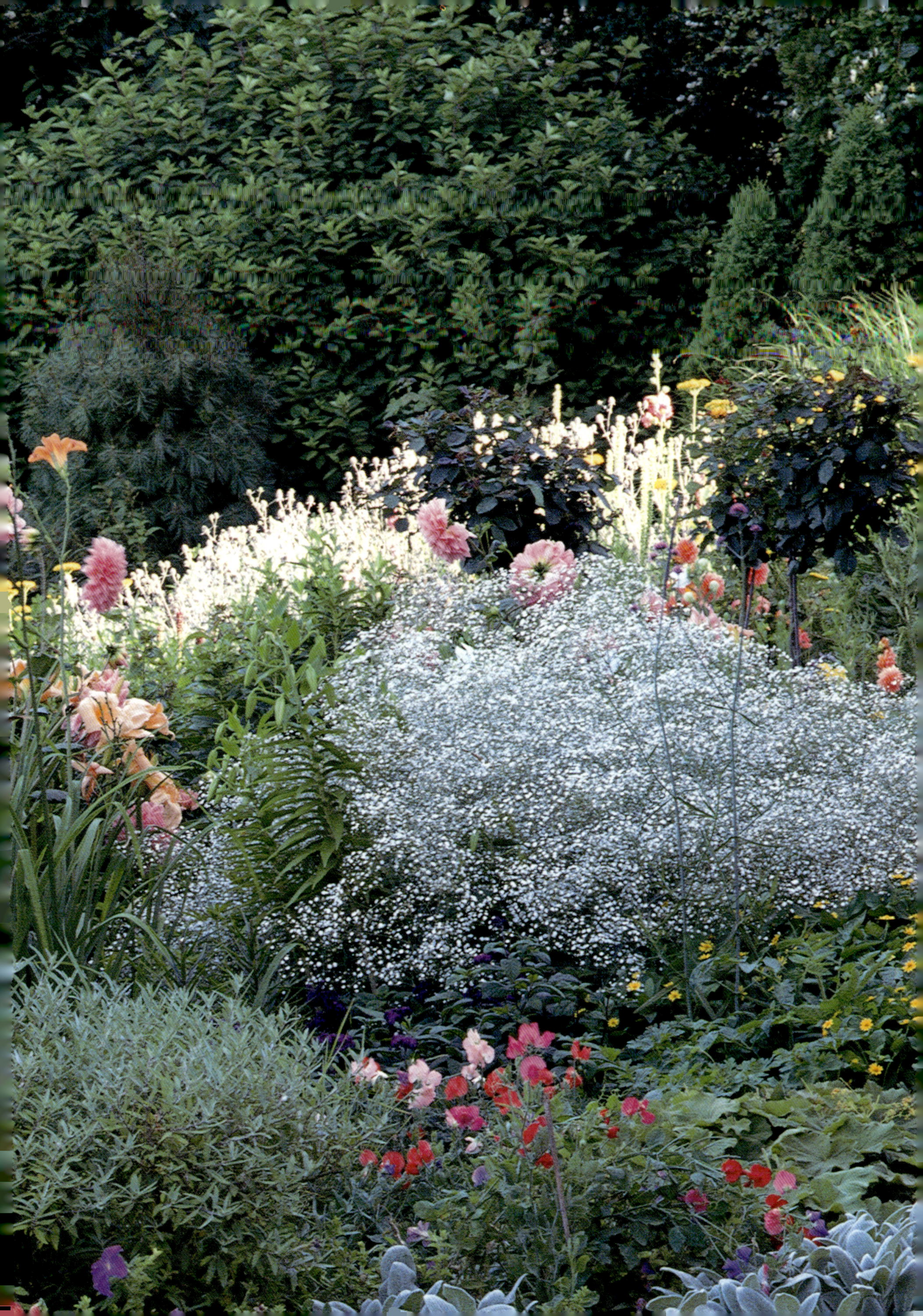

Preceding pages: *Old-fashioned gardens were softer in color and less vibrant than the traditional Victorian garden, but their most distinguishing characteristic was scent. Thus, sweet peas, above, a colonial favorite known for their sweet lingering perfume, were a staple in the 19th-century old-fashioned garden.*

with a touch of feminine elegance: gentle lilies, tubs of oleander that could be moved indoors with the first frost, fuchsias with their shaded petals—but not the humble marigold. Because of this slightly precious aspect, Victorian children were never allowed to romp and play in these gardens. Despite their determinedly old-fashioned flavor, the flowers that bloomed in these precious little plots had a formal "company" feeling compared to the robust varieties that flourished at the side of the house or the kitchen door. Located in the front yard, the old-fashioned garden was traditionally fenced to protect delicate flowers from being trampled by cattle, which in the early years of the century still often wandered free at night.

During the last quarter of the century, many people became interested in the revival of this type of garden—even though gardens filled with self-consciously old-fashioned flowers could still be found in more conservative communities and rural backwaters, primarily in New England, New York State, and Pennsylvania. "Its readoption is advised with handsome dwellings in England, where ground-space is limited,—and why not in America, too?" asked in 1901 noted garden writer Alice Morse Earle, an avid proponent of its nostalgic charms. Well-tended, a front dooryard garden was actually considered a mark of good breeding. Since the garden was usually small, it was relatively easy to keep free from weeds.

One of the most appealing attributes of the flowers in the old-fashioned garden was that they generally could be grown successfully by the amateur gardener. This appealed to many Victorians, weary from the labor of bedding out. "They require no coaxing, no coddling, as so many of the newer kinds do. Give them a moderately rich soil and keep the ground about them free from weeds and you are reasonably sure of a bountiful crop of bloom," said expert Rexford in 1899. The Victorians willingly complied.

For gardeners today who want to revive the revival—that is, plant an old-fashioned garden that would have appealed to Victorian sensibilities—the key thing to remember is that the distinguishing characteristic of the old-fashioned garden was scent. Many of the colonial favorites (sometimes the Victorians fondly called them "old ladies' flowers") were admired because they had a sweetness not found in "modern" flowers; hence the popularity of bachelor's buttons, violets, clove-scented cottage pinks, sweet William, sweet peas, columbines, mignonette, and other generations-old plantings. A typical placement would be against a nostalgic backdrop of tall hollyhock. Daffodils and narcissus in early spring, scarlet and yellow tulips, hyacinth, phlox, Canterbury bells, snowdrops, lilac, and hosta all qualify as old-fashioneds. In 19th-century gardening books, what we know today as hosta was briefly also known as day lily. This can be confusing, since we call another plant day lily today. The latter was especially admired for its beautiful and decorative leaves. Lily of the valley, popular in colonial gardens before the 1700s and often carried in Victorian bridal bouquets (it was a symbol of the old-fashioned virtues of purity and humility), was also grown.

The other notable difference of the old-fashioned garden was that its flowers tended to be softer in color and less flamboyant-looking than the traditional Victorian favorites. The old-fashioned garden, in other words, was hardly the place for exotics like cannas. If the front-yard garden was in full bloom and its pinkish-orange tiger lilies clashed "vilely" with crimson-

Narcissus, below, the "daffodil of the poets," came in an astonishing variety of shapes and colors. In 1903, they were recommended for planting grouped along borders of shrubbery, at the foot of rockeries, or under trees.

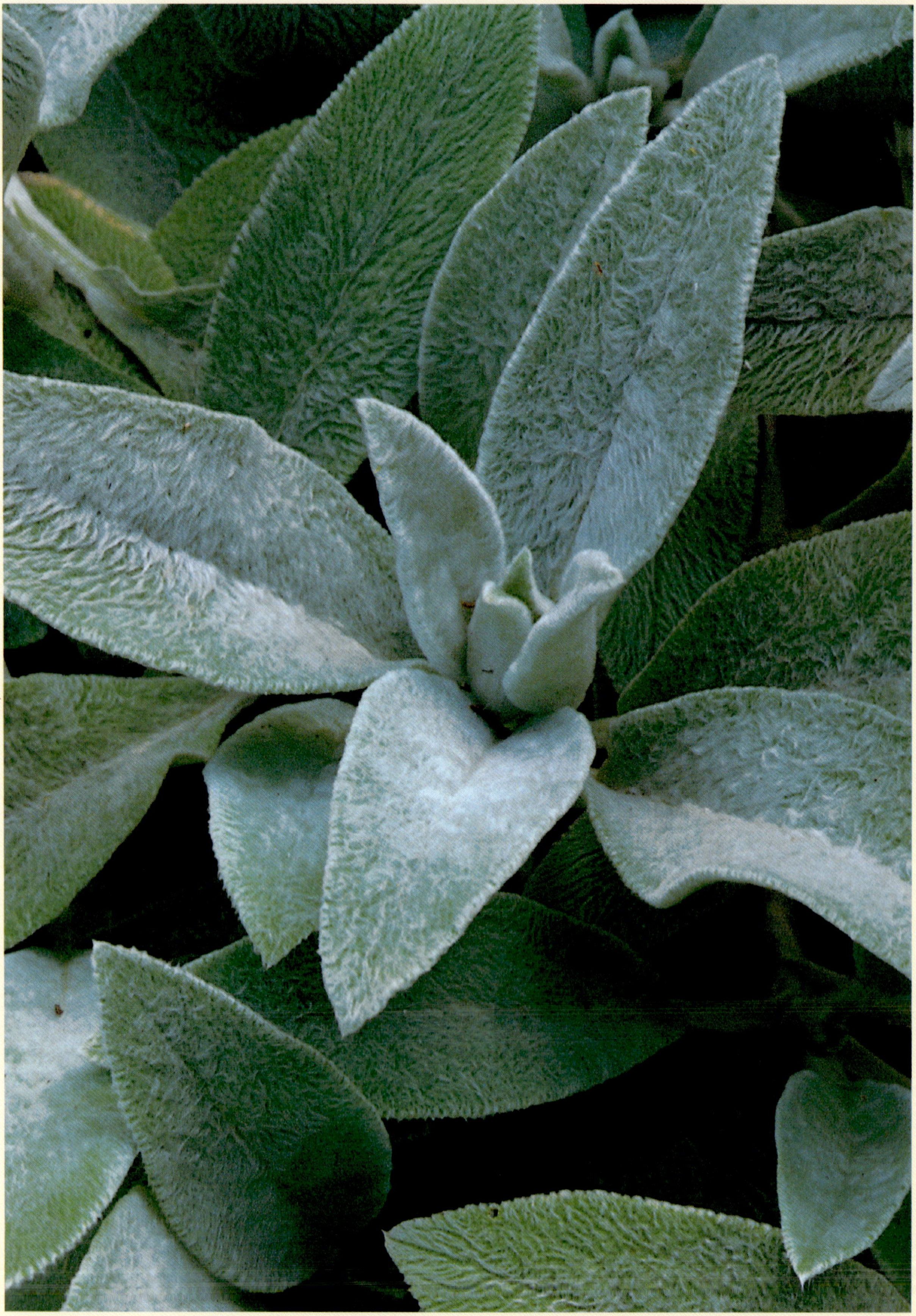

purple phlox and glowing scarlet London pride, one was advised to replace the crimson variety with white, for a more "harmonious" effect.

■ The exception to this rule was the early red peony, one of the most popular flowers in an old-fashioned garden. "I hear people speaking of it with contempt as a vulgar flower—flaunting is the conventional derogatory adjective,—but I glory in its flaunting," defended Alice Earle. She particularly admired the peony for its "exceeding trimness and cleanliness. The plants always look like a well-dressed, well-shod, well-gloved girl of birth, breeding, and of equal good taste and good health," she said, "a girl who can swim … skate … ride, and play golf."

■ Garden schemes for old-fashioned gardens were relatively free from rules. Arbors and trellises, for example, were popular effects, particularly when covered with richly blooming roses. In one greatly admired grandmother's garden planted in 1899, roses, smoke bush, and snowballs flourished on the fences, porch, and roof, while the rest of the garden included randomly planted cherry trees and wisteria and mingled beds of white and purple spotted lilies, larkspur, Canterbury bells, and bachelor's buttons. Myrtle, also known as periwinkle, grew in this particular garden, as did sweet-scented stock. Picturesquely named spice flowers, candleberries and ambrosia are also mentioned, all difficult to identify today.

■ Boxwood was often used to edge the garden paths of the fashionably well to do, and clipped into simple, natural shapes on either side of the doorway. In between the chinks of brick paths and around the box, Johnny-jump-ups blossomed. A simple wooden bench or garden seat was often an important element.

■ One traditional effect that strongly suggests an old-fashioned garden is planting snowberry bushes and snowballs by the garden gates, or edging the front path with white or colored pinks. As a final touch, arbors, screens, or verandas can be covered with fragrant, fast-growing morning glory, with its trumpet-shaped flowers of white, pink, rich blue, or rosy violet.

Moonlight Gardens

When gardeners today think of white gardens, inevitably they think of Vita Sackville-West's Sissinghurst, one of England's legendary romantic gardens of the post-Victorian age. But the gardeners of the 19th century created white gardens, too.

■ A moonlight garden—which was how 19th-century gardeners referred to a garden planted exclusively with white or silvery flowers and foliage—was considered one of the most romantic of all the specialty gardens. Even today, few sights compare to the

A romantic view of a garden in moonlight, above, features a rustic bridge. Lamb's ear, opposite, with its silky, silvery "fur" and faint applelike scent, is an ideal choice for a moonlight garden.

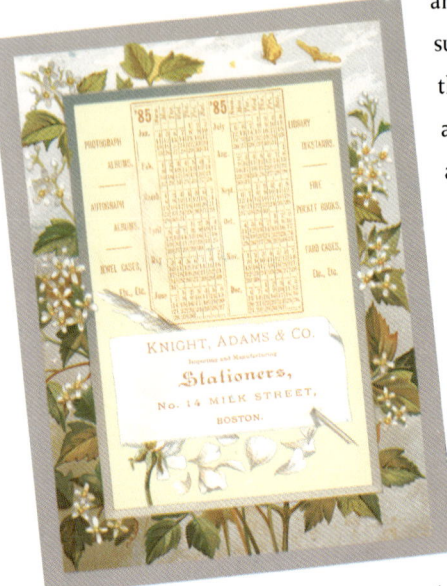

Above, delicate, moon-pale blossoms adorn this vintage calendar. In 1896, the magnificent flowering Ipomoea noctiflora, *below, was called the true magnolia-scented moonflower. In full bloom on a summer evening, this nocturnal relative of the morning glory is a spectacular sight.*

almost celestial shimmer of such a pure white garden as the sun retreats from view and the nighttime mist appears, luring sleepy moon-washed blossoms awake. "A garden in the moonlight, consecrated by the ineffable serenity of the still-hour, and breathing an intenser fragrance in the cool freshness following upon a day of heat and sun, verily murmurs of love," wrote one enraptured 19th-century garden writer. Not surprisingly, it was frequently in the moonlight garden that courting couples pledged their troth.

❈ Although there were many all-white gardens, the singular feature that distinguished a true moonlight garden was that it was planted mostly with fragrant blossoms in whites that ranged from cream to silvery-white to pale lavender-white hues, most of which opened at twilight and bloomed at midnight, bathed in moonlight, mist, and dew. Typical flowers included night-scented stock, whose petals open at twilight, white columbine, an old-fashioned favorite, white iris, and silvery lamb's ear and other whitish-gray foliage plants. Fragrant, white, vanilla-scented heliotrope, tuberoses, and verbena, whose heavy scents attracted bees, butterflies, and hummingbirds, were also planted in moonlight gardens, and of course the white moonflower glory, which opened in the evening.

❈ Pure white or bluish chalky-white flowers were preferred, but other pale shades found their way into the moonlight garden as well. Night-scented stock, a pale gray mauve-lavender flower, was probably planted more for its scent than its color. Gardeners today, for example, can also include white flowers with a faint pink or yellow cast or with green veinings. For example, old-fashioned single or country pinks, which were known as snow pinks, were sometimes used as an edging for the borders of a moonlight garden, giving a charming grayish effect that the Victorians found quaint and beautiful, especially by moonlight. Cool white marble statues and pale vases, pedestals, and garden seats can be used to enhance the garden's otherworldly effect.

❈ The subtle, silvery white ranges of gray-green, gray-blue, and silver-gray foliage were also considered to be especially luminous and beautiful in a moonlight garden. One of the best loved of Victorian silvery plants, for example, was lamb's ear, soft and woolly and covered with tiny, silky silver-white hairs that caught the light—an unusually effective element in a white or moonlight garden. (Lamb's ear was also considered an appropriate edging for rose beds.) The Victorians also liked gray-leafed dusty miller, silvery carpets of lavender or catmint, as well as clouds of baby's breath, gray-green sage, and lady's mantle.

Most moonlight gardens were designed to be small and intimate and frequently were surrounded by deep green hedges and trees, which tended to enhance their eerie and compelling nature. Occasionally, though, they sprawled. One early Victorian moonlight garden, for example, planted in 1833, had a double flower border 700 feet long, with a boxwood-edged path through its center and a flower border 12 feet wide on either side.

In addition to their night-blooming charms, white gardens in general could be radiant in sunlight. A traditional selection for an all-white garden might include an edging of soft, pure-white candytuft, spring snowflakes, star of Bethlehem, narcissus, white-flowered shrubs like spiraeas and Deutzias, double-flowered cherries, and old favorites such as Saint Peter's wreath (bridal wreath). Other white favorites that bloomed in winter window gardens were white tulips, hyacinth with its exquisite bells on slender spikes, old-fashioned lily of the valley, snowdrops, and everblooming calla.

Children's Gardens

It was a well-known tenet of the age that the child who loved to garden would become a superior adult. Developing and tending a flower garden was wholeheartedly regarded as a valuable educational activity for children, teaching the value of hard work and patience and acquainting them with nature's cycles. "Put a child into a garden, and with a little instruction and no trouble, you make him healthy, happy and quite wise enough," one garden expert expounded. "How better can you educate his sense of beauty and order or cultivate in him a perception of natural laws?"

From all sides, children—and their parents—were indoctrinated into the world of gardening with repeated garden images, garden poetry, and garden lore. An engraving in an 1885 edition of the children's magazine *The Pansy* depicts three children diligently tending the overflowing plants and prop-

The burden of flowers is a slight one, to lay on young shoulders, and will broaden and straighten the alert young bodies, not bow them down.

1911

Childhood innocence was depicted in a prettily staged garden photo, above left, and in a *posy-picking young lady, above.*

> *Make your earliest school-room the garden and you are not likely to regret it.*
>
> **HILDEGARDE HAWTHORNE, 1911**

ping a small trellis in "a winter garden" on their windowsill. Victorian children who read this moral magazine—in which they were frequently admonished to be like the pansy and do their best in the little spot where God's hand had placed them—were addressed by the editor as "Pansies" or "dear Blossoms." They belonged to The Pansy Society, and regularly corresponded with the magazine about their pastimes, problems, faults, and play. "My Dear Pansies," wrote the magazine's editor, Mrs. G. R. Alden ("Pansy") of Carbondale, Pennsylvania, "I am very glad that this wintry weather which has made so many blossoms droop their heads, seems to agree with you all. I think I have never seen our bed in more vigorous bloom."

In 1869, two of the foremost oracles of the Victorian household, Catharine Beecher and her sister Harriet Beecher Stowe, also championed the value of gardens in training the young. "Every child should cultivate flowers and fruits to sell and to give away, and thus be taught to learn the value of money and to practice both economy and benevolence," they wrote in *The American Woman's Home*. Other prominent Victorian garden enthusiasts fondly recalled their early introduction to gardening. Mrs. S. O. Johnson, for instance, was "an enthusiastic lover of flowers from childhood . . . having cultivated them ever since the use of the hands was learned." In 1851, seedsman Joseph Breck, who was also the former editor of *The New England Farmer* and *The Horticultural Register*, rhapsodized that no person "blessed with parents that indulged themselves and children with a flower-garden can forget the happy, innocent hours spent in its cultivation."

A typically Victorian children's garden—and one that children today would also enjoy—would include brightly colored, big seeded, and easy-to-grow flowers and vegetables. Sunflowers, poppies, marigolds, petunias (which grew luxuriously and profusely), radishes and carrots (which have short growing cycles), and cucumbers, lettuce, and easy-care beans all fit the bill. Another typically Victorian plant that particularly delighted children was phlox—in white, pink, scarlet, and mauve. Not only was it bright in color and a good bloomer, but it was relatively inexpensive. Some people even considered

Below, *an authentic reproduction of Joseph Breck's famous children's garden of 1833 (described opposite), as re-created by the garden staff of Old Sturbridge Village, Sturbridge, Massachusetts.*

BRECK'S CHILDREN'S GARDEN

IN 1833 JOSEPH BRECK, then superintendent of the horticultural garden in Lancaster, Massachusetts, wrote The Young Florist, in which he described in extraordinary detail the making of an ideal children's garden in hopes of attracting young people to the wholesome benefits of the cultivation of flowers. Because of the size and complexity of the garden, however, one may well suspect that his aim was to sell seeds as well.

BRECK'S CHILDREN'S GARDEN was both colorful and fanciful. Consisting of a combination of 100 different varieties of annuals, perennials, and native wild plants, it was arranged something like a maypole, with concentric circles of flowers, topped by a rustic arbor of birch poles on which flowering vines were trained. Although it may not be possible to duplicate all the plants that Breck required (not all are identifiable today), the following is a sampling of just some of the flowers he suggested.

CENTRAL CIRCLE: White, blue, purplish red, and scarlet morning glories (each about 10 feet high); colored lemon gourds; starry ipomoea; scarlet and white flowering beans.

SECOND CIRCLE: Sweet peas; cypress vine; balloon vines; yellow Mexican ximenia; deep orange nasturtiums, each about 4½ feet high.

THIRD CIRCLE: Red and violet zinnias; red and yellow four-o'clocks; white and yellow chrysanthemums; prince's feather; yellow immortelle; variegated euphorbia; red and white lavatera; blue commelina; old-fashioned flowers like larkspur and love-lies-bleeding.

FOURTH CIRCLE: Grand-flowering argemones; night-flowering primrose; amaranthus; zinnias in many colors; African hibiscus; African marigolds; deep crimson cockscomb; red opium poppies.

Each successive circle in this historic children's garden became progressively lower in height, with no two flowers of the same shape or color placed next to each other. Blue fennel flowers, red and white quilled asters, white catchfly, lemon balm, sweet basil or lavender, African roses, white fringed poppies, and yellow hawkweed were added in the fifth circle; the sixth and outer circle, lowest to the ground, was filled with tiny, dwarf plants, special child-pleasing favorites like sweet alyssum, purple and white candytuft, daisy-leaved catchfly, yellow and white evening primroses, mignonette, scarlet cacalia, forget-me-nots, purple jacobaea, and pansies, along with ice plants and curious plants like the sensitive plant.

Drummond phlox (not to be confused with garden phlox) the ideal children's plant because its colors and markings were so soft and varied; one might try for hours and not find two plants alike. Also recommended for children's gardens are balsam, a tallish plant with flowers as large as tea roses (little girls were said to enjoy arranging these bright flowers in saucers), asters, ten-week stock (also known as gillyflower), pansies, portulaca, sweet peas (for hedges and fragrance), nasturtiums, and whole beds of calliopsis for a "brilliant and child-pleasing" burst of color. Victorian children also liked mignonette, not so much for its appearance but for its sweet fragrance. It was also considered a very proper flower "to give grandma."

The Victorians tried to instill the love of gardening in their children, above; children were encouraged to compete for prizes for tending the prettiest bed and raising the choicest flowers or vegetables.

▦ Children also were attracted to "odd" or "curious" plants, as well as those that bloomed quickly. One turn-of-the-century Michigan woman, Anna Lyman, recommended a background of gourds in a children's garden. "Children are always delighted with the pretty nest eggs, dipper and serpent varieties," she said. Other plants that fell into this category were four-o'clocks, because of their interesting seed vessels and the fact that they did indeed open in the late afternoon; the pink sensitive plant (mimosa), which curled its leaves and withdrew when touched (children were said to love to show visitors to the garden how quickly its leaves would close); ice plant, which had icelike crystals adorning its succulent leaves, and "snails, horns, hedgehogs and caterpillars," all of which were plants with "curious" pods.

▦ Frequently on large English estates a portion of land was set aside for a separate children's garden, with as much attention paid to its arrangement as to the decoration and furnishing of the children's rooms. In addition to a small plot where fruits, flowers, or vegetables could be raised, these gardens usually contained a lawn for a playground, trees to be climbed, a pavilion or summerhouse where lessons could be studied or games played on rainy days, and a stretch of turf for tennis or croquet. While the smallest plots, belonging to the youngest children, may have appeared rather ragged as far as gardens went, in general these privileged Victorian children were said to been entranced by gardening, often competing for prizes for the prettiest bed, the choicest flower, or the finest vegetables.

▦ Middle-class families, whose gardens hardly approached the acreage of the great estates, were also encouraged to reserve a bit of them for the children, or at least to let the youngsters into their own gardens. "Let them live close to its flowers, even though a small foot treads over the borders now and then," parents were urged. "Give them a pair of scissors and let them help cut the blossoms for the house, or snip off the dead ones; teach them to weed, to transplant, to train vines. You will be surprised how well a child becomes a garden, how much lovelier each is for the other."

In fact, it was through gardens like these that the Victorians hoped their children would become lovers of natural history, attuned to the appearances of green grass and blossoming buds. Tiny toy spades, hoes, and rakes were manufactured and sold. Even schools, seeing in gardening a way to teach the rewards of planning, effort, and patience, began to include gardening in their curriculums. "The teacher can stimulate interest by letting each class have a small flower bed, or, if they are not *very* quarrelsome scholars each could have a tiny bed of his or her own," suggested *The Mayflower* in 1900. More and more, good children were depicted in children's books industriously working their gardens or gathering wildflowers—an activity that seemed to have special appeal for young folk. "Don't you know the wild flowers?" little Effie asked her brother in *An Easter Story*, published in 1885. Instead of conservatory "roses and lilies and such things," which would have cost money the children didn't have, there were "lovely violets and May-flowers, and pussy-willows, and lots of pretty things. . . . We could get loads of them in woods back of Mr. Benton's lot."

As for city children who could not tend their own garden plots, a plant of their own could sometimes suffice. "Let it be a plant that bears gay blossoms and lots of them and they will never question you as to its value. They will choose the bright Geranium—value, a few cents—and never the stately Palm, that cost you many times as much," advised "Hepatica," one Midwestern garden expert. Sometimes children were satisfied by a few petunias, particularly those in rich, velvety colors. Generally, Victorian children chose flowers by color rather than fragrance. "They will cull the bright ones that have no perfume before they will take the sweetest ones if they are of a more sober hue," it was said. "How often we see baby hands filled with Dandelions."

THE FAIRY GARDEN

Although no formal mention appears throughout dozens of Victorian how-to garden guides, it is commonly believed today that among the charming little specialty gardens in which Victorian gardeners indulged was the fairy garden. This would have been a diminutive garden, situated in a secluded corner, perhaps surrounded

In the poet's imagination, elfin sprites with flowers for souls, above, peopled many Victorian gardens, giving rise to the fanciful concept of the fairy garden.

Following pages: Fanciful flowers and tiny shoes suggest the fantasy of a Victorian fairy garden.

FLOWERS ARE THE FAERY SOULS OF LONG AGO.

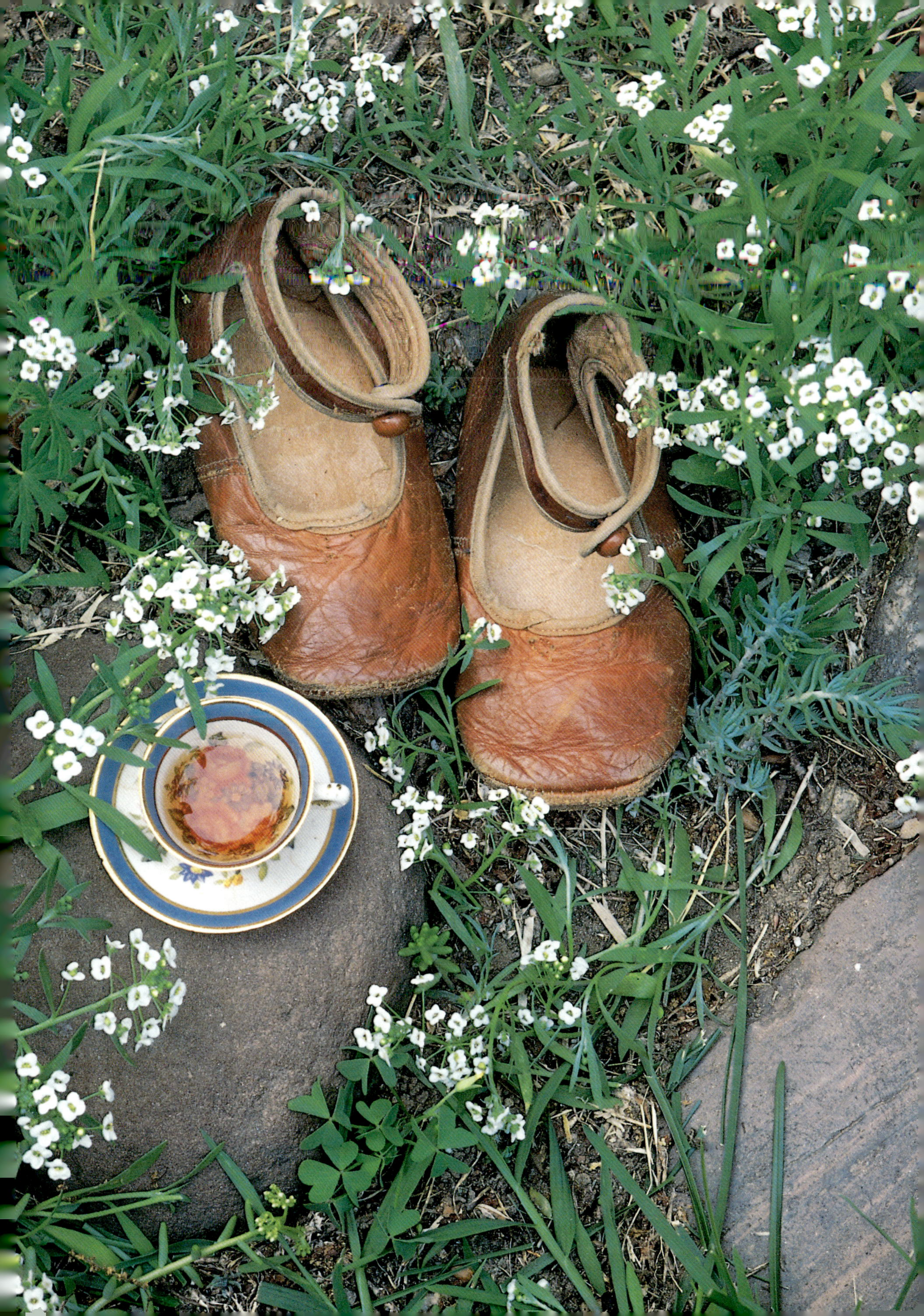

> ### FAVORITE PLANTS FOR OUTDOOR FERNERIES, 1896
>
> **Front row:** *Black maidenhair spleenwort, Rue fern, Common maidenhair spleenwort, Green-stemmed spleenwort, Moonwort, Scaly spleenwort, Bladder fern, Oak fern, Beach fern, Limestone, and Common polypody*
>
> **Center:** *Parsley fern, Lady fern, Hard fern, Male fern, Mountain buckler fern, Rigid buckler fern, Marsh fern, Harts tongue fern*
>
> **Back:** *Broad buckler fern, Royal fern, Hard prickly shield fern, Soft prickly shield fern, Bracken hay-scented fern, Parsley*

by a nest of ferns or a grove of wildflowers, in which one placed a fanciful assortment of miniature "fairy furniture" handcrafted from "found" garden elements. Purportedly it was created to attract wee folk—fairies—a gentle fantasy nurtured by people who had a romantic and picturesque way of viewing the life of the garden and what might possibly go on there after dark.

Did the 19th-century men and women who look out at us so soberly from their sepia photographs truly believe in the existence of fairies cavorting among their flowers by night? Perhaps some did. Who but the Victorians—Sir Arthur Conan Doyle and Lewis Carroll among them—would actually attempt to use one of the tools of technology, the camera, to charmingly prove fairy existence with actual photographs, created by tinkering with the negatives of the film. After all, some Victorians marveled, how could a camera dissemble? To be sure, many Victorians possessed a childlike naiveté peculiar to that time; poised on the brink of the modern world, they still clung to the folklore and legends of the previous centuries.

But most likely, fairy gardens, if not fairies, did exist—as a cherished childhood tradition, like that of Santa Claus or Jack Frost, with which the Victorians fostered both their children's imaginations and their own sense of wonder. It was a romantic notion of a romantic time to people one's gardens with elfin sprites with flowers for souls, who made cloaks from petals and crowns from stamens, and who perched in cowslip cups and sheltered themselves in anemones during a sudden shower. Moreover, it was a literary tradition, at a time when books were a major source of entertainment. "Fairies use flowers for their charactery," wrote Shakespeare—and the Victorians remembered. Robert Louis Stevenson's childhood rhyme "There are fairies at the bottom of my garden./I know for I have seen them there" was an oft-quoted Victorian favorite. So it was that in fern-shaded corners and at the garden's edge, they probably did create fairy gardens, paeans to their delight in the mysteries of nature.

Those looking to re-create the fancy of a fairy garden in the Victorian spirit have only to look to their imaginations. Designed to captivate visitors to the garden with its whimsy and charm, the ideal place for its setup would be in a half-hidden garden corner, at the bank of a stream, or at the point where the cultivated garden meets the untamed edge of the forest (for woods fairies, after all, would not be so bold as to venture into the garden proper). There, one could place diminutive handcrafted chairs fashioned from bark, twigs, and maple leaves, held together with twisted grapevines and upholstered in moss, or fragile tilting tables covered with gossamer-soft leaf cloths, holding teacups made from acorns and dishes from tiny petals. There might even be a white birch bark rocking chair draped with a lap robe stitched together from violet petals. Fairy cheese could be made from fruit of the mallow; tiny cup mushrooms could be fairy purses.

FERNERIES

There was a point, both in America and England, during the 1880s and '90s when "fernmania"—the fern craze—was rampant. It is probably safe to say that nearly every respect-

Palms and ferns were essential for homes of refinement and culture. Above, a bell jar converts an outdoor garden urn into an elegant fernery for an 1870s parlor. Opposite, an advertisement promotes Boston fern, "the best of all ferns for house culture," and cocos palm, "artistic and beautiful."

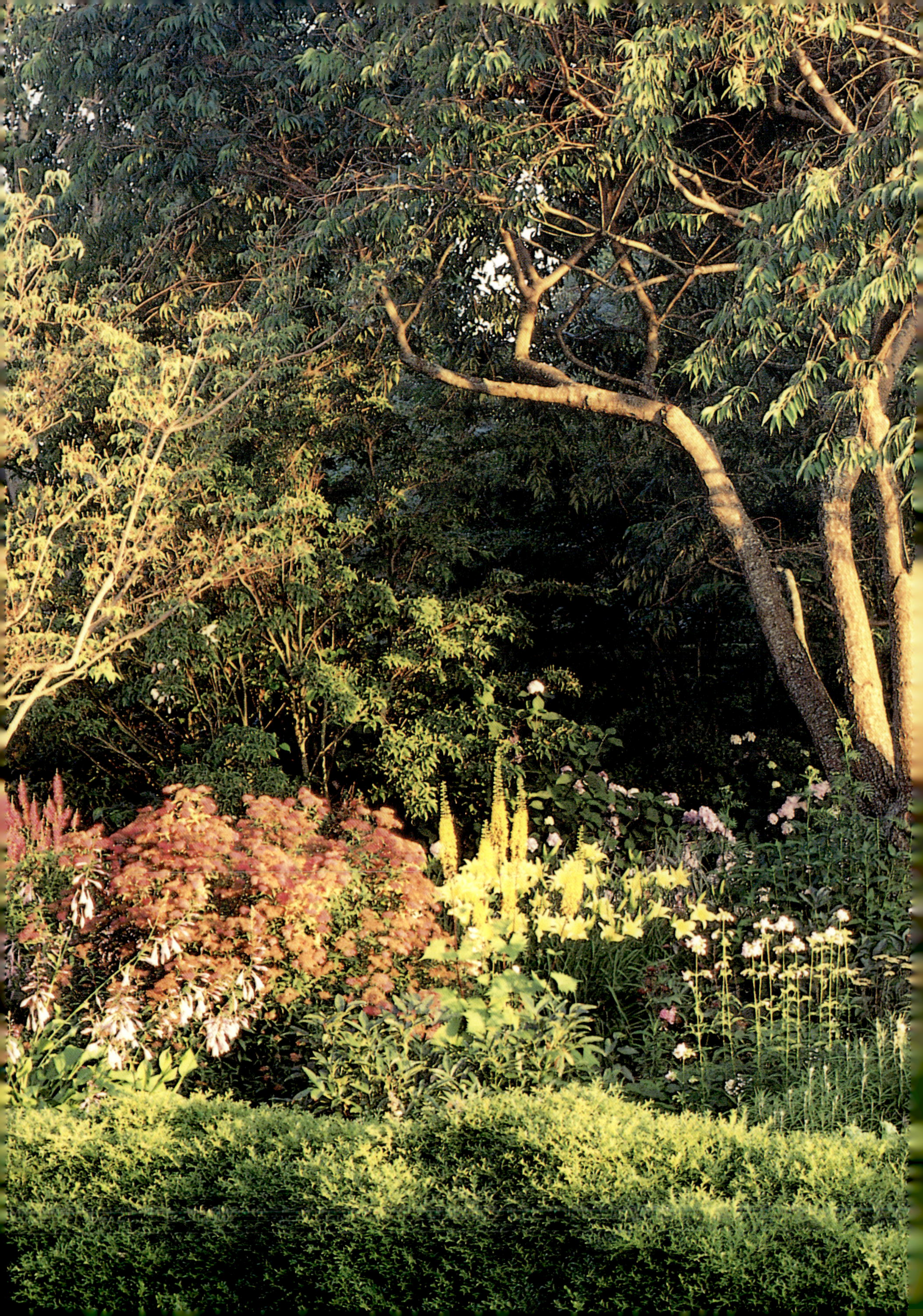

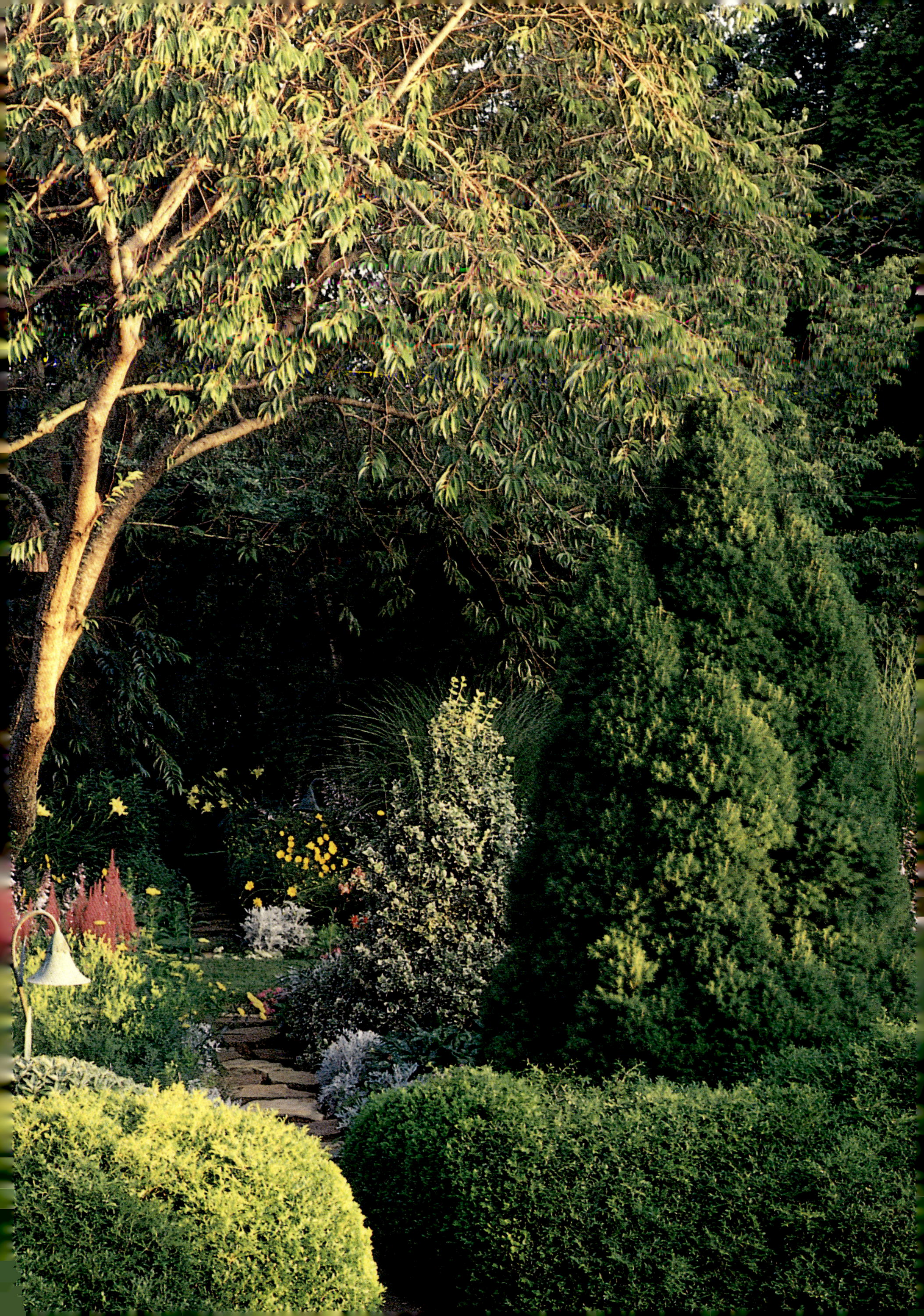

*Preceding pages:
This mature garden of old favorites, with its boxwood hedges, represents the unabashedly romantic side of the 19th-century garden. Originally intended as an American-bred English garden, it has strayed, like many, from its original intent.*

Below, maidenhair (lower) and ostrich ferns (taller) thrive outside the studio of late 19th-century sculptor Daniel Chester French, at his home, Chesterwood.

able homeowner of middle-class pretensions had a feathery-textured fern garden, also known as a fernery, to call his own. To supply these leafy gardens, both indoors and out, Victorian fern hunters frantically scrambled through woodland glades and up and down moist, mossy stream banks, in search of choice specimens.

▦ Indoors, feathery, filmy ferns too delicate for outdoor culture flourished under the glassy protection of handsome Wardian cases or bell-glasses set up in the conservatory or parlor. For gardeners today, potted aspidistra (known as the cast-iron plant because of its hardiness and ability to survive the low light of Victorian parlors, as well as little care), Boston fern (considered one of the most decorative), and sword fern were along the favorite Victorian house ferns that were especially easy to grow, as well as asparagus fern, not a fern but actually a relative of asparagus.

▦ Outdoors, the Victorians built fern houses—greenhouses devoted exclusively to fern culture. A well-furnished outdoor fern house was considered the perfect rustic accent, besides being one that took a comparatively small amount of labor and skill.

▦ But there was also another kind of fern garden—an outdoor fernery in the wild, unenclosed by any sort of lean-to or structure. These flourished by the banks of streams, at the edges of ponds, or in any cool, shady locale. "A beautiful and luxuriant group of ferns may be had for the entire summer by anyone who has a large tree or shady place where they can be planted," said May Perrin Goff in 1882. "If there is a wet and unsightly place that can never be made to look well, all the better; choose that spot for your ferns. An airy place, shaded by the house, will do nearly as well."

▦ To create a typically Victorian fern bed, begin by setting up bark-covered stakes, each about $2\frac{1}{2}$ feet long and $1\frac{1}{2}$ inches in diameter, in a circle or oblong. Stakes should be driven into the ground so they stand 12 to 18 inches high. Wrap or weave the stakes, basket fashion, with grapevine, until the enclosure resembles a rustic basket, filling the bottom with sod or earth. Plant the ferns in the basket center, then ornament by slipping seeds of cypress vine into the soil around the stakes. As they grow, these can be trained around the basket, for what the Victorians considered "a very dainty and exquisite" effect.

Ferneries such as these, especially when created at the banks of streams or near water, might also be enhanced by the addition of stones, tree roots, and burrs, to create corners in which the various kinds of ferns could be embedded. This was thought to perfect a suitably appealing and natural appearance. Particular attention was also to be paid to space for thorough drainage, proper soil mixture, and soil depth before planting. "Some ferns require a greater depth of soil than others, and some again, such as the Common Polypody and Harts-tongue fern, will grow admirably on a wall, which shows that they require but a minimum of soil in which to root," explained *Beeton's*.

In planting the ferns themselves, the tallest fern varieties were placed at the back of the bank and the smallest, dwarf varieties toward the front. Shade and moisture were their two requirements for growth, so they were able to thrive in comparatively dark and gloomy situations unsuitable for flowering plants.

THE SHAKESPEARE GARDEN

Another truly authentic garden period piece was the literary garden, a creation the Victorians dearly fancied. These might be Spenserian gardens, Chaucerian gardens, or even a garden representing all the flowers and foliage mentioned in the poetry of Shelley. Shakespeare gardens were, however, the most admired. In such a garden, which was usually designed as a border, every flower, tree, or shrub—and there were over 200 in number—was one named in Shakespeare's work. Because such a garden was a symbol of one's culture, erudition, and familiarity with great works, each plant would have been labeled with a tiny pottery sign, with an appropriate quotation and a reference to the planting.

Typical flowers in a Shakespeare garden were willow, as a symbol of unfortunate love, mentioned in *The Merchant of Venice*; primroses, rosemary, and saffron (from autumn crocus— "saffron to colour the warden pies") mentioned in *The Winter's Tale*; and violets, widely regarded as Shakespeare's favorite flower. The Bard also called upon the elegant, fragile cowslip, with its slender stem and drooping plume of blossoms, in conjuring up the beauty of the court of the Fairy Queen:

The cowslips tall her pensioners be,
In their gold coats spots you see:
Those be rubies, fairy favours,
In those freckles live their savours.
I must go seek some dewdrops here,
And hang a pearl in every cowslip's ear.

The creation of a literary garden, most often a Shakespeare garden, was a common Victorian pastime. The Victorian trade card, above, depicts two Shakespearean revelers.

Shakespeare wrote frequently of pansies "purple with love's wound"; "there are pansies: that's for thoughts," and under the name of "love-in-idleness," in *A Midsummer Night's Dream*.

Another favorite of the poets was the fragrant May-blooming hawthorn bush with its glossy green leaves, bright scarlet berries, and delicate white blossoms blushed with pink. Shakespeare mentions it in *Henry VI, Part III*, asking,

Gives not the hawthorn bush a sweeter shade
To shepherds looking on their silly sheep
Than doth a rich embroider'd canopy
To kings that fear their subjects' treachery?

The blossoms of the hawthorn were often lyrically referred to as "scented snow"—an image that appealed to the Victorians' sentimental tastes—because of the way the wind scattered its petals over green pathways and roadsides.

The use of the sentimental "language of flowers" reached a high point during the Victorian decades, becoming a mainstay of 19th-century flirtations, coquetry, and courtship. That Shakespeare availed himself of the symbolic meanings of flowers fascinated 19th-century men and women. Shakespeare was considered a master of "florigraphical" images, according to John Ingram in *Flora Symbolica, Or, The Language and Sentiment of Flowers*, a popular book of 1875: "He constantly strove to prove his acquaintance with floral symbolism order to depict the passions of humanity." An example is the coronal wreath Ophelia makes in *Hamlet*, from "crow-flowers" (a species of lychnis or meadow campion), nettles, daisies, and "long purples," which can be translated thus: Crow-flowers signified "fair maid"; daisies, the purity or springtide of life; long purples (not identifiable today) were commonly known as "dead men's fingers"; and nettles needed no comment. The resulting word-picture:

Crow-flowers	A fair maid
Nettles	stung to the quick
Daisies	her youthful bloom
Long Purples (eggplant)	under the cold hand of death

TOPIARY GARDENS

Imagine strolling in a garden and being confronted by an enormous ivy-covered bird, a teapot, an elephant, or a horse. Or turning the corner in a maze of boxwood and feasting one's eyes on a leafy pig or swan. How clever, decorative, and wonderfully artificial, the Victorians must have thought. Topiary, an art of the 17th and 18th centuries, was perfect for 19th-century sensibilities. Raising these forms took time and great patience; one had to trim, train, and continually tie up unruly greenery to keep it growing to shape. Doing so

The curious Gothic topiary shapings, above, were suggested for a garden gate. The engraving, center, shows an example of topiary in progress.

either marked one's skill as a gardener or suggested that one was wealthy enough to hire a retinue of professional topiary trimmers and shapers.

The Victorians loved topiary dogs, ducks, bears, and deer, but believed there was no limit to the sort of effects one could produce. In 1870, Frank Jesup Scott even suggested employing topiary as a substitute for costly iron gateways and fences, recommending that a pair of hemlocks be planted on either side of the gateways of ordinary footwalks and pruned to form charming arches over the entry. "With patience and annual care, these can be perfected within about ten years, but they will also afford most pleasing labor from the beginning," he said. And when topiary was exhibited at the Philadelphia Centennial Exhibition in 1876, the much-talked-about masterpiece featured was even more astounding—a topiary steam locomotive!

In the most elaborate topiary constructions, verdant pavilions were created by bending treetops toward the center, some closed but others with a circular six-foot opening in the ceiling in the manner of a skylight. In these tree houses one had a cool summer resort for smoking or reading, a children's playhouse, or a teahouse. Indeed, during its heyday, creative topiary represented modern man's ultimate control over nature—with stunning possibilities for the garden.

For topiary today, English hawthorns, the double flowering scarlet thorn, some varieties of pine, sassafras (which naturally assumes a parasol-like top), Judas or redbud trees, white-flowered dogwood, striped-bark maple, the paper mulberry, the weeping Japan sophora, and occasionally weeping elms are all suitable. For simple topiary hedges and screens, yew can be shaped into geometric forms no more than 10 or 12 feet high (no taller than a man on the ground could easily trim and tend). For more decorative topiary creations, any small-leafed evergreens can be used that are dense and slow-growing, including English ivy, Swedish ivy (vines that can be trained over metal forms), yew, boxwood, or other clinging plants. Larger topiary creations were generally grown on metal frameworks, smaller ones on wire forms, around which the vines were trained.

While Japanese contemplative gardens were a short-lived Victorian trend, flowers like these richly colored Japanese chrysanthemums were continually popular, above. A collection of six varieties, a 75-cent value, were offered by McGregor's Floral Gems for 42 cents.

There is no form in which the rose grows so gracefully as when rambling over rocks and climbing up trees or trelliswork, or over the alcove. In the garden, well-planted pillars (covered with roses) may become objects of great beauty.

1896

The Japanese Garden

Commodore Matthew Perry opened Japan to American trade in 1845, and by the 1870s, the arts and culture of Japan played a strong role in the decorative arts of the Victorian home—from ultrafashionable accessories like parasols and fans to the silks and textiles that draped the curves of its furniture, to Anglo-Japanesque motifs in wallpaper and fabric designs, on teapots and tableware—and, no surprise, in gardens.

The few Japanese gardens that appeared about the same time were largely contemplative enclaves, rather than beds or borders for flower growing, and relied on costly and specialized props in order to achieve their mood. Waterfalls and pools, quaint lanterns and statues, touches of wisteria or iris, a pagoda-roofed teahouse, an arched footbridge, and other traditional artifacts were just some of the superficial elements that evoked Japanese style. Aesthetically placed stones and a large bronze Buddha would have made such a garden a place for quiet introspection, an unusually subtle manifestation of the Victorian character and not one whose popularity was widespread.

The Victorian Rose Garden

Whether a small arbor ablaze with climbers or a full garden filled with a rich and varied assortment of old-fashioned varieties, any period garden demands some sort of homage to the rose. Regarding them almost reverently as the queen of flowers, the Victorians planted roses around their walkways, in the center of their flower beds, and even used them to decorate their lawns. Most important, they nourished them in scented and colorful separate rose gardens, known as rosariums or rosaries. "The rose is the sweet perfume which the mouths of the gods exhale; the joy of mortals, the loveliest ornament of the Graces in the flowery season of love, and the dearest delight of Venus," wrote nurseryman Thomas Rivers in 1846 in *The Rose Amateur's Guide*, just one of the books devoted entirely to the cultivation of this single flower.

With rose growing documented for literally thousands of years—going back farther than the ancient Greeks and Romans, who also adored the rose—serious rose growers have many sources and societies to call upon for information, as well as literally thousands of rose varieties from which to choose. Even in the 19th century, there were many rose hybrids.

When gardeners talk about the simple elegance and beauty of "old garden roses," they are referring to the types grown before the introduction of the hybrid tea rose in 1867. Of the older roses grown prior to the 19th century's horticultural experimenta-

Roses, Queen Victoria's favorite flower, above, were used to decorate every conceivable article. Below, a vintage label once adorned a bottle of rose-scented toilet water. Opposite, an old rose climbs a stone wall at Sonnenberg Gardens.

One of the many varieties of Victorian tea roses, 'Marie Lambert' (about 1893), above, was also known as 'Snowflake'. Through classical pillars at the Sonnenberg Rose Garden, Canandaigua, New York, opposite, the climbing rose is 'Blaze'; the pink one 'Fashion'. Below, lush roses were favorite subjects for Victorian scrap art.

tion, some of the most popular include the *gallica* or French rose, the *centifolia* or cabbage rose, and the moss rose, which grew alongside "new" roses even in the late 19th century. Autumn damask, *gallica*, damask, *alba*, *centifolia*, and moss roses are the old European roses; new roses were developed when these were crossed with China and tea roses from the Orient. Some of the new roses were Bourbon, Portland, hybrid perpetual, hybrid musks, and finally the hybrid tea.

▨ From the closing years of the 18th century and the beginning of the 19th—when the earliest rose breeding in North America is said to have taken place—horticulturists began their copious experimenting with plant breeding. Many attempts were made to develop the so-called perfect rose, with rose breeders trying for an expanded range of color as well as fragrance, hardiness, resistance to disease, and a longer flowering season. Rose experimentation, which began in earnest in the early part of the century, took off in the 1820s and was in full bloom by 1840. On the whole, while many of the earlier 19th-century roses were climbers or shrub roses, by mid-century the rose, like every other Victorian favorite, was well on its way to becoming a popular bedding plant, with the emphasis strongly on color. Roses used in bedding schemes were more than likely some sort of shrub rose until hybrid teas came to dominate in the early 20th century.

▨ In addition to rose breeders who created many new strains by marrying Asian and European varieties, the world of roses was also widened by the discoveries of Victorian explorers. In 1809, for example, explorers brought back the everblooming China rose, which soon become a Victorian favorite, admired for its delicate foliage and loose blossoms. Park's yellow tea rose followed in 1824, and in Shanghai in 1849, intrepid British explorer Robert Fortune is said to have found the *Rosa rugosa*.

▨ For many years, the beautiful damask rose, with its distinctive perfume, was one of the most admired of Victorian roses. Harrison's yellow rose, which originated in America in 1830, was another, as was *semperflorens* (Slater's crimson China/old crimson China was the preferred name), whose distinctive new shade of red strongly influenced the color preferences of the Victorians. Species of roses came in every color but blue— pink predominated certainly, in ranges from pale to deep; the European roses were various pinks; and roses from the Orient were yellow and orange. Other choice Victorian roses included dwarf noisettes; and in 1840, Bourbons in clear, bright colors.

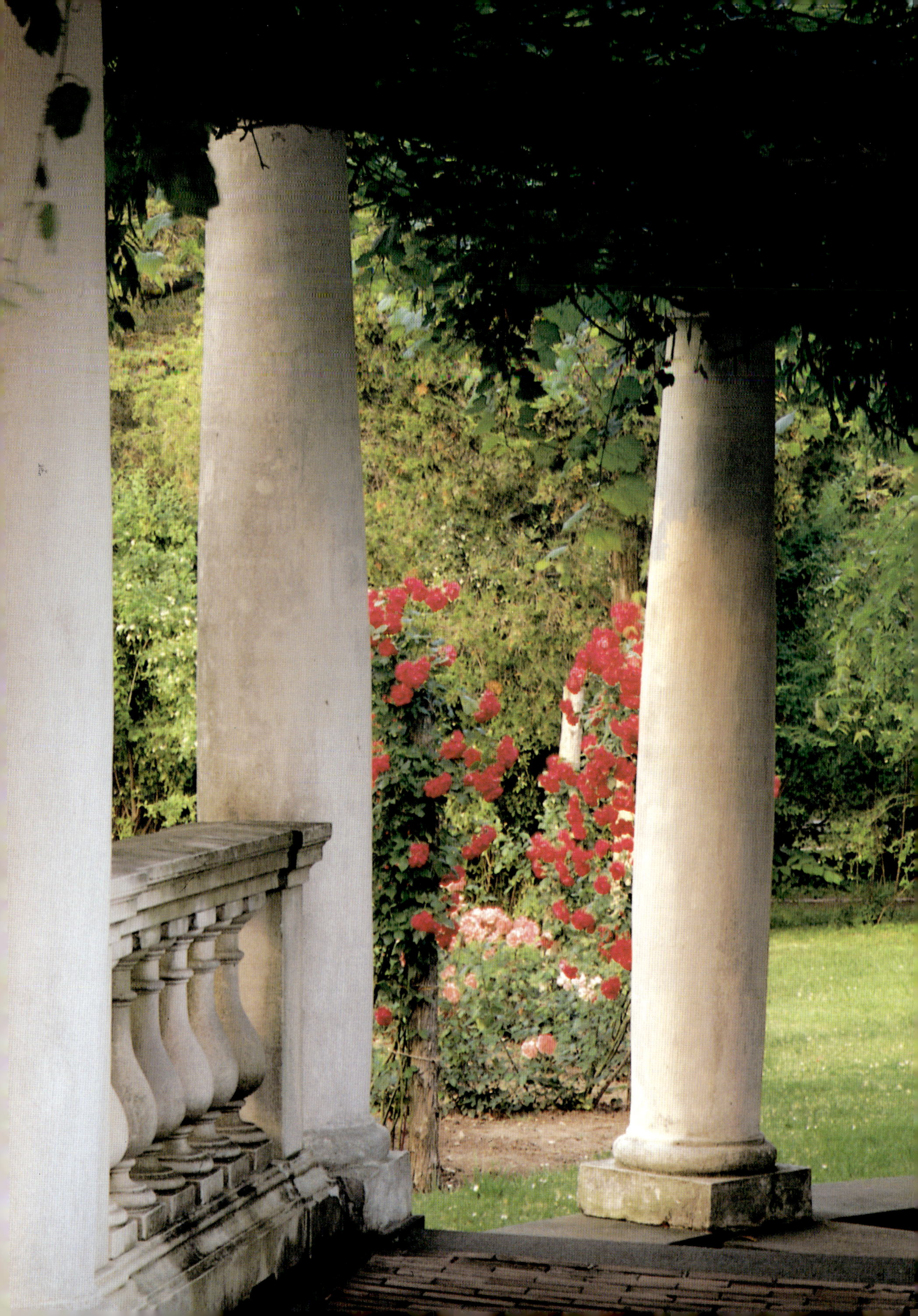

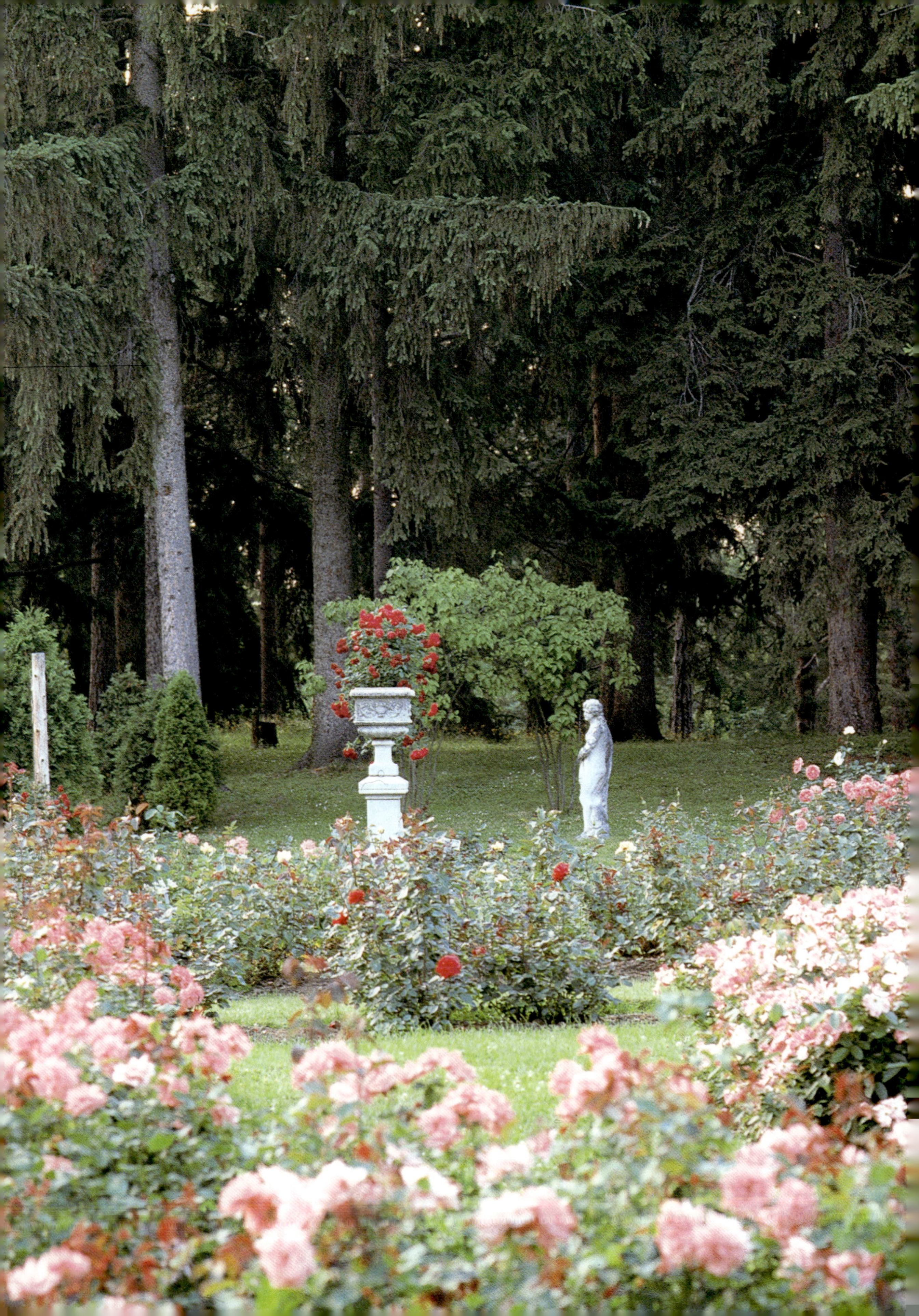

◼ Tea-scented roses from China, especially recommended for planting in conservatories, for walls in arcades, or in England outdoors on heated walls covered with glass, were especially prized. The Victorians even felt that tea-scented roses rivaled the elegant camellia for beauty of color, and nothing was believed to compare with its natural perfume, which reminded one of tea. Tea roses were also admired for the subtleties of their color range—in ivories, pinks, and after 1900 in apricots. Since tea roses are not as hardy as hybrid teas, these were generally grown under glass in cooler parts of the country until the introduction of the hybrid tea.

◼ All of these roses, however (with the exception of the hybrid tea), were eclipsed with the introduction of the hybrid perpetuals, a class that did not even exist at the onset of the era. By 1857, for example, in deference to this shift, *The Rose Amateur's Guide* had reduced the number of pages devoted to mosses and hybrid Chinas from 15 pages each to 11, *gallicas* from 12 pages to 7, and damasks from 6 to just 3.

◼ Because roses were grown by all classes of homeowners, from humble cottager to great lady, rose gardens also varied greatly in form. They were grown in hedges and in baskets, in pots and on arbors. Because of the degree of social cachet and prestige attached to roses, some people felt that an excellent place for planting rosebushes was right in the front yard, prominently displayed. When an entire separate rose garden—a rosary—was planned, it was seldom placed in view of the windows as were many other Victorian gardens, and most often it would be set well apart due to the fact that the many varieties bloomed only once a year. But since roses thrived in the sun, a sunny aspect was a constant.

◼ Sizes of the Victorian rosary varied. It could be anything from a modest festoon of blossoms clinging to a simple arch, to romantic bowers or arches covered with climbing roses, to the more complicated square, rectangular, or especially the circular rosaries which the Victorians adored. One traditional plan to consider, probably for hybrid teas, all of uniform height, is a hedge-enclosed oval rosary which starts with a central "maypole" surrounded by small beds of roses planted in pie-shaped sections and bisected by paths. One of the most important characteristics of a rosary, it was felt, was its pathways, which were generally made of gravel or patterned brick. These permitted visitors to the garden to be able to walk through and inspect the different roses close up. Naturally, the smallest rosebushes were planted closest to the paths and the taller ones in the back.

◼ The Victorians also favored evergreen hedges to enclose their rosaries; these were said to contain the scent somewhat, allowing admirers to enjoy a fragrant atmosphere.

Statuary and fountains adorn this view of the Sonnenberg Rose Garden, opposite. In the background is a pinetum, a planting of coniferous trees. 'American Pillar', a variety of roses originally planted at Sonnenberg, climb a wall bordering an old-fashioned garden. Roses bloom on a confectioner's card, above.

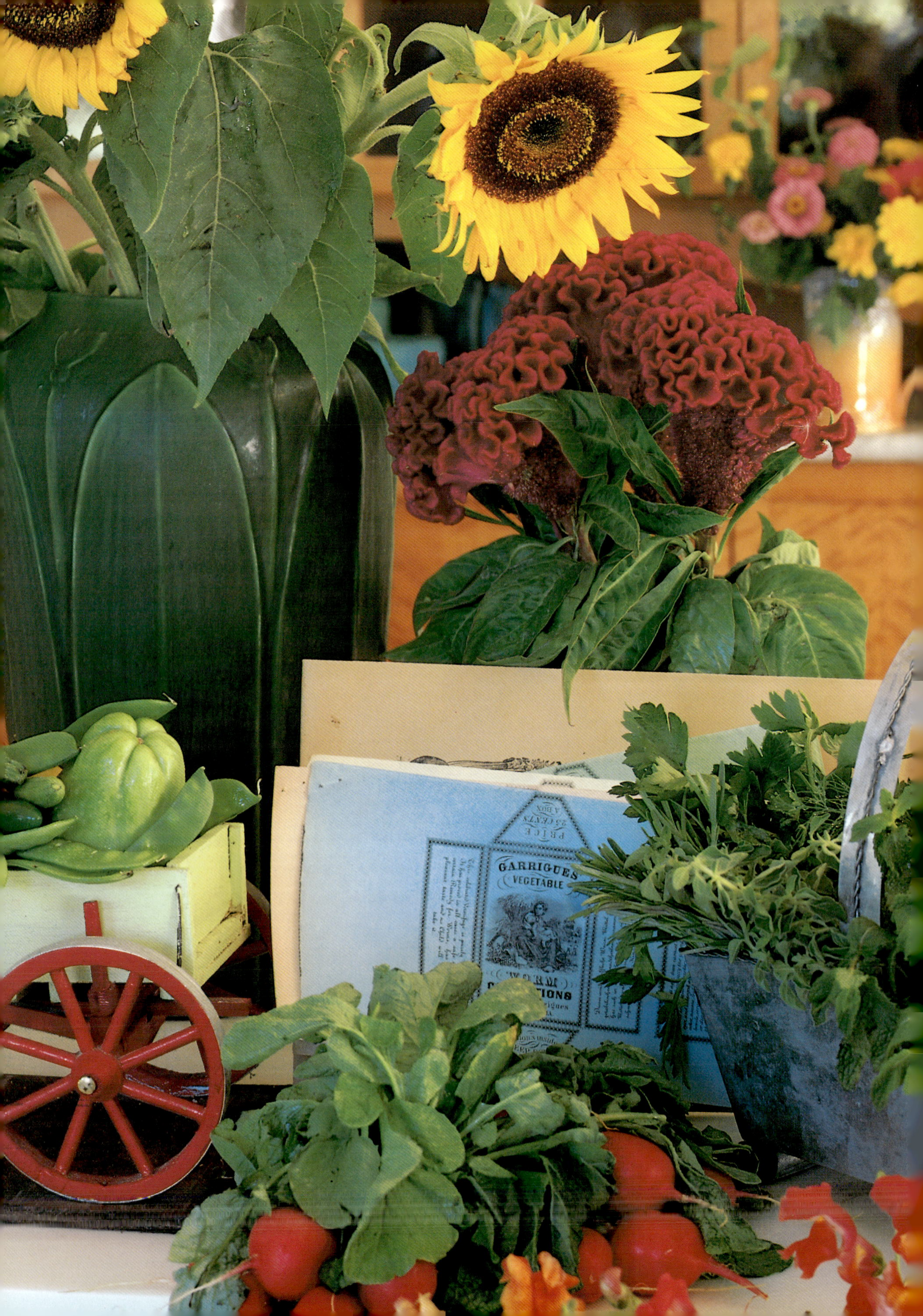
PRICE 25 CENTS A BOX
GARRIGUES
VEGETABLE
WORM

The Kitchen Garden

BEING THE LAYOUTS AND TYPES OF PRODUCE, BOTH ORNAMENTAL AND FUNCTIONAL, TO PLANT IN KITCHEN GARDENS, INCLUDING CUTTING GARDENS, HERBARIUMS, MEDICINALS, AND MORE

At the height of the Victorian era, at the time of the fall harvest, a well-tended kitchen garden would have been a delight to behold. Dense rows of fragrant herbs ready for snipping and luxuriant, leafy stalks weighted with ripening vegetables foretold the promise of savory winter meals ahead. Here and there, cheerful spots of floral color from the adjoining cutting garden brightened the scene, while graceful trailing vines, heavy with deep purple grapes, leaves tinged an ochre

Kitchen gardens were traditionally planted and tended by women, while men worked the orchards and fields. Fruits and herbs fresh from the kitchen garden, right, infuse vinegars with natural flavors and glowing color. Below right, a larger view of the same kitchen shows a Victorian window alcove full of plants and kitchen accessories.

hue, caught the final moments of sunlight, warmth, and growing time. Strictly speaking, kitchen gardens, set aside for the nurturing of culinary, medicinal, and other useful plants, went back to the earliest days of the Republic. Based on colonial precedent, the 19th-century kitchen garden was a functional plot—utilitarian and practical rather than ornamental, albeit with a few subtle ornamental additions. And on the whole, the style and form of the original colonial kitchen gardens held fast into the Victorian age. Thanks to its simple bounty, the Victorians welcomed the seasons with a plentiful supply of fresh and preserved homegrown fruits, berries, vegetables, and tender herbs and spices.

▪ Here were sorrel and dandelion for salads, Sweet Mountain peppers to flavor pickles, and tangy bilberries and raspberries to enliven desserts. Lavender sprigs were gathered to scent stacks of well-washed linens as well as to make the favorite summertime beverage, lavender lemonade. Carrots flavored soups, but also supplied feathery green leaves to adorn dishes of flowers and fill out vases. "The value of a well-filled vegetable garden to the busy housekeeper is inestimable," observed Ella F., a Flanders, New York, homemaker of the 1890s, writing to one of her favorite gardening magazines. "To fully appreciate the fine fresh vegetables from one's own garden, it is sometimes necessary to have been dependent upon an ill-stocked market."

▪ In addition, according to tradition going back to the 18th century, it was in the kitchen garden that medicinal plants and herbs were grown—as opposed to a separate herb garden (see page 153). A necessity in rural areas, where doctors were few, kitchen gardens supplied chamomile for stomachaches, parsley leaves to sweeten the breath, and oregano to soothe the twinges of toothache, as well as raspberry leaves for pots of steaming raspberry tea, which was a blanket pain remedy recommended for all "women's problems," including the labor of childbirth.

Generally located close or adjacent to the kitchen back door, for the cook's easy access, the first American kitchen gardens were traditionally tended by women, while men took care of the orchards and fields. Even when it came to large estates with extensive kitchen gardens and perhaps orchards as well—all of which were cultivated by professional gardeners and servants—the women of the house were still expected to oversee their planting and care. The example of such capable colonial women gardeners was frequently held out as inspiration for earnest but hesitant Victorian wives who were encouraged to admire the rural virtues of their wholesome great-grandmothers. In the October 1889 *Homemaker* (reprinted May 1890), for example, the demeanor of the elder Mrs. Washington, the mother of George Washington, was praised. More than a century earlier, in 1784, clothed in modest homespun, wearing a broad straw hat, and with garden tool in hand, she calmly received none other than the Marquis de Lafayette in her Fredericksburg garden.

During the 19th century the kitchen garden became even more firmly ensconced as a feminine stronghold. "The care and oversight of the vegetables as well as the flower garden, frequently devolves upon women," admitted one 1870s gardening manual. But ever solicitous of the refined fastidiousness of their ladies—not to mention presumed female physical and intellectual limitations—the Victorians did offer concerned precautions: "A good kitchen garden requires labor and some brains to run it—but children will often supply the former, and the housewife must not lack the latter." As with other gardens, the so-called hard work of kitchen

> *Nothing is a greater source of usefulness and profit to a family than a good-sized systematically kept kitchen garden. The family can draw upon it almost every day in the year for a supply of healthful food. The American people will be much better off when they appreciate the garden as the English do.*
>
> **THE MAYFLOWER, SEPTEMBER 1896**

During the winter, families gathered around the table, as in the engraving, left, perusing seed catalogs, engaged in the pleasant chore of deciding what to plant.

Following pages: Victorian seed catalogs and seed packets offered a vivid promise of bounty for the kitchen.

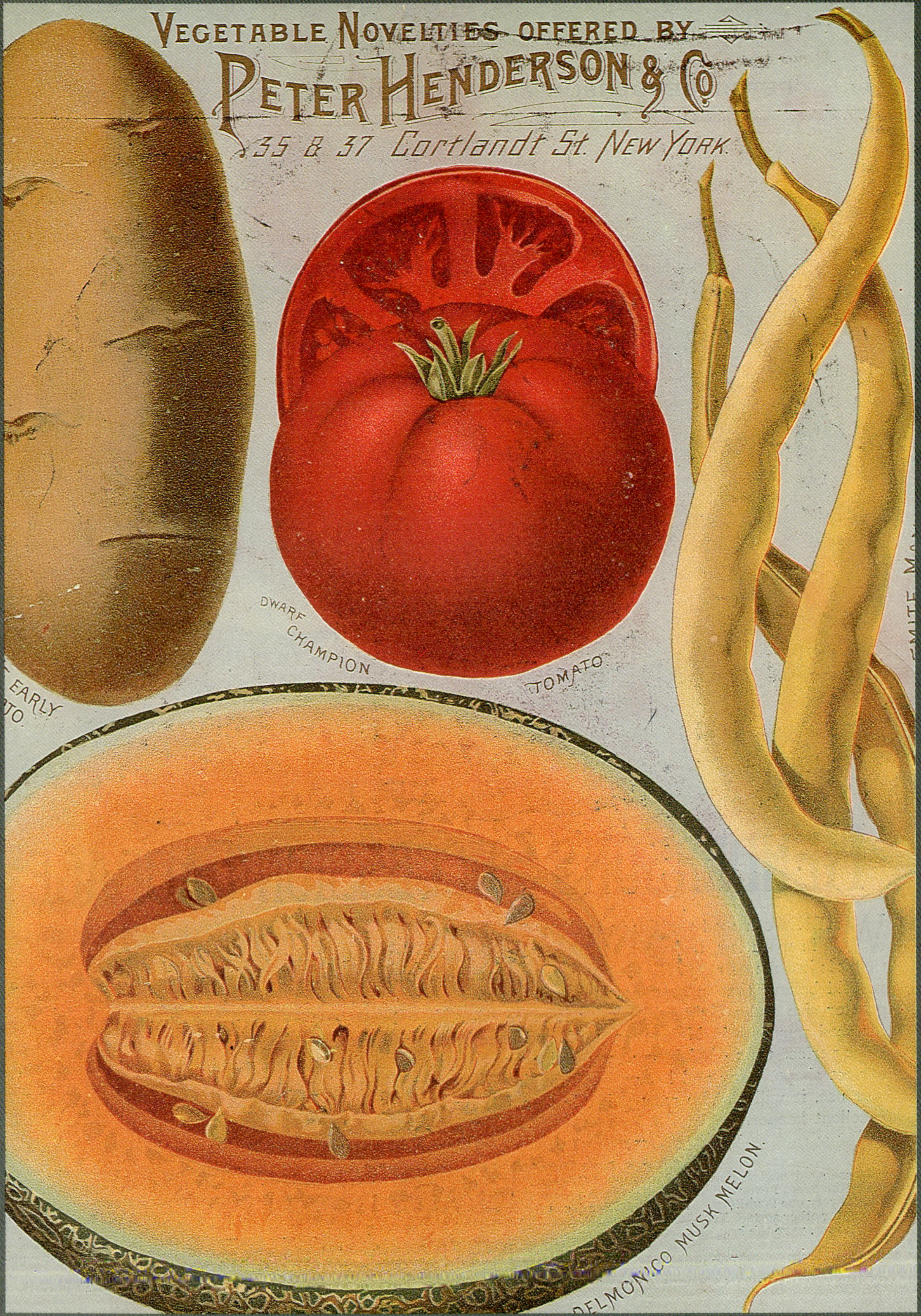
VEGETABLE NOVELTIES OFFERED BY
PETER HENDERSON & Co
35 & 37 Cortlandt St. New York.
DWARF CHAMPION TOMATO
EARLY
DELMONICO MUSK MELON.

CUCUMBER
WILD

THE PAGE SEED COMPANY
GREENE, N.Y.

ONION
Small Pickling

THE PAGE SEED COMPANY
GREENE, N.Y.

A little patch of ground set aside for the kitchen garden will pay for itself and will yield a continuous supply of fresh vegetables far superior in quality to those bought in the market, to say nothing of the pleasure of cultivating them and eating your own produce.

THE DELINEATOR, MARCH 1897

gardening—taking care of paths and preparing the soil—was considered men's chores; planting seeds and pulling weeds, women's. If men did their jobs, however, "we, of the weaker sex, can surely do the rest—if we please so to do," encouraged one lady gardener. She cited the example of an elderly acquaintance who, despite being reduced to walking with a crutch, purportedly tended one of the finest vegetable gardens in the vicinity. Her garden was always ahead of all her neighbors'. "She was a lady, delicate, refined and lovely, and her flowers and strawberries fully equaled her vegetables. Will not our fair sisters strive to imitate her example?"

Winter was the season for planning vegetable gardens, an activity eagerly anticipated by the whole family. Since seeds from peddlers' carts and country stores were often scorned—"they are not so certain to be pure and fresh"—purchase from the new mail-order catalogs was advised. For weeks, these colorful catalogs were amassed—each detailing hundreds of horticultural varieties that the hybridizers had developed—to be avidly inspected when the entire family gathered around the fireplace to engage in the pleasant task of determining what to plant. It was generally felt that seeds from catalogs were superior to those gathered at random from fields and gardens.

In the course of perusing the catalogs and planning the kitchen garden, the merits of all the newly developed strains of vegetables were sure to be debated. Suggestions from popular horticultural guides were thoughtfully considered. "This vegetable is a cross between a Turnip and a Cabbage in flavor and makes a nice dish," suggested Mrs. Johnson, describing kohlrabi (then known as kohl rabi or turnip-rooted cabbage). "The Early White Vienna is the best variety... Be sure and plant some cabbages for winter salad. They are unsurpassed for this purpose, and far more nutritious if eaten uncooked." Cabbagy tastes were particular Victorian favorites, and cauliflower was believed to have a place in every garden.

Planning the kitchen garden meant determining not only what to plant but when to plant it. Rapid advancements in agriculture had resulted in improved strains of vegetables, ones that could be planted earlier, yielding early crops, or later in the season for late crops. Gardeners striving for variety in their daily meals selected from hardy strains and chose fruits and vegetables that naturally ripened at different times of the year. Strawberries, for example, were an early crop; Brussels sprouts showed themselves as late as

In 1886, this Flat Dutch "Cabbage-head," below, was used to advertise the Henry A. Peck Co., a New York dealer in fertilizer established in 1850.

The Victorians liked the formality of raised beds where plants could be groomed and tended with ease. Left, in the Costanzo/Tuff kitchen garden in Cape May, New Jersey, herbs of short to medium height lend themselves to neat, well-defined rows. Metal markers with hand-lettered names give each variety an identity or tell what herbs will (hopefully) sprout in a particular location.

November. Certain types of kale as well as some herbs like winter savory might last well into the coldest months of the year, lightly covered with salt hay for insulation.

▣ Through the vehicle of the popular garden magazines, sharing experiences with growing different strains of fruits and vegetables was common in the 19th century, as it is today. "For the three years past, we have planted Child's Honey Dew Sweet Corn, and all who have partaken of it at our table pronounced it the sweetest and most delicious corn they ever tasted. And that is our own verdict," one reader informed the *Mayflower* in February 1900. "And I wonder how many readers of the Mayflower cultivate the Salsify or Vegetable Oyster?" asked Mrs. G. W. of Flanders, Maine. "Our garden would not be complete without this healthy and most delicious vegetable; for an oyster stew we prefer it to real bivalves, and it is nice cooked in several other ways."

▣ Home remedies for gardening ills were exchanged as well. Should cutworms attack the tomatoes, for instance, peers advised the troubled gardener to "boil some oatmeal, make it very sweet and mix this with a very little Paris green. Lay at each plant a little lump of this mixture, repeat three or four days and that will settle the cut-worms." And of course the garden writers and seedsmen constantly touted their own recommendations.

▣ For the most part, 19th-century kitchen gardens retained the simple

Yearbook U. S. Dept. of Agriculture, 1904. PLATE LIV.

PERFECTION CURRANT.

IN VEGETABLE SOCIETY

*The leek and the lettuce were fuming at fate,
Which started a sort of salad debate.
"They care for us, yes," said a green cabbage glum,
"Because they can use us when other days come."*

**Ormsby A. Court, Massachusetts,
The Mayflower, October 1898**

Preceding pages, left: *'Perfection' currants from the 1904 Department of Agriculture Yearbook; right, an early Jersey Wakefield Cabbage, introduced in this country in 1840, grows at the Richardson Parsonage, Old Sturbridge Village, Massachusetts.*

Three recipes accompanied the 1889 trade card, below—for "cold" slaw, stuffed cabbage, and cabbage fried with cream. The Premium Flat Dutch cabbage was promoted in a 1906 catalog.

> *In Southern States fall is the proper time to sow seed of many of our leading garden vegetables, and our readers in that section of the country will do well to give the matter immediate attention. Lettuce seed may also be sown in Northern gardens in the fall.*
>
> **THE MAYFLOWER, SEPTEMBER 1896**

square or rectangular layout, crossed by one or two main walks, of the previous century. "No better form can be devised for a kitchen garden," confirmed *Beeton's New All About Gardening* in 1896. Even at that late point in the century, as kitchen gardens gained in cachet and their maintenance became less a source of sustenance and more of a status symbol and recreational activity, resulting in more herbs and cutting flowers than vegetables, most still retained the familiar geometric shape of early American times with long boundaries to the east and west and shorter ones to the north and south. With its straight lines and neat subdivisions, it was practical—easy to lay out with just a reel of string, and easy to work in neat rows.

After the Civil War, although this form dominated, the Victorians did manage to add their own particular stamp to this basically functional garden. For the wealthy, the simple rectangular plot might be enhanced with fancy starburst patterns, with trellises or curving walkways. Occasionally the garden might even be moved from its practical right-behind-the-kitchen location in the back of the house to the side of the home or some other more prominent site.

Initially, even as gardeners indulged in all sorts of experimentation with new strains and varieties of fruits and vegetables, they still tended to prefer produce with which they were most familiar, and that could be dried or preserved most easily. As the century advanced, however, certain items began to acquire subtle, subliminal meanings. One might be imbued with an air of sophistication and worldliness, for instance, by aspiring to the cultivation of more exotic vegetables such as broccoli or asparagus, as opposed to the more mundane peas, corn, and beans. Another indication of prestige was the ability to produce early crops. The gardener who harvested the earliest peas or lettuce was a gardener of uncommon prowess, certainly to be admired and congratulated.

The tentative introduction of ornamental plants and flowers into the ever-practical kitchen garden was another modification of the Victorian age. From the 1860s onward, references to ornamental plants in the kitchen garden begin to appear. The April 1889 *Mayflower* pointedly mentions that "some of the [pepper] plants are handsome enough to raise as ornaments, with the added advantage of having the fruit to use when the season is over." Another issue adds that one of the handsomest plants for table decoration was the recently introduced Coral Gem Bouquet pepper. "The shape of the plant was perfect," the writer enthused. Soon the Kaleidoscope and Celestial varieties were discussed as being "very ornamental" as well as extra-fine quality for the housekeeper's use. Eventually, plants like asparagus, purple and white kale, sea kale with its silvery-gray foliage on ivory stems, and even pumpkins were sometimes raised for aesthetic reasons alone.

Along with the cabbagy tastes that Victorians adored, peas and beans were regarded as one of the staple crops a vegetable gardener could grow. Rhubarb was also a favorite, for its taste (called pieplant, it could double for apples in lieu of apple pie) as well as for its medicinal qualities (it was said to have made an excellent tonic when mixed with Castile soap!).

Herbs were chosen for their varied textures, height, and color, as well as for eventual kitchen use. In the background, left to right, shrubby lemon thyme, silvery-gray artemisia, and the fine hairy leaves of chamomile. The traditional brick pathways, nicely aged with moss, are ideal both for impeding weed growth and insuring a firm and level walking—and working—surface.

CLOVES
Caryophyllus aromaticus.

Fig 1. Clove tree.
" 2. Fruit enlarged.

SACHETS FOR DRAWERS

Ingredients — ½ lb. of lavender flowers, ½ oz. dried thyme, ½ oz. dried mint, ¼ oz. cloves, ¼ oz. carraway seeds, 1 oz. common salt. *Mode* — the lavender flowers must be rubbed from the stalk, the thyme and mint reduced to powder, and the cloves and carraway seeds bruised in a mortar. The whole should then be mixed with the salt, which must be well dried before it is used.

THE YOUNG ENGLISHWOMAN, 1880

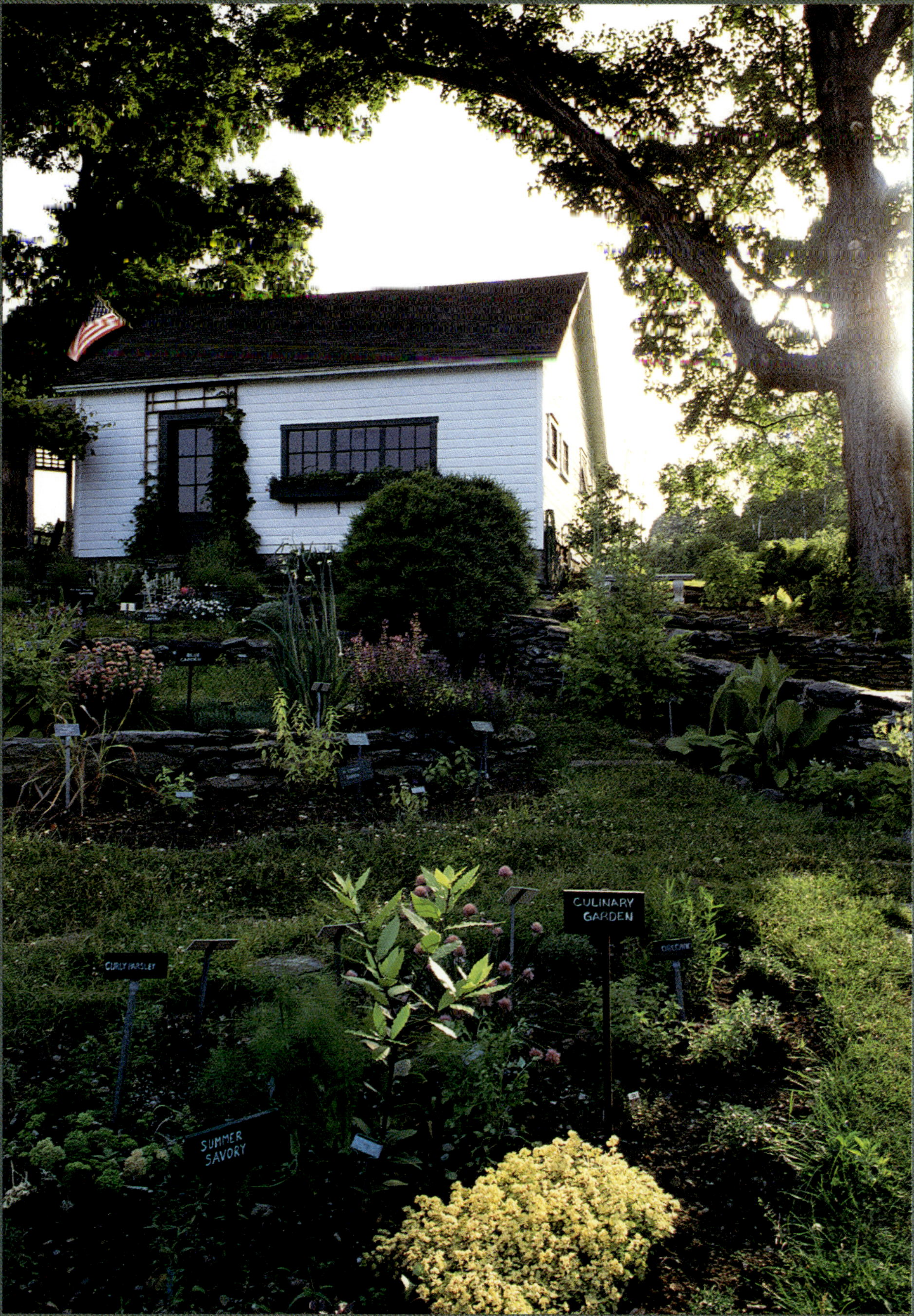
CULINARY GARDEN
CURLY PARSLEY
SUMMER SAVORY

Preceding pages, left: A trade card for cloves; right, a terraced culinary garden with old-fashioned charm, including markers for each bed.

Black and red raspberries like these, right, grew in Florence Holmes's turn-of-the-century garden in Canada.

Some plants went in and out of style. Garlic, for example, was eliminated from some Victorian kitchen gardens when anti-French sentiment ran high, due to the political ups and downs of the Second Empire during the 1840s and '50s, and again in 1870 during the Franco-Prussian War.

The Victorians also gave a good deal of thought to where in the garden each type of vegetable should be planted. For example, main crops such as cabbages, cauliflower, potatoes, and beans were planted in the central plots, usually in rows going from north to south to allow each an equal amount of sunlight. The sunniest, most open spots in the garden were reserved for currants and strawberries.

The warmer south border of the kitchen garden traditionally was planted with early crops like lettuce, radishes, peas, new potatoes, carrots, and turnips. Since this area remained warm at the end of the regular season, late crops like French beans or spinach were also grown there.

As for size, depending on the needs of the household, kitchen gardens varied greatly: there were small plots; there were manageable, medium-sized gardens; there were the vast rows of plantings of the wealthy, frequently supplemented by greenhouses to supply exotic out-of-season produce for the household table. Since it was crucial that the garden be well-maintained, it was considered best that the kitchen garden not be *too* big. According to one contemporary study of the re-creation of a historic kitchen garden, the average affluent family would have maintained a garden of just under an acre—about as much as one gardener could manage.

Yet gardens could also be much smaller. Florence Holmes, a turn-of-the-century Canadian housewife, cultivated a fairly traditional vegetable garden, which, though small—she had only a quarter of an acre of ground for her house, shed, barn, hen yard, and garden was remarkably productive, especially as all the front was taken up with a little lawn and flower garden. Holmes and her family made the most of their limited space, growing tomatoes, black and red raspberries, strawberries, cabbages, peas, beans, corn, and cauliflower. They planted grapes on the south side of their barn, and even toyed with the idea of growing climbing cucumbers and watermelons.

There was not much external embellishment in the Victorian kitchen garden. At most there might have been a trellis at each end of the center walk covered with honeysuckle vines or some other flowering climbing plant. Perhaps a bench or a table might be set out or there might be a small shed in which gardening tools, implements, and baskets were stored. This would provide just enough visual interest during the occasional walks that the gentleman of the house would take to show off the productivity of his bountiful plot.

There, while extolling the virtues of gardening in general, stopping to marvel at the pearly, waxen whiteness of a certain strain of potato piled in a rustic basket on the side of the garden path, or pausing to examine a juicy cluster of grapes on the vine, our Victorians felt certain that they were experiencing the good life, productive, wholesome, healthful, and refined.

VICTORIAN CUTTING GARDENS

As the interest in and need for decorative home flowers increased, kitchen gardens, once limited to just fruits, herbs, and vegetables, expanded in scope and a full-scale cutting garden entered its boundaries. In 1899, for example, Mrs. S. E. Kennedy of Rhode Island recalled her grandfather's kitchen garden: "On the right of the vegetable garden of which I have been speaking, was a pretty old-fashioned flower garden, the dividing line between a flourishing row of Currant bushes which bore such beautiful clusters of fruit that my mouth waters at the remembrance."

Unlike the formal vast flower gardens the Victorians loved so well, the Victorian cutting garden was a less formal affair whose purpose was to provide flowers for the bouquets and arrangements of the home. Typically, on a large estate it would have been tucked along the pathways of the kitchen garden, because, as with vegetables and herbs, flowers were often gathered daily.

The cutting garden, which was adjacent to the kitchen garden, was less formal than the other flower gardens of the 19th century and was used to supply flowers for the table and for bouquets, baskets, and vases throughout the home, above. Below, children gather flowers from a typical cutting garden.

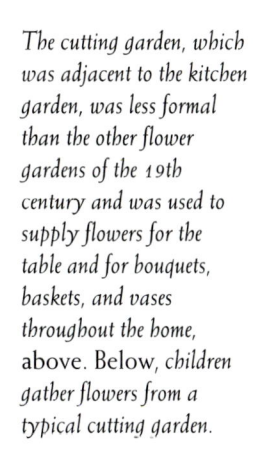

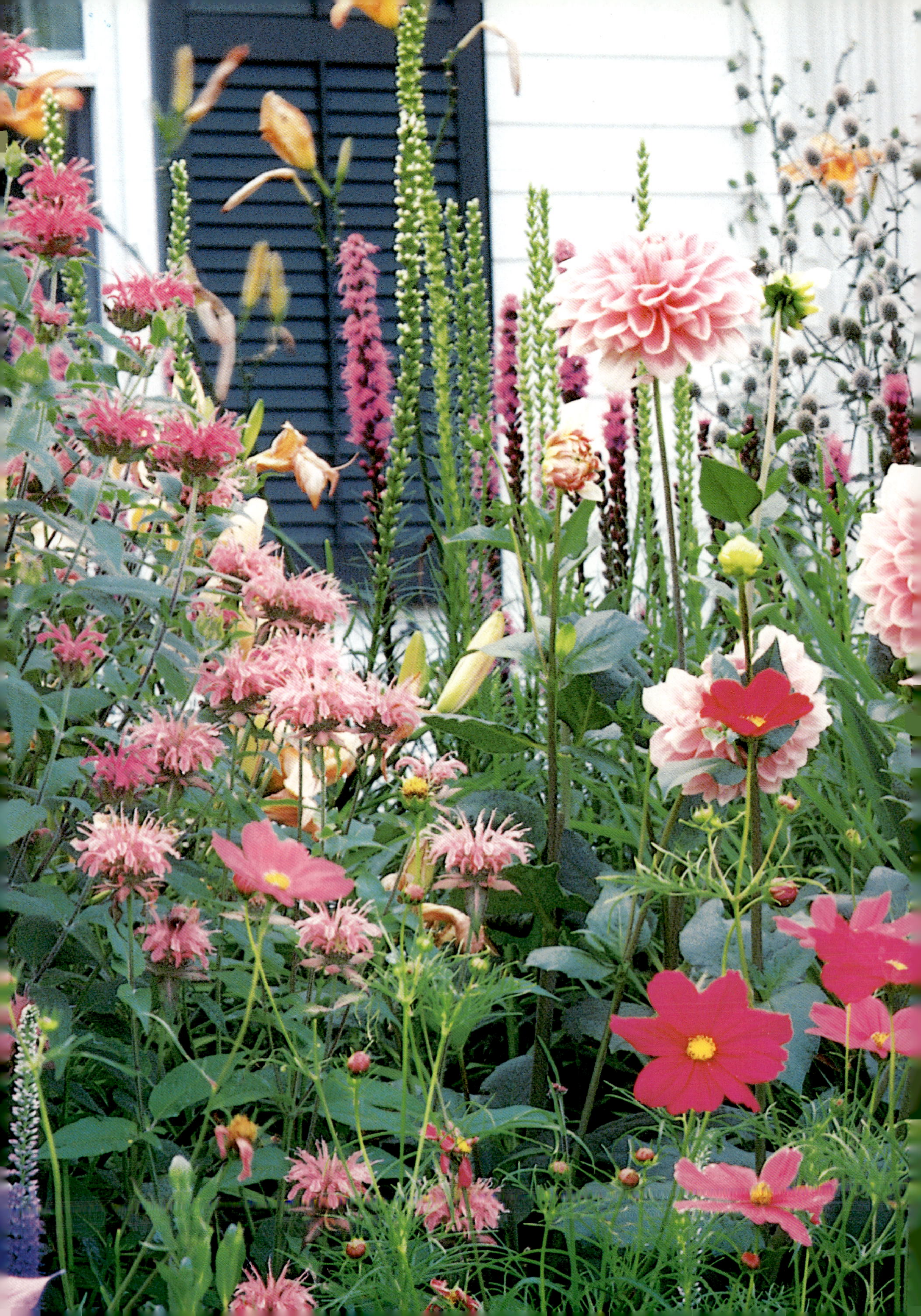

> ### VICTORIAN CUTTING GARDEN FAVORITES
>
> *Asters   Bishop's flower   Wild foxglove*
> *Feverfew   White yarrow   Single gaiety garden pink   Hollyhock*
> *Sweet sultans   Love-in-a-mist*
> *Spider flower   Red Oriental poppy   Sweet scabiosa*
> *Oxford blue   Lily of the valley   Sweet peas*
> *Pansies   Larkspur   Phlox   Candytuft   Fuchsias*

In some cases, the cutting garden was intended to provide the household with the same flowers found in the formal gardens, without depleting the formal beds. Lacy ferns and brightly colored, sweet-scented flowers were needed for the ladies' hand bouquets and tall, dramatic, preferably unscented flowers for the vast centerpieces of the dining room sideboard, while tiny nosegays of pansies and anemones might be slipped beside each place setting at the table. The cutting garden supplied stems of brilliant larkspur and other large florals for the oversized display vases of the parlor or hallway, which had to be regularly filled, as well as fragrant sweet peas for tiny cut-glass vials that graced feminine bedchambers. And in the summer, brightly colored flowers in shades of orange or purplish crimson were cut and put aside to dry until, mingled with evergreen and dried ornamental grasses, they were used to fill the sitting room vases during the winter season, before yielding to the first flowers of early spring.

THE HERB GARDEN

Herbs and spices were an essential part of every kitchen garden and the Victorians managed to enjoy these aromatic seasonings year round. Fresh herbs were of course usually available throughout the late spring, summer, and early fall. In the winter, some herbs, like sage, parsley, and winter savory, could still be harvested. Others, if grown in pots, could be brought inside when the weather got cold, while still others were dried and kept in the pantry. Herbs were also used for medicinal and beauty purposes, as well as for fragrant and ornamental additions to small bouquets and flower arrangements.

Cutting gardens included a wide variety of flowers, from old-fashioned favorites to the same flowers found in the home's more formal flower beds. The charming cutting garden, opposite, includes cosmos, dahlias, and beebalm. Even if the flowers cut were a simple bouquet of roses, above, the garden was a source of indoor as well as outdoor beauty.

HERBAL REMEDIES FROM THE 19TH-CENTURY GARDEN

Chamomile *Spearmint* *Basil* *Coriander* *Sage*

- The scent of crushed fresh angelica leaves helps nausea and refreshes stale air.

- Rose hip tea, drunk regularly, will help keep colds away.

- The soothing effects of chamomile tea are good against insomnia (use before bedtime), and for stomachaches.

- For a toothache, chew on an oregano leaf.

- For diaper rash or any skin irritation, try a compress of comfrey.

- Stress headaches and depression may be relieved with lavender tea.

- For "women's problems" of all kinds, raspberry leaf tea is recommended. If taken in the last months of pregnancy it will make labor easier.

- For burns and sunburn, use the gel from an aloe vera plant.

- Caraway seeds chewed or infused in a tea will stimulate the appetite after sickness and is mild enough for children.

- Spearmint and sage tea are good for children troubled with worms.

- The leaves of the geranium are an excellent application for cuts. When the skin is rubbed off, and for other wounds of the same kind, one or two leaves must be bruised and applied on linen to the part, and the wound will become cauterized in a very short time.

- A nice wash for the delicate skin of infants is made by obtaining maple twigs. Put a small amount of alum in and boil with the twigs. Wash the tender places with this in lieu of water.

- If any are troubled with bronchitis or asthma, smoke dried mullein leaves two or three times a day. Use a common clay pipe and smoke night and morning, oftener if necessary. Severe cases of bronchitis, and of several years' standing, have been cured by smoking these leaves.

- For snakebites, roll plantain leaves and bruise them; tie them on the bite and drink a quantity of whiskey.

- For canker sore mouth, use common cranesbill root steeped and sweetened with honey, as a mouthwash. Use frequently; or wash the mouth with a tea made from the fruit of the staghorn sumac (Rhus typhina); at the same time take a teaspoonful internally. Repeat every few hours until a cure is effected.

Among the culinary herbs the Victorians found most indispensable were thyme, sage, bay, sweet marjoram, sweet basil, chives, savory, chervil, fennel, dill, and all sorts of mint like spearmint or peppermint. Lemon thyme was also admired—an essential in every garden "on account of its delicious flavor," according to *Beeton's*. Parsley was perhaps the most essential Victorian herb of all, as a mealtime garnish, as seasoning, and for small bouquets. Borage and balm were grown for the Victorian claret cup and champagne cup, two highly popular warm weather drinks, and for making balm tea and balm wine.

The six essential herbs that the French called *les fines herbes* were sweet basil, chervil, sweet marjoram, thyme, rosemary, and tarragon. While many Victorian women followed French fashion, they also tended to rely on specific herbs for each course: sage for stuffing, dill and fennel for fish, horseradish for roast beef, chives—preferred as being less strong than onions—tarragon, and other herbs chopped over fresh salad.

In colonial times, a special section of the kitchen garden was routinely set aside for a simple geometric design of herbs of all kinds. During the 19th century, some women still adhered to this classic herb garden design, particularly as the nostalgia for their rural origins grew. More women, however, simply incorporated the herb garden into the vegetable garden itself, generally planting herbs and spices as a border, close to the pathway so they might be easily picked. Another option was to plant the herbs on a separate strip of ground halfway between the kitchen garden and the cutting garden, which too kept them easily accessible to the cook or mistress of the house on a daily basis.

But herbs also moved into other parts of the garden. Their attractive leaves and flowers were appreciated by the Victorians on an aesthetic level as well as a practical one—a luxury that set Victorian women apart from their earlier counterparts. Parsley and lavender, for example, made wonderful border plants and were often found in formal flower gardens. Thyme and other small-leafed herbs were frequently placed in rock gardens. Using herbs for their ornamental beauty and fragrance in landscaping was often recommended to Victorian gardeners.

PARSLEY

Herbs were used as fragrant additions to bouquets, as well as for flavoring and seasoning. Mint, below, was an essential in any 19th-century herb garden. Low-growing varieties of thyme, mint, and other small-leaved herbs were frequently placed in rock gardens as well. Using herbs in landscaping for their ornamental beauty and sweet fragrance was often recommended to Victorian gardeners.

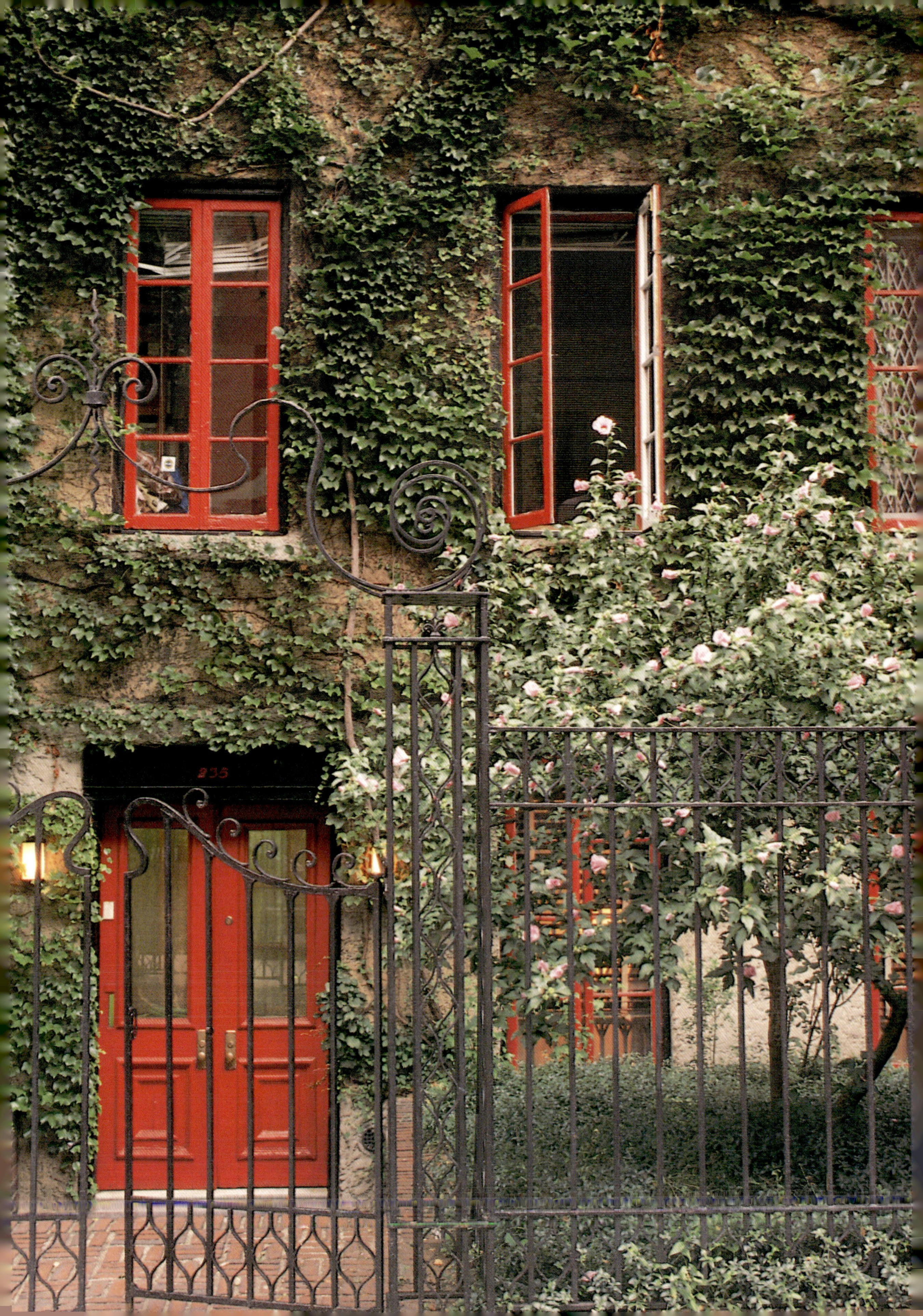

City Gardens

BEING THE MANNER IN WHICH THE VICTORIANS COPED WITH THE URBAN DEARTH OF NATURAL BEAUTY; ALSO HANGING BASKETS

With all the excitement and interest in gardening, how did city gardeners fare? The fact is, faced with such formidable obstacles as small to nonexistent plots as well as smoke and soot rising from thousands of domestic chimneys, well known as being highly "prejudicial to vegetable life," they nevertheless coped admirably with the city's lack of greenery. Their dark green window boxes bloomed with small purple heliotrope, blue and white lobelias, snowy white alyssums and yellow-orange

The window garden, right, lauded by Catharine Beecher and her sister in The American Woman's Home, *1869, featured an ivy vine surrounding the window, a simple Wardian case, a potted calla lily, and potted fuchsia, as well as ferns and flowers in hanging baskets. Below, These Lady Washington geraniums are from a c. 1906 catalog. An ornate fence, profuse flowering vines, and a touch of the picturesque in the wall sculpture make this an ideal city garden, opposite.*

PELARGONIAS

nasturtiums. Pots of geraniums and petunias were artfully positioned. In small front-yard plots, veiled in smoky urban shadows, they patiently cultivated beds of ferns, violets, pansies, and impatiens. Building fronts were blanketed in ivy and other vines. "I would have flowers somehow and somewhere if I lived in the attic of a ten-story tenement," declared I. Wood of Massachusetts, writing in *The Mayflower* at the turn of the century. "I would get an old tin can if I couldn't afford a flower pot and I would beg a slip of a Geranium from one of the gardeners in the park.…I would!"

Owners of 19th-century row houses were the most able to indulge their taste for outdoor gardening, since row houses usually possessed a small front-yard garden—sometimes scarcely more than a patch of land—usually grassed over and enclosed by a decorative iron fence. Because of the cheek-by-jowl positioning of the houses, there were no side yards; the rear of the house was a workspace off the kitchen for laundry, access to the alley, and other tasks. Yet in 1898 a Michigan man who lived in a house that had little garden space but a backyard about six feet wide, three feet of which were taken up by a walk, commented that there is always a nook or corner that could be used for floriculture. "My wife and I determined to have some Asters and undaunted by the unpromising nature of the soil or the lack of space, I thoroughly dug over a bed three by six feet, put in some fertilizer and sowed the seed." By about 1915, the rear yard first began to be adapted to accommodate small vegetable and flower beds. Rather than have the back drawing room or parlor look out on bare walls and dirty pavement, city dwellers made every effort to create a pleasant vista with a garden.

Surprisingly, small front-yard city gardens were generally simple in design. City dwellers, as well as those with small-sized gardens, were urged to forgo elaborate flower bed shapes such as diamonds or stars in favor of plain circles or ovals. A garden with a curving or undulating edge—called an "arabesque" by Downing—was also recommended for small properties, as it was thought to give the illusion of greater space.

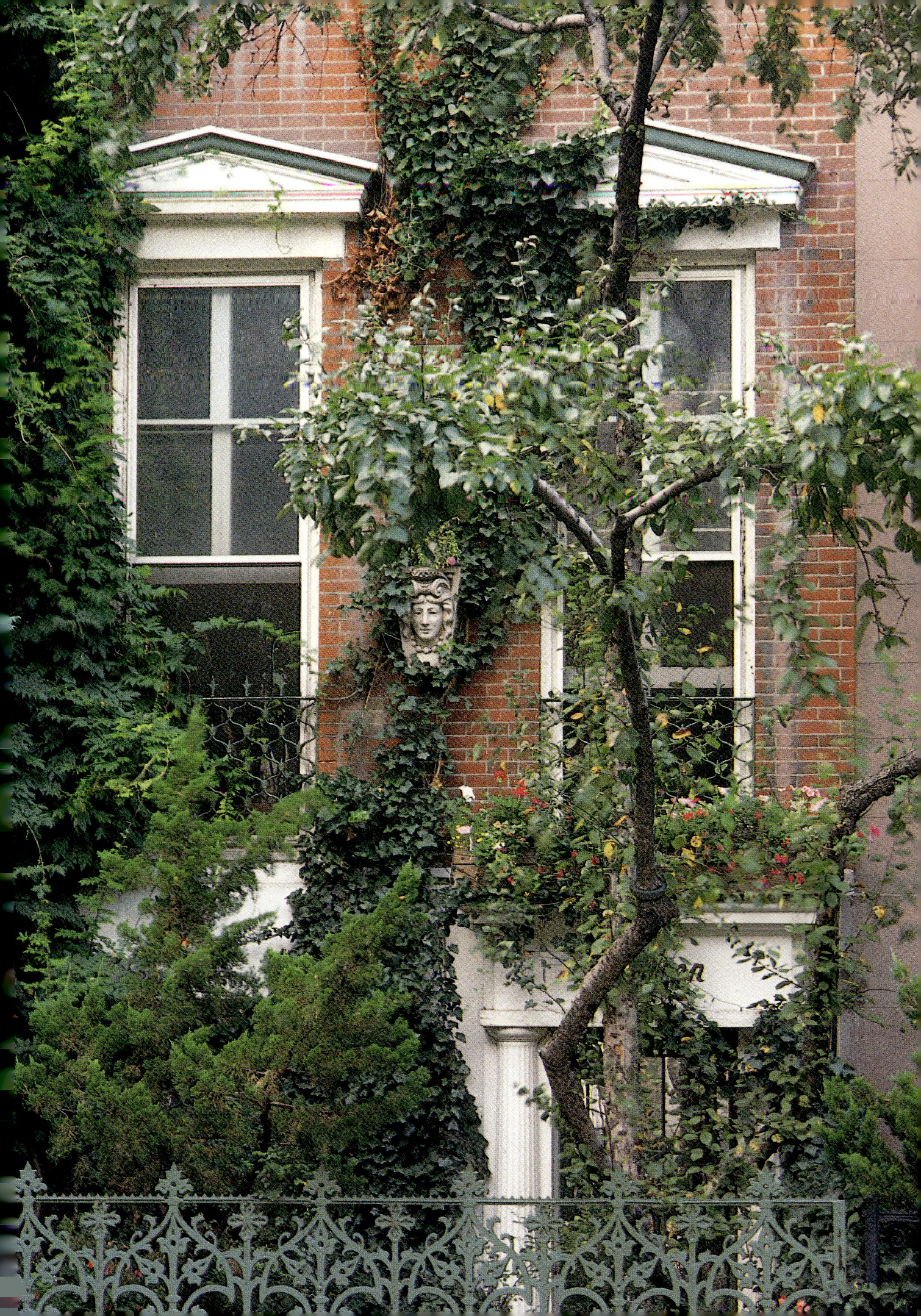

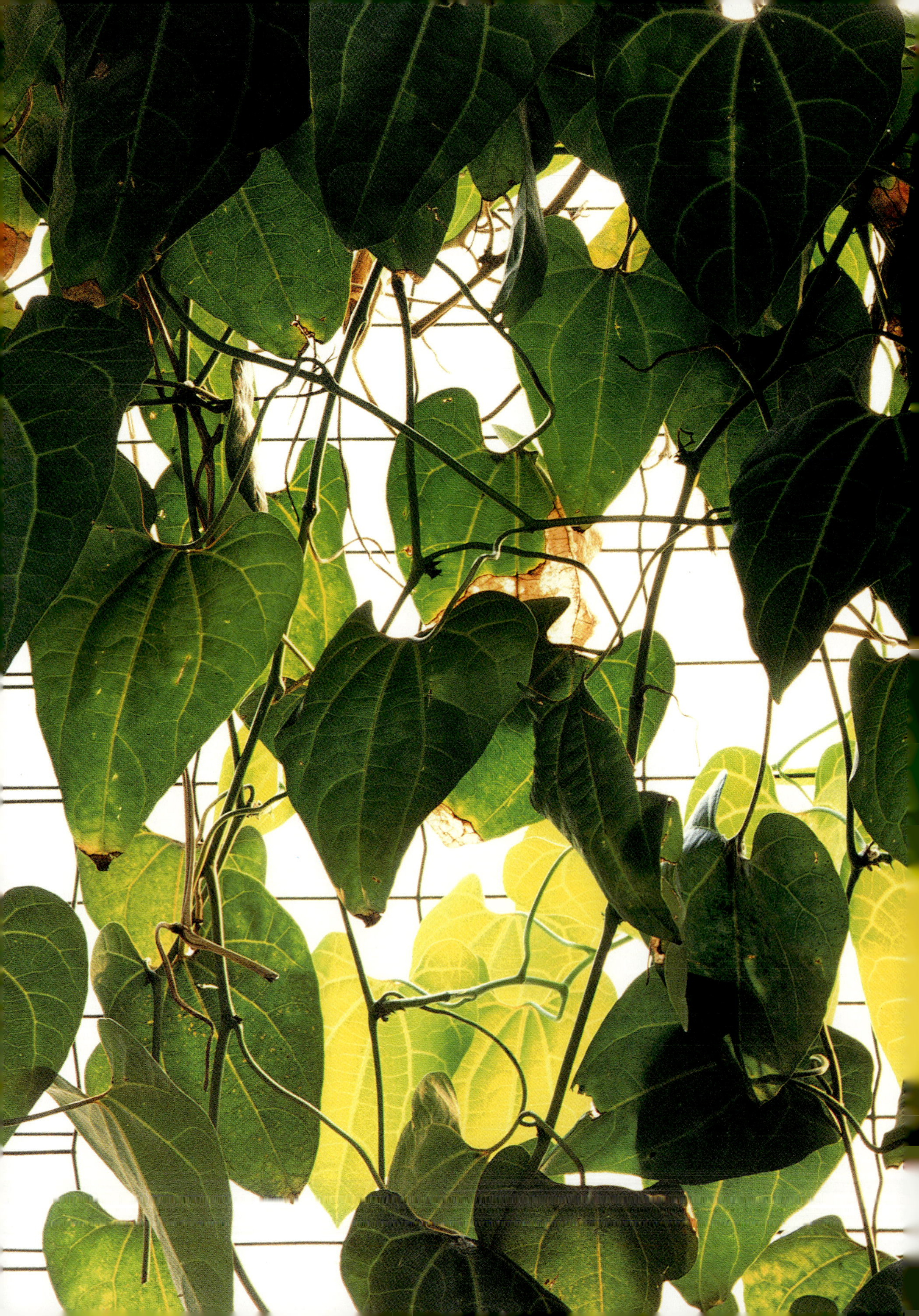

In creating a small front-yard city garden today, a simple and authentic treatment is to keep the center of the garden plot clear—done in grass or stone—with flower beds forming a straight, narrow border around the outer perimeters. If there is room for a pathway, it should curve, to avoid angles that might draw attention to the squareness of the space, and to trick the eye into believing the yard is actually larger than it is.

Another typical way to handle a front yard would be to plant a small patch of grass surrounded by border beds, and in the center place an ornament such as an urn or fountain overflowing with ivy or a flowering vine. This could all be enclosed with a decorative iron fence. Alternatively, the central urn could be replaced with a small, circular bed of flowers.

In Victorian times borders, which lent a neat edge to flower beds and walkways, were thought to be particularly important in small city front-yard gardens, where neatness was important and the appearance of even a single fuzzy little edge would be magnified. Typical border plantings included variegated ground ivy; violets (popular in the South, since they retained their dark green foliage all year round); white alyssum; hardy, clove-scented pinks; double-curled parsley ("as dainty as a piece of lace work"); golden feverfew; and the many varieties of dusty miller. English ivy was also said to make a handsome and striking border for a large circular bed, while irises planted as a border would prevent beds from washing out in heavy rains.

For most small-sized or city beds, gardeners chose the tiniest, daintiest flowers, in the softest colors. "In a small yard, the coarser flowers give an unpleasant and *bizarre* effect," commented *The Mayflower*. And perspective was a consideration. Flowers that would look well in the "faraway" corners of large gardens, for instance, would be inappropriate in a small one, since such corners were virtually nonexistent. "One is quite near to all the flowers and for that reason they should all be sweet and dainty," it was reasoned. Large flowers like hollyhocks, overly bright flowers like marigolds or zinnias, or even those that were dramatic or striking in appearance, like sunflowers, were therefore appropriate only in larger gardens. Big trees and big flowers would only draw attention to the smallness of the surroundings, confirmed *The Household*. A city garden should be dainty and neat, without being prim.

As for color, what were termed "near" colors, such as bright yellow,

A romantic veil of ivy was an important addition to a city home, opposite. Above, *a moss-covered hanging basket lends this garden special charm.*

Above, *city gardeners could consider a low-growing phlox for a sunny window box.*

should be avoided; shades that give a "faraway" look, like a small border of blue flowers, were preferred. Thus, a typically small front-yard garden might include shrubbery such as everblooming roses, a few tall lilies, a row of gladiolus, and a dwarf dahlia here and there—red in a shady corner, lilac and white in the sun. A border of blue ageratum would add to the desired faraway look, thereby widening the entire space.

For narrow beds that run under windows, gardeners can plant purple heliotrope, white and pink geraniums, a border of white alyssum, and a spring border of blue violets—all traditional treatments. Coleus is another authentic choice, planted along the front fence and interspersed here and there with a few choice bedding plants. For walkways leading to the front door, the Victorians traditionally liked pansies and crocuses in the spring and later a border of lobelias or verbenas—or "anything that is delicate and pretty that will keep close to the ground, but avoid mixtures." If your garden has a shady corner, you can also add a fern nook, or a few delicate potted chrysanthemums in the fall.

A common problem for city gardeners was lack of sunlight. Many garden periodicals went out of their way to recommend plants and flowers that would thrive in the shadows of tall city buildings. Pansies, violets, forget-me-nots, lily of the valley, tuberous begonias, impatiens, and greenery such as ferns and ivy were all considered suitable for shady city gardens. Benjamin F. Albaugh, author of *The Gardenette or City Back Yard Gardening* (1915), suggested planting hardy ferns (not parlor ferns) in the city garden's damp, shady nooks or corners, especially on the north sides of buildings. Ferns and vines planted in tubs were also used as portable fillers.

For city dwellers who lacked a front-yard garden or even the smallest

---

If the tiny garden is sweet and trim and tasteful, nobody will think of saying: "Such a small crowded place!" It will be a dainty gem and make up in quality what it cannot give in quantity. It will differ from a large and handsome garden just as a dainty corsage bouquet differs from a hall decoration.

ELLEN FRIZELL WYCOFF, NORTH CAROLINA,
THE MAYFLOWER, MARCH 1900

grassy plot, there were other options to pursue. Some resorted to planting flowers in urns, pots, tubs, and even wheelbarrows. A flower-filled wheelbarrow was considered new, quaint, and pretty, and highly suitable for those flower lovers who might not have the usual posy beds. Gardeners might consider filling up a rustic wheelbarrow with nasturtiums, with a few taller plants in the center, as suggested by *The Mayflower* in May 1898. Geraniums were also popular for urns, as were pansies surrounded by borders of smaller flowers such as alyssum or mignonette, with vines draping over the sides. Hyacinth and other bulb beds were options for the spring, to be replaced with annuals later in the season. These were frequently grown in the 1890s by city gardeners who were reduced to doing their planting in barrows and tubs.

▦ Climbing vines that dramatically covered the exterior walls of the house—just as textiles and drapery modestly covered its interior tabletops and windows—were another important part of a city garden landscape. Ivy, morning glory, and wisteria were the most popular choices, concealing unsightly walls or unattractive fences. For small screened-in porches or verandas, clematis, ipomoea, Dutchman's pipe, climbing roses, and honeysuckle were considered appropriate. If the vines were not what the Victorians called "of the runaway sort," which they eschewed for their "smothered, swallowed-up appearance," greenery along the walls could add the illusion of size and space. And if the vine-covered "green wall" could be grown in a single summer, so much the better. Gardeners today can try morning glories, or if something more delicate and sheltered is preferred, thunbergia, admired by the Victorians for its lovely cream and yellow flowers. Note that since the Victorians were hesitant about having too much yellow in their gardens, the use of thunbergia—and nothing else in that color—was thought to be just right.

▦ Ever ingenious, city Victorians found many other ways to make their lives green. "In a city back-yard, it sometimes happens that there are shady corners, or narrow strips of ground along boundaries or fences, especially on shaded sides of buildings, which may be devoted to the growing of wild or native flowers," pointed out one garden expert. One city gardener, for example, managed to grow just such a wildflower collection on a very narrow strip of ground three feet wide, five or six yards long, on the north side of her house, bordered on one side by a walk and the other by an iron fence. Since this bed was planted with flowers she picked up at picnics, on visits to the country, or in rambles over hills and along the

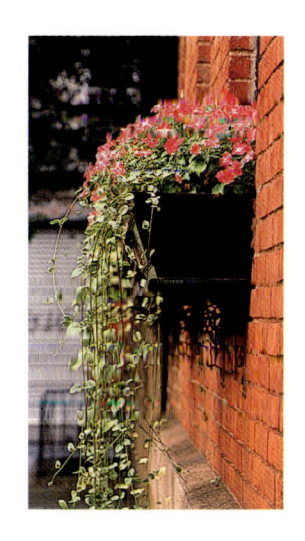

Often, the only garden possible for a city dweller was a window box like the one above, spilling over with colorful flowers and trailing foliage.

HANGING BASKETS

While a suspended plant basket, usually made of wire and covered with moss, was an acknowledged part of indoor window gardening, it was also a graceful and most necessary ornament on the veranda or porch during the hot summer months.

Hanging baskets were cause for much discussion and creativity in the household guides of the day. Although wire and moss baskets were considered by far the ideal, many other kinds were experimented with. Rustic baskets, for instance, made from rough knotty twigs and branches, were consistently admired—"so popular and beautiful," praised The Household. Branches were soaked or steamed in hot water until pliable, stained with brown staining or black varnish, then bent around a plain wooden bowl until the whole surface was covered, and nailed securely in place. Catharine Beecher and Harriet Beecher Stowe came up with the unique variation of suspending half a coconut shell, filling it up with soil, and planting it with flowers and vines, while Peter Henderson in Gardening for Pleasure advocated making baskets covered with laurel roots twisted in grotesque shapes.

Hanging baskets that were used on shaded verandas or in shady rooms were filled almost exclusively with mosses and ivies, as well as with ivy-leafed geraniums and also impatiens, all of which would trail over the sides or could be trained to climb on trelliswork placed in the basket. In the center were placed upright plants such as dracaenas, caladiums, echeverias, and ferns. Sunny baskets held plants with flowers and greater brilliancy of leaves, including lobelias, nasturtiums, and petunias to drape and trail over the basket edges, with coleus, begonias, or any small, brightly flowered plant in the center.

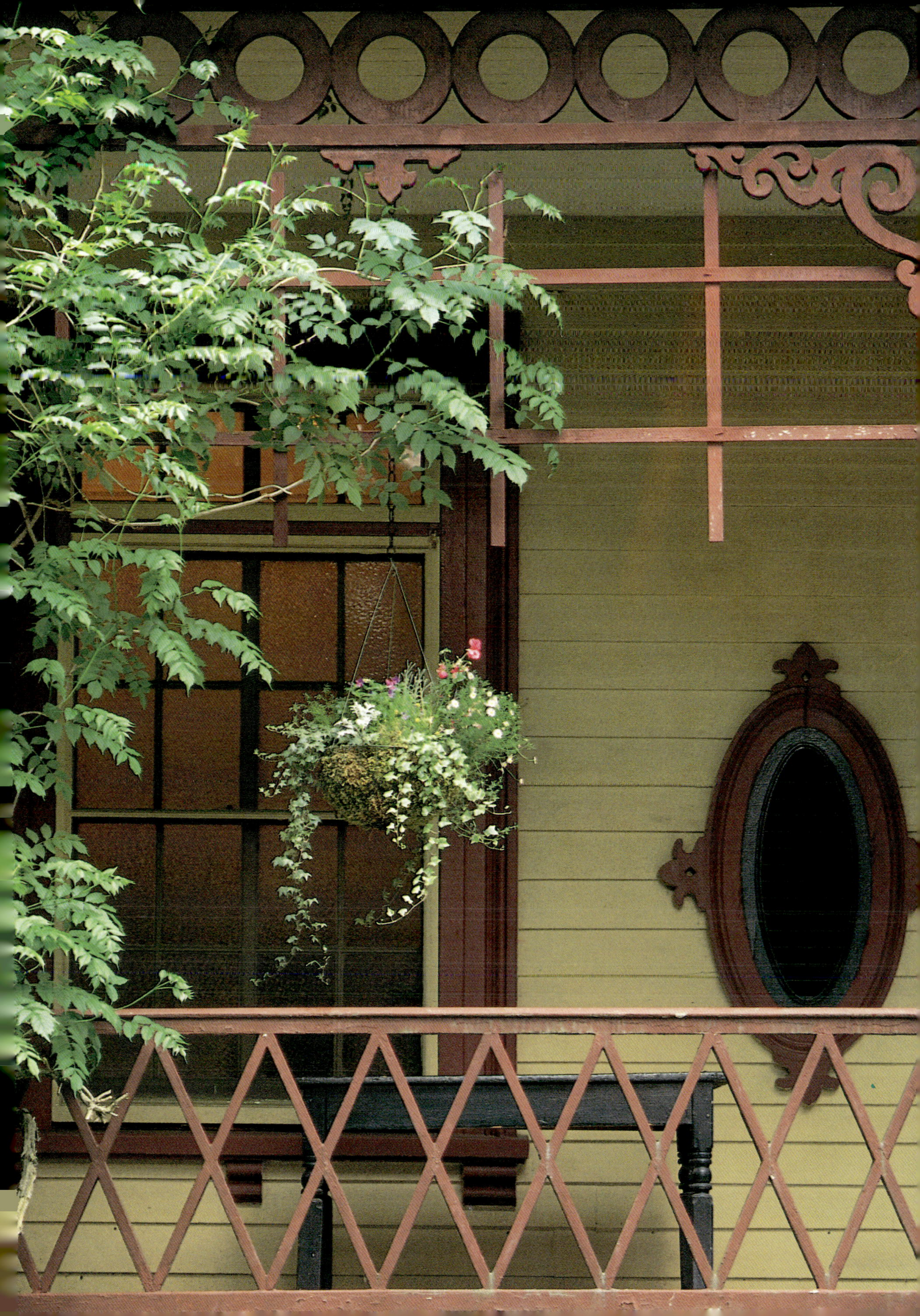

Preceding page: *The authentic hanging basket at Acorn Hall is filled with typically 19th-century plants, including ivy geranium, browallia, brachysome, and Dahlberg daisy. Herbs for such a basket would include santolina, clove, and thyme.*

Hanging baskets, right, *were not only decorative, they were handy—during inclement weather they could move indoors or to another part of the porch.* Below, *a container decorated with shells was a doorway option.*

river, she called it her "souvenir garden." "Only choice specimens were taken, and only one or two of a kind," she qualified. Although these flowers were planted "promiscuously," the results were thought to be most pleasing. (Today, such foraging in the wild is known to have harmful effects on the environment and is discouraged, but wildflower gardens certainly can be grown from nursery-raised plants.) In 1899, a Minnesota woman recalled a small but ingenious city garden in a box, fastened to the railing at the top of a flight of outdoor stairs and planted with nasturtiums, pansies, and other annuals. A second box, fastened at the side of the stairs a few feet down, contained thriving sweet peas. And as a crowning touch, morning glories, planted in the ground and trained to cover the entire side of the stairs, formed an elegant archway.

▪ Vegetables presented more of a challenge, but one source recommended cutting small holes all around halfway up the side of a small barrel and filling it up first with stones, then with soil to the top. Plants or seeds were placed in the soil, one type to a barrel (if melons or cucumbers were planted, they could be tied up against a wall) and watered through the holes by submerging the barrel in a wet tray, keeping the stones in water all the time.

▪ Even for city dwellers who lacked ground-floor access, there was still room for the window box. "In the cities especially, where space is economized by placing story upon story, and the buildings are so close that there is often no room for even a spear of grass to be grown, the only garden that is possible is one that is formed in a box on a window sill," sympathized Peter Henderson in *Gardening for Pleasure* in 1887. Window boxes were preferred for convenience (less watering) and attractiveness and were available in a wide variety of forms and materials. Made of zinc, tin-lined wood, terra-cotta, or iron, depending on the taste and means of their owners, window boxes were limited in space: usually only four or five feet in length, eight to ten inches in width, with room for about six to ten inches of soil. Nevertheless, they provided the opportunity for city folk to participate in the gardening craze. A good wooden box, painted an inconspicuous green, could be fastened to the window with metal mounts, then filled with flowers. Gardeners were duly warned that the box should be securely set in place so it would not threaten the heads or lives of unwary passersby.

▦ As the boxes were usually overhead (too high to allow for close examination) and draped with overhanging plants, ordinary, inexpensive pine boxes were also used, as long as they were put together firmly to withstand exposure to weather and the weight of the soil. Zinc linings tacked onto the wood, with spaces left in the bottom to allow water to pass through, were advised. More costly boxes (often seen in London and Edinburgh) made of wood, lined with zinc or tin, and then covered with ornamental encaustic tiles were also available, as were cheaper but still attractive imitations.

▦ During the 1880s, at the height of the passion for ornamentation, many different ways were concocted to ornament these window boxes; despite the fact that the ornamentation was sure to be obscured by plant growth. Patterned oilcloth designed to imitate tilework, brightly colored geometrically designed cloth, and even wallpaper (storks, palm trees, and tropical designs were preferred) were pasted, glued, or tacked onto the sides of the boxes and trimmed with a narrow molding. Boxes were also faux-painted to resemble walnut or stone, adorned with pasted-on acorns, horse chestnuts, pinecones, shells, or dry tendrils of grapevines, then coated with common varnish. Some suggestions were of dubious attractiveness. For example, *The Household* suggested splitting prune seeds in two and glueing them on the box "in fantastic shapes. . . . Spread a coat of thick glue on intervening spaces, and sprinkle on rice while the glue is yet soft. After all is thoroughly dry, paint the rice carefully and varnish the whole box."

▦ For a Victorian-style window box, start with vines like ivy or climbing nasturtiums along the front and sides and fill in with flowering plants. Some Victorian experts preferred setting pots in the box rather than planting them directly. That way, they could be turned to the light as needed, and any plants that failed or went out of blooming season could be removed without disturbing the rest. For sunny spots, strong, vigorous plants such as petunias, geraniums, heliotropes, and begonias were preferred. For shady boxes (all of which should have a southern exposure) the Victorians liked mignonette, sweet alyssum, phlox, and portulaca.

Victorian window boxes could be unusually decorative, adorned with tiles, stencils, or natural ornaments. The ones here are from Rustic Adornments for Homes of Taste *(1870).*

peony	foxglove	sunflower
poppy bud	sweet alyssum	bugleweed
purple coneflower	day lily	globe thistle
orchid	poppy	peony

The Victorian Garden
Directory

SELECT BIBLIOGRAPHY
—170—

GLOSSARY
—171—

GUIDE TO HISTORIC GARDENS
—177—

SOURCES FOR HISTORIC
SEEDS AND PLANTS
—181—

INDEX
—183—

SELECT BIBLIOGRAPHY

Should you wish to explore the world of Victorian gardens further, listed below are some of the primary source books that were most helpful to me. Some are early editions, which have their own charm; others are facsimiles, more and more of which are being reprinted today, to the delight of modern-day gardeners.

Beecher, Catharine E., and Harriet Beecher Stowe. *The American Woman's Home.* Watkins Glen, N.Y.: The American Life Foundation, 1979. Originally published New York, 1869.

Beeton's New All About Gardening, A Popular Dictionary of Garden Work. London: Ward, Lock & Bowden, 1896.

Breck, Joseph. *The Flower Garden; or Breck's Book of Flowers.* Guilford, Conn.: Opus Publications, 1988. Originally published Boston, 1851.

———. *The Young Florist.* Cambridge, Mass.: Applewood Books, 1989. Originally published Boston, 1833.

Buist, Robert. *American Flower Garden Dictionary.* New York: Orange, Judd & Company, 1854.

Downing, Andrew Jackson. *Victorian Cottage Residences.* New York: Dover Publications, 1981. Originally published as *Cottage Residences; or A Series of Designs for Rural Cottages and Cottage Villas and Their Gardens and Grounds,* 1842. Adapted to North America in 1873 ed.

Durand, Herbert. *Wild Flowers and Ferns.* New York and London: G.P. Putnam's Sons, 1923.

Earle, Alice Morse. *Old-Time Gardens, A Book Of the Sweet O' the Year.* New York: The Macmillan Company, 1901.

Goff, May Perrin, ed. *The Household of the Detroit Free Press: A Cyclopaedia of Practical Hints for Modern Homes.* Detroit: The Detroit Free Press, 1882.

Hawthorne, Hildegarde. *The Lure of the Garden.* New York: The Century Company, 1911.

Heath, Francis George. *Garden Rockery, How to Make, Plant and Manage It.* London: George Routledge & Sons, 1908.

Henderson, Peter. *Gardening for Pleasure.* New York: Orange Judd Company, 1887.

Hibberd, Shirley. *Rustic Adornments for Homes of Taste.* London: Groombridge & Sons, 1870. Originally published in 1856.

Johnson, Mrs. S.O. ("Daisy Eyebright"). *Every Woman Her Own Flower Gardener.* New York: Henry T. Williams, 1873.

Loudon, Jane. *Gardening for Ladies; and Companion to The Flower Garden.* Ed. A.J. Downing. New York: John Wiley, 1860.

Maling, E. A. *A Handbook for Ladies on In-door Plants, Flowers for Ornament, and Song Birds.* London: Smith, Elder & Company, 1870.

Rivers, Thomas. *The Rose Amateur's Guide.* New York: Earl M. Coleman Enterprises, 1979. Originally published London, 1846.

Scott, Frank Jesup. *Victorian Gardens.* Watkins Glen, N.Y.: American Life Foundation, 1982. Originally published as *The Art of Beautifying Suburban Home Grounds of Small Extent,* 1870.

GLOSSARY

The following list includes those plants most commonly used in Victorian gardens. Where there are common names, those are listed first, followed by the contemporary botanical name.

Acacia. *Acacia* sp. Family of shrubs with delicate yellow flowers.

African marigold. *Tagetes erecta.* Brilliant orange or yellow flowers, often used in bedding schemes. Annual. *T. patula* is the French marigold; *T. signata pumila* is the Mexican marigold.

African violet. *Saintpaulia.* Houseplant popular for abundant purple, pink, and white flowers with hairy green leaves. Not related to violas.

Ageratum. *Ageratum* sp. Dwarf blue variety introduced in second half of 19th century. Popular bedding plant.

Alpine aster. *Aster alpinus.* A low-growing plant for rock gardens.

Ambrosia. *Ambrosia artemisiifolia.* Today known as ragweed; appreciated in Victorian times for its tall golden sprays.

Anemone. *Anemone coronaria.* Also known as windflower. Member of buttercup family, with similar flowers but various bright colors.

Angelica. *Angelica archangelica.* A tall plant with bright green leaves and round, hollow stems, with celerylike flavor. The stems are often candied.

Artemisia. *Artemisia annua.* Small white or yellow flowers and fragrant foliage. One of many sorts usually grown for its silvery foliage.

Aspidistra. *Aspidistra elatior.* Popular houseplant grown for ornamental foliage. Called cast iron plant by the Victorians for its hardiness and need for minimal care.

Aster, Michaelmas daisy. *Aster* sp. Victorian favorite, fall-blooming daisy-like flower with yellow center surrounded by petals of different colors.

Baby's breath. *Gypsophila paniculata.* Clouds of tiny white flowers dry well.

Bachelor's button. *Centaurea cyanus* (annual) or *C. montana* (perennial). Also known as cornflower or bluebottle. Loved for its delicate blue flowers.

Bamboo. *Bambusa* sp. Often used in gardens for exotic, dramatic look.

Banana plant (Abyssiman banana). *Musa ensete.* Tropical plant grown in Victorian greenhouses for large ornamental leaves and tropical effect.

Bee balm. *Monarda didyma.* Brilliant red blossoms. Lemon-scented leaves can be used as a substitute for tea.

Black-eyed Susan. *Rudbeckia hirta.* Bold yellow-orange petals with dark center; was a familiar sight in all Victorian gardens.

Bleeding-heart. *Dicentra spectabilis.* Introduced from Japan in the late 1840s, this intensely Victorian flower has unusual pink and white heart-shaped flowers that hang like lockets from their branches.

Bougainvillea. *Bougainvillaea glabra.* Tropical vine with bold, brightly colored flowers.

Bouncing Bet. *Saponaria officinalis.* Pale pink flowers that bloom throughout the summer.

Boxwood. *Buxus* sp. Popular hedge or border shrub with small waxy leaves. Often used in Victorian gardens to outline the bedding-out areas.

Cacalia sagittata. *Emilia sagittata* var. *lutea.* Also called tassel flower. Loved for bright golden flowers.

Caladium. *Caladium bicolor.* Tropical foliage plant, popular as a houseplant for unique patterning on large leaves. Also for summer bedding.

Calceolaria. *Calceolaria crenatiflora.* Part of the snapdragon family; has bright colored, slipperlike flowers. Also called pocketbook plant.

Calendula. *Calendula officinalis.* Bedding plant with bright orange-yellow blossoms. Sometimes called pot marigold. Annual.

Calliopsis. *Calliopsis drummondii.* Also called *Coreopsis.* Popular bedding plant with daisylike yellow flowers.

Camassia. *Camassia* sp. Spring bulb with dainty blue or white flowers. Member of the lily family.

Camellia. *Camellia japonica.* Brought from the Orient in the mid to late 19th century, camellias have feathery roselike flowers on shrublike plant. Pink and white, singles and doubles.

Campanula. *Campanula medium.* Also called bellflower. Bell-shaped flowers range from blues and violets to whites and pinks. There are about a dozen species of campanula. *C. medium* is Canterbury bells; *C. persicifolia* is peach-leaved bellflower; *C. isophylla* has starlike flowers, usually blue.

Canary-bird flower. *Tropaeolum peregrinum.* Vine with feathery, deeply cut yellow flowers.

Candleberry. *Myrica pennsylvanica.* Member of myrtle family, another name for bayberry.

Candytuft. *Iberis sempervines.* White flower perennial with a sweet scent. Commonly grown as an edging plant. Globe candytuft comes in lavender, crimson, and red, but white is most popular.

Canna. *Canna ehmanni.* Striking bright yellow flowers on tall stalks; a Victorian favorite.

Canterbury bells. *Campanula medium.* Singles and doubles. Originally in dark blue or white (pink was a 19th-century development). Sometimes called cup-and-saucer plant.

Caraway. *Carum carvi.* The seed of this herb is widely used in cooking, most familiarly in rye bread. Chewed by Victorian ladies to sweeten the breath.

Carnation. *Dianthus caryophyllus.* Popular for tight clusters of petals and delicate clove scent. For borders or cutting.

Carpet echeveria. *Urbinia agavoides* or *Echeveria agavoides.* Red flowers with yellow tips make this variety good for bedding schemes.

Castor bean. *Ricinus communis.* Also called castor-oil plant or Palma Christi. An exotic tropical plant used as a centerpiece in beds of annuals. Grows to 10 to 12 feet with 2-foot-wide leaves.

Catchfly. *Silene carolinia.* Related to "pinks," catchflies boast clusters of red, pink, or white blossoms. This is a wildflower. *Lychnis viscania* or *L. viscana vulgaris* is the catchfly (perennial) in cultivation.

Chamomile. *Matricaria chamomilla* (German annual); *anthemis nobilis* (Roman perennial). Tiny daisylike flowers have a delicate scent and flavor and are widely used in soothing teas for stomachaches or insomnia.

Chervil. *Anthriscus cerefolium.* Delicate aromatic leaves with slight licorice flavor are wonderful in salads.

Chilean bellflower. *Lapageria rosea.* Vine with red, bell-shaped flowers. Difficult to grow, requiring frost-free winters and cool summers.

China aster. *Callistephus chinensis.* Loved for bright blue, red, pink, or white flowers. Annual bedding favorite.

Chinese pinks. *Dianthus chinensis* or *D. sinensis.* Wonderfully fragrant variety.

Chives. *Allium schoenoprasum.* Similar to but more delicate than the onion in foliage and flavor, chives are widely used in soups and salads.

Chrysanthemum. *Chrysanthemum indicum.* Classic autumn garden plant, grown in greenhouses till after WWI.

Clematis. *Clematis jackmanii.* Vine with lively star-shaped flowers originally from China. One of the large flowered hybrids used in the 19th century.

Climbing hydrangea. *Hydrangea anomala petiolaris.* Clinging vine with large clusters of flowers.

Cobaea. *Cobaea scandens.* Vine with purple bell-shaped flowers. Annuals.

Cockscomb. *Celosia cristata.* Ostentatious and richly colored unusual flowers. A Victorian favorite.

Coleus. *Coleus blumei.* Loved for its colorful foliage. For annual bedding.

Columbine. *Aquilegia canadensis.* Dainty yellow flowers with red spurs.

Commelina. *Commelina coelestis.* Also called dayflower. Bright blue flowers added splashes of color to the garden.

Common foxglove. *Digitalis purpurea.* Tall spires of thimblelike flowers are another classic from the old-fashioned garden.

Common polypody fern. *Polypodium vulgare.* Good fern for rockeries.

Cornflower. *Centaurea cyanus.* Also called bachelor's button and bluebottle.

Cottage pink. *Dianthus plumarius.* A strong, hardy perennial with subtle shades of white, lilac, and pink and a strong clove scent. Suitable for edging and in rock gardens.

Cowslip. *Primula veris.* Yellow flowers with orange centers. A member of the primrose family.

Crocus. *Crocus vernus.* Its early bloom often indicates the coming of spring.

Crowfoot. *Ranunculus.* Also called buttercup. Delicate yellow flowers.

Cyclamen. *Cyclamen persicum* or *C. indicum.* Pink or white flowers bloom on stalks with heart-shaped leaves.

Cypress vine. *Quamoclit pennata.* Vine with slender, red flowers.

Daffodil. *Narcissus sp.* Beloved springtime bulb.

Dahlias. *Dahlia.* Popular, with wide variety of sizes and colors. *D. pinnata* is the common or garden dahlia; *D. merchii* is the bedding dahlia.

Dandelion. *Taraxacum officinale.* Usually considered a weed, dandelions were appreciated for both the bold yellow flowers and silver seed puffs. Greens were often used in salads.

Dead nettle. *Lamium sp.* Low-growing plant often used in rockeries.

Delphinium. *See* Larkspur.

Deutzia. *Deutzia grandiflora.* Large clusters of white flowers that bloom in springtime.

Dill. *Anethum graveolens.* Feathery green foliage of dill has a mild taste that is especially good with fish and cucumber, as in dips and pickles.

Dusty miller. *Centaurea gymnocarpa.* Lavender flowers on almost white, "dusty" foliage. Grown for foliage rather than flowers (perennial).

Dutchman's pipe. *Aristolochia durior.* A classic vine, popular in old-fashioned gardens, with large heart-shaped leaves and a drooping flower that resembles a pipe. Grown for foliage.

Echeveria. *Echeveria gibbiflora.* Blue-gray leaves with bright red flowers. Often used for bedding.

Eglantine. *Rosa eglanteria,* also *R. rubiginosa.* Also called sweetbrier. A hardy rose with apple-scented foliage.

Elephant's ear. *Colocasia antiquorum.* Grown for large, ornamental foliage that resembles elephants' ears. Used in tropical bedding schemes.

Euphorbia. *Euphorbia corollata.* Also called flowering spurge. Used both in bedding schemes and cutting gardens. (This is just one of a number of different kinds—there are another half dozen commonly in cultivation.)

Fennel. *Foeniculum vulgare.* Resembles dill in its foliage but tastes slightly of licorice; good with salads or seafood.

Fennel flower. *Nigella damascena.* Plant with tiny blue or white flowers.

Feverfew. *Chrysanthemum parthenium.* Pretty, daisylike flower with strong scent. Fresh leaves were thought effective in controlling headaches.

Fleur de luce. *Iris purpurea.* Old-fashioned French name for a certain iris going back to the 17th century.

Forget-me-not. *Myosotis scorpioides.* A low-growing beauty with blue petals and white centers.

Forsythia. *Forsythia suspensa* (this is the weeping form), *F. fortunei* (more erect). Sprays of soft yellow flowers popular with Victorians (these were not the only sort grown).

Four-o'clock. *Mirabilis jalapa.* Colorful, fragrant trumpet-shaped flowers that open late in the afternoon. Ideal for children's gardens.

Freesia. *Freesia refracta.* Fragrant yellow and white flowers.

Fringed gentian. *Gentianopsis crinita.* Bold blue flowers with delicately fringed petals.

Fuchsia. *Fuchsia hybrida.* Brightly colored flowers that bloom in the garden throughout the summer. In mild climates these can survive outside all year, but in the U.S. are essentially grown as pot plants.

Geranium. *Pelargonium hortorum.* Best beloved bedding plant, with colors ranging from pure white to salmon pink to bright scarlet.

Gladiolus. *Gladiolus gandavensis.* Soft, feathery flowers on tall stems that make dramatic arrangements.

Globe amaranth. *Gomphrena globosa.* Brightly colored flowers often used in cutting gardens.

Gnaphalium. *Gnaphalium obtusifolium.* Small flowers on tall spikes.

Golden feverfew. *Chrysanthemum parthenium aureum.* Golden-leafed version of common feverfew used for bedding.

Grape hyacinth. *Muscari botryoides.* Small delicate towers of deep purple flowers.

Great bellflower. *Campanula latifolia.* A perennial deep purple beauty and a substitute for Canterbury bells (biennial).

Hart's-tongue fern. *Phyllitis scolopendrium.* Fern with long, leathery green fronds.

Hawkweed. *Hieracium aurantiacum.* Also called devil's paintbrush for spikes of red or orange flowers. Has escaped cultivation and is now found on roadsides and in fields.

Hawthorn bush. *Crataegus crus-galli.* Shrub with white flowers and red berries. One of many hawthorns in cultivation. Usually thought of as a small tree with a single trunk.

Heliotrope. *Heliotropium arborescens.* Deep purple clusters made up of masses of tiny blossoms with a rich vanilla scent; a Victorian favorite.

Hibiscus. *Hibiscus moscheutos.* Shrub with brightly colored, ornamental flowers. This is the northern sort, common rose mallow. *H. rosa sinensis* is the tender or southern variety.

Holly. *Ilex* sp. Distinctly shaped green leaves and red berries of this shrub are indispensable in holiday decorating.

Hollyhock. *Althaea rosea.* No old-fashioned garden would be complete without a nostalgic backdrop of this tall showy flower.

Honesty. *Lunaria annua, L. biennis.* An old-fashioned favorite with small, pinkish-purple flowers. Originally colonial. Common for seeds. Also called moneyplant or satin flower.

Honeysuckle. *Lonicera caprifolium.* Vine with sweetly scented yellow and white flowers. Also woodbine or Dutch honeysuckle, *L. pericyclamenum;* trumpet honeysuckle, *L. sempervirens;* Hall's honeysuckle, *L. japonica* var. Hallian.

Horseradish. *Armoracia rusticana.* The sharp flavor of this root was indispensable with roast beef. A member of the mustard family also said to be good for rheumatism.

Hosta. *Hosta plantaginea.* From China, one of the few available in the 19th century; with white trumpetlike flowers and glossy heart-shaped leaves. Also called plantain lily.

Hyacinth. *Hyacinthus* sp. Spring bulb with large, strongly scented clusters of purple, pink, or white flowers.

Ice-plant. *Mesembryanthemum crystallinum* or *Cryophytum crystallinum.* Low-growing plant with tiny white or pink flowers. Grown for foliage. *Sedum maximum* is also called ice plant.

Impatiens. *Impatiens petersiana.* Shade-loving annual with delicate flowers.

Iris. *Iris versicolor.* Most common variety of this flower has blue petals with a splash of yellow in center. (This is only one variety, a wild sort found in the northern U.S. There are many more grown in the garden.)

Ivy. *Hedera helix.* Classic vine with shiny green leaves. Victorian symbol for friendship, fidelity, and marriage.

Jack-in-the-pulpit. *Arisaema triphyllum.* Known for decorative foliage and almost-green flowers. Suitable for wildflower gardens.

Jacobea. *Senecio jacobaea.* Small yellow flowers in the daisy family. Jacobea in English gardens is *S. elegans,* a dwarf annual with purple, crimson, or white flowers.

Japanese quince. *Cydonia speciosa.* Flowering low-growing shrub with bright red flowers.

Jasmine. *Jasminum officinale.* Also called jessamine. Loved for fragrant white flowers. Tender.

Johnny-jump-up. *Viola tricolor.* The forerunner of the modern pansy, these are miniature, with primarily dark purple faces and yellow markings.

Kenilworth ivy. *Cymbalaria muralis.* Small purple flowers with yellow centers, part of the snapdragon family. A creeper; not grown for its flowers.

Lady's mantle. *Alchemilla vulgaris.* Wonderfully ornamental herb with soft green leaves with pleats that mimic the folds in a lady's cloak. Not generally used for culinary purposes, its small yellow flowers were often used in floral arrangements.

Lady's slipper. *Impatiens balsamina* (Balsam). Slender pink, rose, white, or carmine flowers set between waxy green leaves and resembling a moccasin or slipper. About 10 inches tall.

Lamb's ear. *Stachys byzantina* or *S. lanata.* Leaves of this plant are woolly, resembling a lamb's ear.

Lantana. *Lantana camara.* Popular houseplant with clusters of red and yellow flowers. Also a pot plant.

Larkspur. *Delphinium ajacis.* Annual, for bedding and cutting. Old-fashioned name for delphinium. Stately and striking in all shades of blues and purples, making a rich background for a perennial border. Delphinium Belladonna (perennial) was used for Victorian bouquets.

Laurel. *Laurus nobilis.* Leathery green leaves often used in wreaths and garlands. Grown in warm, southern gardens; a pot plant in the north.

Lavatera. *Lavatera trimestris* or *L. rosea.* Flowers on tall stems similar to hollyhocks.

Lavender. *Lavandula angustifolia.* Delicate purple flowers often dried to scent linen cabinets and keep away moths. This is the current botanical name for "English" lavender, but in 19th-century sources, *L. spicata* is English lavender, *L. stoechas* is French or Spanish lavender.

Lavender-cotton. *Santolina chamaecyparissus.* Low-growing plant with gray leaves and tiny yellow flowers.

Lemon balm. *Melissa officinalis.* This herb's fragrant lemon-scented leaves are a wonderful addition to soups, salads, even iced tea. The scent was said to lift the spirits.

Lilac. *Syringa vulgaris.* Shrub with clusters of fragrant white or purple flowers. Scent especially popular for ladies' toilet waters.

Lily. *Lilium sp.* A Victorian symbol of purity. Some 19th-century lilies are *L. tigrinum*, *L. speciosum* (turn of the century), *L. auratum*, and *L. pardalinum*.

Lily of the valley. *Convallaria majalis.* A colonial flower and symbol of purity, often carried in small bouquets by Victorian ladies.

Lobelia. *Lobelia erinus.* Lush and low-growing plant with blue flowers makes this a classic bedding plant.

London pride. *Saxifraga umbrosa.* Deep pink flowers, very popular in England. Smaller varieties often used in rockeries.

Loosestrife. *Lythrum sp.* Deep red-purple flowers on tall wispy stems. Has escaped cultivation and is now considered a weed.

Love-in-a-mist. *Nigella damascena.* Named for fine, mistlike foliage but grown for its flowers.

Love-lies-bleeding. *Amaranthus caudatus.* Long, drooping, distinctive dark red tassels.

Lupine. *Lupinus perennis.* Clusters of blue, white, or pink flowers on long stalks. Part of the pea family. While this may have been grown in the 19th century, *L. harlwegi* and *L. polyphyllus* are the most common now.

Lychnis. *Lychnis coronaria.* Also called Rose Campion. Red flowers on downy, almost-white foliage.

Madonna lily. *Lilium candidum.* Old-fashioned favorite with large, pure white flowers.

Mallow. *Althaea officinalis.* Marshmallow. Pink flowers borne on very tall stems—up to six feet. There are a number of different mallows—hibiscus, althaea, lavatera, malva.

Maurandya. *Maurandia scandens.* Vine that flowers in winter in a cool greenhouse.

Mayflower. *Epigaea repens.* Common in woodlands of eastern U.S., a plant with small pink or white flowers. Pilgrims supposedly named it after their ship. Also called trailing arbutus.

Mignonette. *Reseda odorata.* Unassuming in appearance, but wildly popular during the 18th century because of its lovely fragrance, it enjoyed a revival in 19th-century old-fashioned gardens. Sent from Egypt by Napoleon to Empress Josephine.

Mimosa. *Mimosa pudica.* Also called sensitive plant for its leaves that curl up at the touch. Southern.

Mimulus. *Mimulus luteus.* Also called monkey flower. Yellow flowers with colorful markings.

Mint. *Mentha spicata.* Spearmint is considered the most common variety of this herb; others include peppermint, orange mint, and lemon mint. It provides delightful fresh flavor and is used in a variety of foods—and mint jelly and mint juleps.

Monarda. *Monarda didyma.* See bee balm.

Moneywort. *Lysimachia nummularia.* Also called creeping Jenny or creeping Charlie; a climbing plant with small yellow flowers. For damp, shady corners.

Morning glory. *Ipomoea tricolor.* The original, brought to this country between 1776 and 1850, had a single trumpet-shaped blue flower and large, heart-shaped leaves. Annual.

Myrtle. *Myrtus communis.* Fragrant dark green leaves with creamy white flowers. Southern.

Narcissus. *Narcissus sp.* Also called jonquils, daffodils. (Narcissus is the genus that includes jonquils, daffodils, and narcissi.)

Nasturtium. *Tropaeolum majus.* Delicate, edible yellow and orange blossoms.

Nemophila. *Nemophila sp.* Softly colored trumpet-shaped flowers with ornamental leaves.

Oleander. *Nerium oleander.* Evergreen that blooms from late spring through the summer. Tropical. Thrives in a temperate greenhouse in the North.

Orchid. *Cattleya sp.* Favorite exotic plant for Victorian greenhouses. This is only one genus. Many others were grown and collected in Victorian conservatories and glass houses.

Oregano. *Origanum vulgare viride.* A member of the marjoram family; oregano's flavor is more pronounced when dried. Wonderful in sauces.

Oriental poppy. *Papaver orientale.* Known for its huge, magnificent scarlet blooms.

Oxalis. *Oxalis montana.* Also called American wood sorrel. White and pink flowers sprout from pinkish stems. A number of different species are in cultivation, some outdoors, some in greenhouses.

Oxlip. *Primula elatior.* Member of the primrose family.

Pampas grass. *Cortaderia selloana.* Very tall-growing, ornamental grass.

Pansy. *Viola tricolor.* A Victorian favorite. Flowers come in many different color combinations. (The modern pansy is thought to be an offshoot of *viola tricolor.*)

Parsley. *Petroselinum hortense.* Its delicate flavor makes parsley one of the most commonly used herbs in cooking. Often used as a border plant because of its tight green foliage.

Passion flower vine. *Passiflora caerulea.* Vine with delicate blue or white flowers. Conservatory climber.

Penstemon. *Penstemon sp.* Beard-tongue. Bright flowers top the hairy stems of this plant.

Peony. *Paeonia officinalis.* Large ornamental flowers with many feathery petals. Shown at the Philadelphia Exposition of 1876 but popular since colonial times.

Perilla. *Perilla frutescens.* Foliage often has decorative markings. One variety, *crispa*, was often used in bedding for the bronze color of its leaves.

Periwinkle. *Vinca minor.* Running myrtle. Popular ground cover with waxy green leaves and small blue-purple flowers. Vine.

Petunia. *Petunia hybrida.* The common garden petunia is one of the most beloved Victorian bedding plants.

Philodendron. *Philodendron giganteum.* Evergreen known for huge showy green leaves. Greenhouse (tropical).

Phlox. *Phlox drummondii.* Showy Victorian favorite. Annual. For bedding schemes.

Pinks. *Dianthus sp.* Popular variety in Victorian gardens, known for tight tufts of petals and sweet scents.

Poppy. *Papaver sp.* Popular for large, brightly colored flowers.

Portulaca. *Portulaca grandiflora.* Low-growing and creeping. Also called moss rose. Annual.

Primrose. *Primula polyantha* or *P. vulgaris.* A spring flower; many Victorian gardens often had a "primrose path." These are two of the many species.

Prince's feather. *Polygonum orientale.* Small clusters of pink flowers on stems with alternating leaves.

Purple coneflower. *Rudbeckia purpurea.* Petals droop around dark center cones. Attracts birds and butterflies.

Pyrethrum. *Chrysanthemum coccineum.* Also called painted daisy for feverfew. Good as cut flowers.

Ragged robin. *Lychnis flos-cuculi.* "Ragged" petals of this plant made it fit well in a wild garden.

Ranunculus. *Ranunculus asiaticus.* Also called buttercup or crowfoot.

Rose. *Rosa sp.* The Victorians' favorite; many varieties of this flower were loved for delicate folds of petals and sweet fragrance.

Rubber plant. *Ficus elastica.* Popular houseplant, with thick, large dark green glossy leaves.

Rudbeckia. *Rudbeckia fulgida.* Also *R. hirta, R. lacinata.* Also called coneflower. Deep yellow flowers bloom in late summer. Showy and daisylike.

Rue. *Ruta graveolens.* Grown for its gray-green foliage, the small yellow blossoms of this common herb appear in early summer.

Sage. *Salvia officinalis.* The soft gray leaves of the sage plant make it a pretty addition to the garden. Its flavor complements chicken and pork.

Salsify. *Tragopogon porrifolius.* Also known as "vegetable oyster" or "oyster plant" because of its distinct flavor, this root was especially popular during the Victorian era.

Sassafras. *Sassafras albidum.* Flowering tree with leaves and twigs that are fragrant when crushed.

Scarlet bush. *Hamelia erecta* or *H. patens.* Small shrub with red or orange tubular flowers and red berries in fall.

Scarlet runner bean. *Phaseolus coccineus.* Ornamental bean plant with scarlet flowers. Annual.

Scarlet sage. *Salvia splendens.* Dense plant with long, oval leaves and bright red flowers. Widely used annual in Victorian bedding schemes.

Scotch thistle. *Onopordom acanthium.* Prickly leaves covered in a fine, silvery-white down.

Shasta daisy. *Chrysanthemum maximum.* Classic garden flower with white petals surrounding a yellow center. There are also ox-eye daisies, Michaelmas daisies, and painted daisies, among others.

Smilax. *Smilax myrsiphyllum asparagaides.* Climbing vine with blue-black berries.

Snapdragon. *Antirrhinum majus.* Loved in gardens for its wide variety of bright colors on soft green stalks.

Snow-ball. *Viburnum carlcephalum.* Fragrant clusters of white blossoms. This is a modern variety. *Viburnum opulus*, the European cranberry bush viburnum, is the 19th-century snow-ball bush.

Snowberry. *Symphoricarpos racemosus* or *S. albus*. Shrub that produces small white berries.

Snowdrops. *Galanthus nivalis*. Plant with dense foliage and small nodding white flowers.

Sorrel. *Rumex acetosa*. Garden sorrel has slightly lemon-flavored leaves that go well in soups and salads and add delicate flavor to lamb and veal.

Spiderwort. *Tradescantia virginiana*. Has slender leaves with deep blue or purple flowers. About two feet high.

Spiraea. *Spiraea* sp. Shrub with white or pink flowers that blossom in late spring.

Spring snowflake. *Leucojum vernum*. Plant with bell-like white flowers.

Star of Bethlehem. *Ornithogalum umbellatum*. Dramatic plant with a long stalk topped with as many as 20 white starlike flowers.

Stock. *Matthiola incana*. Common in old-fashioned gardens; flowers bloom atop tall stalks. Fragrant.

Summer savory. *Satureja hortensis*. Small narrow leaves give wonderful flavor to just about everything from meats and fish to salads and vegetables. The winter variety is perennial and is often used in rock gardens. Winter savory is *S. montana*.

Sunflower. *Helianthus* sp. The double form was popular in the 19th century, when gardeners had such a love for extravagance.

Sweet alyssum. *Lobularia maritima*. Charming, popular bedding plant. Tiny white flowers and a sweet scent.

Sweet basil. *Ocimum basilicum*. Shiny green leaves of this plant add delightful flavor to sauces, salads, and vegetables. It goes especially well with tomatoes.

Sweet marjoram. *Majorana hortensis* (also *Origanum majorana*). The soft grayish-green leaves have a pleasing flavor that complements salads as well as meats, especially lamb, and fish.

Sweet pea. *Lathyrus odoratus*. An old-fashioned flower with a sweet lingering perfume. Annual.

Sweet rocket. *Hesperis matronalis*. Also called dame's rocket. Delicate white or purple flowers. Scented.

Sweet William. *Dianthus barbatus*. Flower has a wonderful clove fragrance, appropriate for old-fashioned gardens.

Tarragon. *Artemisia dracunculus*. The leaves' distinct licorice flavor makes them a wonderful addition to sauces, salads, chicken, and fish.

Tea rose. *Rosa odorata*. Especially fragrant variety of rose that smells like green tea.

Thunbergia. *Thunbergia alata*. Called black-eyed Susan vine. White or yellow flowers with a purple throat. Used in hanging baskets. Annual.

Thyme. *Thymus vulgaris*. This aromatic herb is an indispensable addition to meat dishes. It is often used in rock gardens as a low-growing green.

Tiger lily. *Lilium tigrinum*. Popular for deep red-orange flowers.

Trumpet creeper. *Campsis radicans*. Vigorous vine with red or orange trumpet-shaped flowers.

Tuberose. *Polianthes tuberosa*. White fragrant flowers bloom in late summer. Tender pot plant.

Tulip. *Tulipa* sp. Bulb is common as a bedding flower. One of a dozen or more species of tulips. There are and were numerous hybrids also available.

Umbrella tree. *Magnolia tripetala*. Variety of magnolia tree with very large leaves and white flowers.

Verbena. *Verbena hortensis*. A popular bedding plant and excellent ground cover. Annual.

Vinca. *Vinca* sp. Also called periwinkle. Perennial vine of different species often used in window boxes and hanging baskets because of its trailing quality. Ground cover.

Violet. *Viola conspera*. A Victorian favorite. Common variety in northern areas has deep purple petals and yellow centers. Bushy heart-shaped leaves make it a good border plant.

Virginia creeper. *Parthenocissus quinquefolia*. Also known as woodbine. Climbing vine with blue berries. Foliage turns red in fall.

Wallflower. *Cheiranthus cheiri*. Popular in England because the wallflower prefers moist climate. Fragrant flowers.

Wandering Jew. *Tradescantia fluminensis*. Used in hanging baskets and window boxes because of trailing greens and small white flowers.

Wiegelas. *Wiegelas*. Shrub with pink or red tubular flowers.

Wisteria. *Wisteria frutescens*. Classic vine with hanging bunches of lavender flowers. American wisteria grown for its foliage rather than its flowers. Also Japanese wisteria, *W. floribunda*, and Chinese wisteria, *W. sinensis*, with much more striking flowers.

Woodbine. *Lonicera periclymenum*. Vine loved for its bright yellow flowers.

Xeminesia. *Verbesina encelioides* or *Xeminesia encelioidas*. Also called golden crown beard. Known for bright yellow and orange flowers. Southern.

Yew. *Taxus* sp. Evergreen shrub with needle leaf and red berries.

Yucca. *Yucca filamentosa*. Dramatic plant with spiky foliage and tall stalks topped by creamy white flowers.

Zinnia. *Zinnia elegans*. Also *Z. angustfolia*. Popular cutting plant with strong stems and brilliantly colored flowers. Both are the basis for the development of the modern zinnia.

GUIDE TO HISTORIC GARDENS

ACORN HALL
68 MORRIS AVENUE
MORRISTOWN, NJ 07960
(201) 267-3465

Restored in 1971, the gardens of Acorn Hall reflect the period 1853–1888 and include a vast array of flower varieties, Concord grape vines running along a picket fence, an herb wheel, and a small "pleasure garden" with a fountain, gazebo, and rustic benches.

BEAUREGARD–KEYES HOUSE
1113 CHARTRES ST., NEW ORLEANS, LA
(504) 523-7257

General Pierre G. T. Beauregard, Confederate leader, lodged in this house for more than a year during the Civil War. The formal garden is comprised of white-blooming flowers, shrubs, and trees around a central courtyard and fountain.

BELLE ISLE PARK
DETROIT RECREATION DEPARTMENT
DETROIT, MI

This island park, designed by Frederick Law Olmstead, was a popular picnic spot in the late 19th century and has formal gardens, woodland trails, and a lagoon. The Anna Scripps Whitcomb conservatory was built in 1904 and houses more than 25,000 plants.

BELLINGRATH GARDENS AND HOME
RT. 1, THEODORE, ALABAMA 36582
(205) 973-2217

Sixty-five of Bellingrath Gardens' 905 acres are landscaped to include impressive displays of annuals and perennials, a rose garden, a Japanese garden, and some of the largest bulb displays in the country. Also on the grounds is a bird sanctuary, where more than 200 species of birds can be seen throughout the year.

BERKSHIRE BOTANICAL GARDENS
STOCKBRIDGE, MA 01262
(413) 298-3926

This lovely 15-acre botanical garden includes a rose garden, terraced herb garden, vegetable garden, wildflower meadow, and woodland trails as well as a "primrose path." Flower festivals are hosted throughout the year.

BILTMORE ESTATE
ONE NORTH PARK SQUARE
ASHEVILLE, NC 28801
(800) 543-2961

Completed in 1895, Biltmore was the country estate of George Vanderbilt. The grounds were laid out by Frederick Law Olmstead and include a wild azalea garden, a rose garden with more than 5,000 plants, a 4-acre walled English garden, and a "palm court" in the conservatory with a fountain in the center.

BLITHEWOLD GARDENS AND ARBORETUM
101 FERRY ROAD, BRISTOL, RI 02809
(401) 253-2707

The land on which Blithewold mansion was built was purchased in 1894 as a mooring site for a millionaire's yacht. The family spent the next 80 years embellishing the gardens, creating a dramatic rock garden, water garden, and an "enclosed garden" that is entered through a small opening in a high wall of shrubbery.

BULLOCH HALL
180 BULLOCH AVE., ROSWELL, GA 30077
(404) 992-1731

This 1840 Greek Revival house is surrounded by 16 acres, which include a heart-shaped driveway, boxwood gardens, herb gardens, and orange trees planted around the sides of the house itself.

CENTURY HOUSE
YUMA, AZ
(602) 782-1841

Planned and executed in 1875, the gardens surrounding Century House incorporate the flora of the Southwest into a Victorian-style garden with palm and citrus trees blending with roses and geraniums. Several aviaries and wandering peacocks reflect the original owner's love of birds.

CHESTERWOOD
STOCKBRIDGE, MA 01262
(413) 298-3579

Sculptor Daniel Chester French summered in this house from 1896 through the 1930s. Its 120 acres are made up of English-style perennial gardens and a superb woodland walk with many ferns, decorated with many of the artist's pieces.

CORAL GABLES HOUSE
907 CORAL WAY
CORAL GABLES, FL 33134
(305) 460-5361

The grounds surrounding this 1899 house once covered 150 acres. Now just under 2 acres, the grounds still manage to frame the house with flowering fruit trees and beds of annuals and perennials, one of which is bedded out each year in the shape of a sundial.

EBENEZER MAXWELL MANSION
200 W. TULPEHOCKEN ST.
PHILADELPHIA, PA 19144
(215) 438-1861

Built in 1859, this stone villa is surrounded by gardens designed by A. J. Downing and Frank J. Scott. Only authentic plants are featured, including lovely groupings of ferns, holly, and azaleas.

ELLWANGER GARDENS
ROCHESTER, NY 14620
(716) 546-7029

In 1867, the Ellwanger Gardens were part of a pear orchard surrounding the property's main house. It was slowly transformed into a private garden and today glorious perennial beds, boxwood hedges, and a "lavender walk" surround a few of the remaining 100-year-old pear trees that still bear fruit. The "roomlike" design is idiosyncratic and typically 19th century. An exceptional garden.

THE GENERAL PHINEAS BANNING RESIDENCE MUSEUM
WILMINGTON, CA 90748
(310) 548-7777

Eucalyptus trees abound in the 20-acre park that surrounds the 1864 Banning residence. There is a wonderful rose garden, as well as wisteria arbors and a "sunken patio" surrounded by ivy.

GRAND HOTEL
MACKINAC ISLAND, MI 49757
(906) 847-3331

The grounds surrounding this 1887 hotel have many picturesque gardens, including the lilac garden, "Begonia Bend," a gazebo, and a greenhouse.

HAMMERSMITH FARM
OCEAN DRIVE, NEWPORT, RI 02840
(401) 846-7346

The site of John F. Kennedy and Jacqueline Bouvier's wedding reception, the gardens of Hammersmith Farm, built in 1897, were landscaped at the turn of the century by Frederick Law Olmstead. The 60 acres of grounds have long lines of allées, a small terrace garden, and a sizable cutting garden with more than 100 varieties of flowers.

HARRIET BEECHER STOWE HOUSE
73 FOREST ST., HARTFORD, CT
(203) 522-9258

The restoration of the gardens surrounding the Harriet Beecher Stowe House used Stowe's own journals, correspondence, and old photos for authenticity. On the grounds are Victorian window boxes, hanging baskets, several color scheme gardens, and a highly textural "round Victorian garden" with variegated plants such as a 10- to 15-foot-tall castor-oil bean plant with 4-foot leaves.

LADEW TOPIARY GARDENS
3535 JARRETTSVILLE PIKE
MONKTON, MD 21111
(301) 557-9570

One of the best topiary gardens in America, the Ladew Topiary Gardens has 15 landscaped gardens on 22 acres, including a rose garden, a cottage garden, and a "Victorian garden" with a stone table and chairs, a fountain, and flowers in blue and mauve.

LINCOLN PARK
2400 N. STOCKTON DRIVE
CHICAGO, IL 60614
(312) 742-7736

This 225-acre park includes a "grandmother's garden," planted in 1893, filled with perennials. The main garden has flower beds, a fountain, and statuary. The conservatory, built in 1891, has a palm house, a fernery, and a permanent orchid display.

LONGWOOD GARDENS
RT. 1, KENNETT SQUARE, PA 19348
(215) 388-6741

Begun in 1906 by Pierre S. DuPont, Longwood Gardens boasts more than 10,000 kinds of plants covering 350 acres. The gardens include many Victorian influences, including cottage gardens; a grotto; and peony, wisteria, and rose gardens. The 5-acre water garden was fashioned from a memory DuPont had of such a display when he was a child at the 1876 Philadelphia Centennial Exposition.

MARTIN FLYNN MANSION
URBANDALE, IA
(515) 278-5286

A living-history museum reflects how wealthy Victorian farm families lived. Small flower beds are surrounded by lawns and farmland.

Maymont
1700 Hampton St.
Richmond, VA 23220
(804) 358-7166

This 1890 mansion is one of the last remaining Victorian homes with all the original acreage intact. The 100 acres include an Italian garden, a Japanese garden, a grotto, and gazebos, statuary, and urns. Special touches are a children's petting zoo and carriage rides around the grounds.

Missouri Botanical Garden
4344 Shaw Blvd.
St. Louis, MO 63110
(314) 577-5100

This 79-acre botanical garden was started in 1859 by Henry Shaw, whose 1850 house is still on the grounds. The gardens include two rose gardens, an herb garden, a rock garden, and a greenhouse that houses their camellia collection.

Mohonk Mountain House
Lake Mohonk, New Paltz, NY 12561
(914) 255-1000

This majestic Victorian inn built between 1879 and 1910 has 7,500 acres of grounds, more than 100 rustic gazebos, trellises, arbors, an herb garden, and impressive yearly displays of bedded-out annuals in intricate carpet bed designs.

Molly Brown House
1340 Pennsylvania St.
Denver, CO 80203
(303) 832-4092

Flower beds filled with bleeding hearts, Johnny-jump-ups, and columbine, and ornate benches provide a serene setting around this 1889 historic house. There is even a yellow rose that bloomed when Molly Brown herself lived here.

Morris Arboretum of the University of Pennsylvania
9414 Meadowbrook Ave.
Philadelphia, PA 19118
(215) 247-5777 or (215) 242-3399

Begun in 1887, this 166-acre arboretum has some of the most beautiful Victorian gardens in the country, including a rose garden, a fernery, a hidden grotto, a "magnolia slope," and a swan pond.

Natchez Mansions
Natchez, MS 39120
(601) 446-6631

Natchez is a town known for its beautiful historic homes and gardens, all within an easy stroll. In particular "D'Evereux," c. 1840, has terraces, reflecting pools, and fountains; and "Stanton Hall," c. 1857, has wonderful courtyards and impressive displays of azalea and dogwood.

Naumkeag
Stockbridge, MA 01262
(413) 298-3239

The grounds surrounding this 1885 Stanford White house provide serene walks amid grass terraces and flower gardens, including a summer "afternoon garden" with shade and reflecting pools.

New York Botanical Garden
Bronx, NY 10458-5126
(212) 220-8700

Comprised of 250 acres of gardens, forests, and rolling hills, the centerpiece here is the Enid A. Haupt Conservatory built at the turn of the century (1901) with 11 greenhouses and a 90-foot-high dome over the "Palm Court," which has palms with 20-foot branches and a beautiful cast-iron fountain.

Olana State Historic Site
RD 2, Hudson, NY 12534
(518) 828-0135

Olana was the country estate of Hudson River School artist Frederic Church, who built it in 1872 and used the landscape as a canvas for the next quarter century. Its 250 acres are descibed as "wild and romantic" with hundreds of wildflowers and a "mingled garden" of herbs, flowers, and shrubs near the house.

Old City Park
Dallas, TX
(214) 421-5141

This 13-acre park has 27 Victorian buildings showing many different styles, surrounded by flower gardens, an herb garden, a gazebo, a fountain, and a bandstand.

Park-McCullough House
West Street
North Bennington, VT 05257
(802) 442-5441

The grounds of this 1865 house have both naturalistic Victorian-style gardens as well as more geometric colonial gardens, all filled with hundreds of annuals and perennials. A lovely herb garden is also maintained.

Queen Anne Cottage
Los Angeles State & County Arboretum
Arcadia, CA 91006
(818) 821-3222

In the historic section of the Los Angeles State and County Arboretum, this 1885 cottage is surrounded by a garden including roses, forget-me-nots, and ferns.

Rockwood Museum
610 Shipley Road
Wilmington, DE 19809
(302) 571-7776

The Rockwood estate was built between 1851 and 1857 and was landscaped to capture the naturalistic style that was popular. Expansive lawns lead to meandering paths through shaded woodlands. A tour of the house itself leads to a wonderful conservatory filled with exotic plants.

Rosedown Plantation and Gardens
St. Francisville, LA 70775
(504) 635-3332

Built in the late 1830s, Rosedown Plantation shows the opulence of the antebellum period. Highlights of the garden include a camellia arboretum, flower gardens, a medicinal herb garden, and several fountains.

Roseland Cottage
Woodstock, CT
(203) 928-4074

Built in 1846, Roseland Cottage boasts beautifully designed grounds with 21 flower beds showing off roses, poppies, petunias, and geraniums, among others. Their yearly bedding out of 4,500 annuals into a low boxwood hedge creates a maze of color and line.

Sam Houston Park
Houston, TX
(713) 655-1912

The oldest city park in Houston, Sam Houston Park has seven Victorian structures, dating from 1823–1905. Each house has an enclosed garden distinctive to its period. A walking tour is a special way to see the progression of gardening styles through the Victorian era.

Shadows-on-the-Teche
317 E. Main St., New Iberia, LA 70560
(318) 369-6446

The semitropical setting in southern Louisiana is a dramatic backdrop for this historic home's three acres of azaleas and camellias growing beneath towering oaks draped with Spanish moss.

Skylands Botanical Garden
Ringwood State Park
Ringwood, NJ 07456
(201) 962-7031

This 125-acre botanical garden includes many picturesque gardens, both formal and informal, such as the peony garden, magnolia walk, "crab apple vista," a wildflower garden, and a heather garden. Pools and fountains are situated throughout the grounds.

Sonnenberg Gardens and Mansion
151 Charlotte St., Canandaigua, NY 14424
(716) 924-5420

Considered one of the most magnificent late Victorian gardens ever created in America, the Sonnenberg Gardens are made up of 50 acres surrounding an 1887 mansion and include nine formal gardens of various styles (moonlight, pansy, Japanese), a conservatory, an arboretum, statues, gazebos, fountains, and ponds. Of special interest is the carpet bedding in the shape of a fleur-de-lis.

Strawberry Banke
Portsmouth, NH 03802-0300
(603) 433-1100

This 10-acre living museum has several historic gardens, including a Victorian garden created from the letters and diaries of a woman who wrote between 1850 and 1890. The garden has bedded-out annuals, a wild garden, an evergreen grove, trellises, and a greenhouse.

Wave Hill
675 W. 252nd St., Bronx, NY 10471
(212) 549-3200

Wave Hill, built in 1843, is the only Hudson River estate within the city limits that has been preserved for the public. The 28 acres of gardens overlooking the Hudson River and the Palisades include formal flower gardens, a "wild" garden, an herb garden, 4 greenhouses, and 4 gazebos.

SOURCES FOR HISTORIC SEEDS AND PLANTS

ABUNDANT LIFE SEED FOUNDATION
P.O. Box 772
Port Townsend, WA 98368
(206) 385-5660

AMBERGATE GARDENS
8015 Krey Avenue
Waconia, MN 55387
(612) 443-2248

ANTIQUE ROSE EMPORIUM
Route 5, Box 143
Brenham, TX 77833
(409) 836-5548

KURT BLUEMEL, INC.
2740 Greene Lane
Baldwin, MD 21013
(410) 557-7229

BLUESTONE PERENNIALS, INC.
7211 Middle Ridge Road
Madison, OH 44057
(216) 428-7535

W. ATLEE BURPEE COMPANY
300 Park Avenue
Warminster, PA 18974
(215) 674-4900

CAPRILANDS HERB FARM
Silver Street
Coventry, CT 06238
(203) 742-7244

CARROLL GARDENS, INC.
444 East Main Street
P.O. Box 310
Westminster, MD 21157
(800) 638-6334

COMSTOCK, FERRE & COMPANY
263 Main Street
P.O. Box 125
Wethersfield, CT 06109
(203) 529-3319

CROWNSVILLE NURSERY
1241 Generalsway Highway
Crownsville, MD 21032
(410) 923-2212

FARMER SEED AND NURSERY COMPANY
818 NW 4th Street
Faribault, MN 55021
(507) 334-1625

FOX HILL FARM
440 West Michigan Avenue
P.O. Box 9
Parma, MI 49269
(517) 531-3179

GARDEN PLACE
6780 Heisley Road
P.O. Box 388
Mentor, OH 44060
(216) 255-3705

GARDENS OF THE BLUE RIDGE
P.O. Box 10
Pineola, NC 28662
(704) 733-2417

GLASSHOUSE WORKS GREENHOUSES
Church Street
P.O. Box 97
Stewart, OH 45778
(614) 662-2142

GURNEY'S SEED AND NURSERY COMPANY
110 Capitol Street
Yankton, SD 57079
(605) 665-1671

HEIRLOOM GARDEN SEEDS
P.O. Box 138
Guerneville, CA 95446
(707) 869-0967

HEIRLOOM SEED PROJECT
Landis County Museum
2451 Kissel Hill Road
Lancaster, PA 17601
(717) 569-0402

HENRY FIELD SEED AND NURSERY COMPANY
415 North Burnett
Shenandoah, IA 51601
(712) 246-2011

THE HERB COTTAGE
Washington National Cathedral
Mount St. Albans
Washington, D.C. 20016
(202) 537-8982

HIGH COUNTY ROSARIUM
1717 Downing
Denver, CO 80218
(303) 832-4026

HILLTOP HERB FARM
Box 1734
Cleveland, TX 77327
(713) 592-5859

HOLBROOK FARM AND NURSERY
Route 2, Box 223B
Fletcher, NC 28732
(704) 891-7790

JOHNNY'S SELECTED SEEDS
Foss Hill Road
Albion, ME 04910
(207) 437-4301

KARUTZ GREENHOUSES
1408 Sunset Drive
Vista, CA 92083
(619) 941-3613

OLIVER H. KELLEY FARM
15788 Kelley Farm Road
Elk River, MN 55330
(612) 441-6896

LAMB NURSERIES
East 101 Sharp Ave.
Spokane, WA 99202
(509) 328-7956

LOGEE'S GREENHOUSES
141 North Street
Danielson, CT 06239
(203) 774-8038

MERRY GARDENS
P.O. Box 595
Camden, ME 04843
(207) 236-9064

MONTROSE NURSERY
P.O. Box 957
Hillsborough, NC 27278
(919) 732-7787

NEW ENGLAND WILD FLOWER SOCIETY
Garden in the Woods
180 Hemenway Road
Framingham, MA 01701
(508) 877-7630

NICHOLS GARDEN NURSERY
1190 N. Pacific Highway
Albany, OR 97321
(503) 928-9280

OLD STURBRIDGE VILLAGE SEED STORE
1 Old Sturbridge Village Road
Sturbridge, MA 01566
(508) 347-3362

PARK SEED COMPANY
Cokesbury Road
Greenwood, SC 29647
(803) 223-8555

PEACEABLE KINGDOM
P.O. Box 313
Washington, TX 77880
(409) 878-2353

PERENNIAL PLEASURES NURSERY
2 Brickhouse Road
East Hardwick, VT 05836
(802) 472-5104

PLIMOTH PLANTATION
P.O. Box 1620
Plymouth, MA 02632
(508) 746-1622

REDWOOD CITY SEED COMPANY
P.O. Box 361
Redwood City, CA 94064
(415) 325-7333

SEEDS BLUM
Idaho City Stage
Boise, ID 83707
(208) 324-0858

SELECT SEEDS
180 Stickney Hill Road
Union, CT 06076
(203) 684-5655

SHEPHERD'S GARDEN SEEDS
6116 Highway 9
Felton, CA 95018
(408) 335-5400

SISKIYOU RARE PLANT NURSERY
2825 Cummings Road
Medford, OR 97501
(503) 772-6846

SOUTHERN EXPOSURE SEED EXCHANGE
P.O. Box 158-C
North Garden, VA 22959
(804) 973-4703

STALLINGS NURSERY
910 Encinitas Blvd.
Encinitas, CA 92024
(619) 753-3079

STOKES SEEDS, INC.
Box 548
Buffalo, NY 14240
(416) 688-4300

SUNNYBROOK FARMS NURSERY
9448 Mayfield Road
Chesterland, OH 44026
(216) 729-7232

TAYLOR'S HERB GARDENS
1535 Lone Oak Road
Vista, CA 92084
(619) 727-3485

THOMAS JEFFERSON CENTER FOR HISTORIC PLANTS
Monticello
P.O. Box 316
Charlottesville, VA 22902
(804) 979-5283

VERMONT BEAN SEED COMPANY
Garden Lane
Fair Haven, VT 05743
(802) 273-3400

WELL-SWEEP HERB FARM
317 Mount Bethel Road
Port Murray, NJ 07865
(908) 852-5390

WHITE FLOWER FARM
Route 63
Litchfield, CT 06759
(203) 567-8789

WHITE SWAN SPECIALTY SEED GARDENS
8030 SW Nimbus Ave.
Beaverton, OR 97005
(503) 641-4477

INDEX

Acorn Hall, 96
Aesthetic Movement, 16
Albaugh, Benjamin F., 162
Alden, Mrs. G. R. (Pansy), 116
Alyssum, 48–49, 53
Amateur Cultivator's Guide to the Flower and Kitchen Garden, 29, 32
Arabesque garden, 158
Arboretums, 71, 73–74
Architectural style, landscaping complementing, 73
Art of Beautifying Suburban Home Grounds of Small Extent, The (Scott), 20

Bartram, William and John, 28, 40
Basket. *See* Hanging basket
Beauté Inconstanté, 13
Bedding, 47–64
 carpet, 57–64
 circular, 54, 56
 designs, 51, 52, 53, 56, 60, 61, 63
 out, 15, 48–49, 57, 63, 66
 patterns, 61, 63
 ribbon, 53–54
 single-species, 48–53
Beecher, Catharine, 24, 27, 44, 45, 116, 158
Beeton's *New All About Gardening*, 53, 78, 127, 146, 155
Blue garden, 15, 103
Borders, 47, 64–67, 161
Boston ivy, 75
Boxwood, 113, 126
Breck, Joseph, 16, 21, 28–29, 116, 117
Breck's Book of Flowers, 21
Breck's children's garden, 116, 117
Bronx Botanical Garden, 42, 91
Buist, Robert, 16, 73
Burpee catalog, 32

Caladium, 54, 56
Carpet bedding, 57–64
Cast iron
 fence, 5
 fountain, 88, 92
 garden furniture, 85, 88–89
Catalogs, 9, 10, 28–29, 32–33, 139, 142
Chatsworth conservatory, 96, 97
Chesterwood, 63, 64, 73, 126
Children
 gardening benefits, 24–25
 gardens for, 115–19
Childs, Mr., 32
China aster, 9
Chrysanthemum, 66, 129
Circular bedding, 54, 56

City garden, 20, 156–67
Clematis, 77
Cleome, 69
Climate, 13
Coleus, 52–53
Color
 blue garden, 15, 103
 city garden, 161–62
 moonlight garden, 15, 113–15
 ribbon bedding, 53–54
 single-species bedding, 48–53
 use of, 49, 56–57, 102–3
Colorado blue spruce, 40
Color gardens, 102–3
Conservatory, 15, 42, 44, 96–97, 99
 greenhouse vs., 42
Cottage garden, 67–69
Cottage Residences (Downing), 52
Cutting garden, 151–53

Dahlia, 54, 65
Day House, 8, 107
Delphinium, 2
Downing, Andrew Jackson, 5, 16, 20, 21, 52, 67, 72, 74, 91, 158
Drummond, Thomas, 40

Earle, Alice Morse, 57, 66–67, 110, 113
Ellwanger, George, 33
Ellwanger Gardens, 5
English ivy, 75, 77
Enid A. Haupt Conservatory, 42
Every Woman Her Own Flower Gardener (Johnson), 24
Eyebright, Daisy. *See* Johnson, Mrs. S. O.

Fairy garden, 119–22
Fences, cast-iron, 5
Fernery, 42, 79, 122, 123, 126
Ferns, 45, 88, 97, 126
Fertilizer, 33
Flora Symbolica, Or, The Language and Sentiment of Flowers (Ingram), 128
Flower Garden, The (Breck), 21
Flowers
 bedding choices, 15, 41, 51
 border, 65–66, 161
 cutting garden, 151–53
 differing names for, 17
 new and exotic, 2, 15
 symbolism of, 2–3, 15, 21, 41, 42, 106, 111
 See also specific names
Fortune, Robert, 16, 41, 77, 132
Fountains, 52, 88, 91, 92

Foxglove, 2
French, Daniel Chester. *See* Chesterwood
Front porch, 77, 84–85, 89
Fuchsia, 15
Furniture, lawn. *See* Garden furniture

Gardener's Encyclopedia, The (Loudon), 16
Gardenette or City Back Yard Gardening, The (Albaugh), 162
Garden furniture, 38, 71, 83
 cast-iron, 85, 88–89
 rustic, 77, 79, 81, 89, 91
Gardening
 attire, 25, 36
 benefits, 5, 21, 24–25, 27–28, 115–16
 books, 16–17, 170
 passion for, 3–4, 15, 45
 plant types, 9, 38–41, 132
 restoration and re-creation, 5, 7, 8–13, 15
 social and moral appeal, 5, 21, 24–25, 27
 tools, 16, 35, 36–38, 119
 women's influence on, 102
 See also specific garden types, e.g., Kitchen garden
Gardening by Myself (Warner), 16
Gardening for Pleasure (Henderson), 16, 61, 96, 164, 166
Garden room. *See* Fernery
Gazebo, 15, 73, 78, 92, 93, 96
Geranium, 67, 158, 163
 bedding, 48, 49, 51
 popularity, 38
Gladiolus, 8
Glossary, 171–76
Goff, May Perrin, 126
Gothic style, 72–73, 74
Grandmother's garden. *See* Old-fashioned garden
Grass. *See* Lawn
Greenhouse, 41–42, 96
 conservatory vs., 42

Hall, George, 41
Hanging basket, 158, 161, 164, 166
Harriet Beecher Stowe Center, 8, 56, 107
Hawthorn bush, 128
Hawthorne, Hildegarde, 56, 116
Henderson, Peter, 96, 164, 166
Henry A. Peck Co., 142
Herb garden, 153–55
Herbs, medicinal, 138–39, 154
Hibberd, Shirley, 85, 89, 93, 95
Historical gardens guide, 177–80
Historical seeds and plants, sources for, 181–82
Holmes, Florence, 150–51

Home decorating
  garden as home extension, 3, 9, 12
  garden motif, 1–2, 20–21, 61
Honeysuckle, 75, 77
Horticulture. See Gardening
Hothouse. See Greenhouse
Hunt, Leigh, 23

Ingram, John, 128
Insecticides, 33, 36, 143
Irving, Washington, 73
Ivy, 75, 77, 160, 129

Jaenicke, Adolf, 99
Japanese garden, 129, 131
Japanese honeysuckle, 77
Jekyll, Gertrude, 57
Johnny-jump-up, 3, 104
Johnson, Mrs. S. O., 16, 24, 27–28, 75, 116, 142

Kennedy, Mrs. S. E., 151
Kitchen garden, 136–55

Lamb's ear, 113, 114–15
Larkspur, 2
Lawn, 36–38, 65
Lawn mower, 16, 36–38
Lewis and Clark expedition, 40
Lily of the valley, 3
Literary garden, 127–28
Little Men (Alcott), 25
Loudon, Jane, 16
Loudon, J. C., 97
Loudon, John, 16, 72
Lyman, Anna, 118

Medicinal plants/herbs, 138–39, 154
Mohonk Mountain House, 61, 63
Montgomery Ward catalog, 33, 35, 36, 89
Moonlight garden, 15, 113–15
Morning glory, 75
Mosseries, 81
Mount Hope Garden and Nurseries, 28, 33

Narcissus, 111
Naturalistic gardening. See Picturesque style
New York Botanical Garden, 42, 91

Old-fashioned garden, 12–13, 107–11, 113
Old Sturbridge Village, 116
Orangeries, 96
Orchid, 16
Osage orange, 40
Outbedding, 15, 48–49, 57, 63, 66
Outbuildings, 77, 78, 84, 92, 93, 96; See also Gazebo

Palm, 99, 123
Pansy, 3, 17, 163
  garden, 15, 103–6
Pansy, The (magazine), 115–16
Parlor gardening, 3, 44
Parry, Charles Christopher, 40
Parterres. See Bedding
Pathways. See Walkways
Paxton, Jos., 96
Peony, 41, 107, 113
Petunia, 48
Phlox, 66
Picturesque style, 72–73, 77–79, 81
Plant names, 17; See also Glossary
Poppy, 3, 30–31
Porch, 77, 84–85, 89
Pyrethrum, 36

Raymond, Reba L., 91
Repton, Humphrey, 21
Rexford, Eben E., 106, 111
Ribbon bedding, 53–54
Rivers, Thomas, 131
Rochester Seed Store and Horticultural Society, 28, 33
Rockeries, 15, 16, 71, 79, 81
Romanticism, 72–73
Rooteries, 81
Rose
  breeding, 16, 132
  garden, 130, 131–35
  popularity, 13, 15
Rose Amateur's Guide, The (Rivers), 131, 135
Royal Botanic Gardens, 96
Ruskin, John, 72
Rustic Adornments for Homes of Taste (Hibberd), 13, 167
Rustic garden furniture, 77, 79, 81, 89, 91

Salvia, 53
Scarlet runner bean, 75
Scott, Frank Jesup, 16, 20–21, 99, 129
Scrollwork, 60
Seeds
  catalogs, 9, 10, 28–29, 32–33, 139, 142
  sources, 181–82
Shaker seed packets, 29, 33
Shakespeare garden, 127–28
Shrubbery, 74–75
Single-species bedding, 48–53
Small gardens, 100–35
Sonnenberg Gardens, 54, 63, 131, 132, 135
Specialty garden, 100
Statuary, 83, 92
Stowe, Harriet Beecher, 24, 27, 44, 45, 56, 116, 158; See also Harriet Beecher Stowe Center
Summerhouses. See Outbuildings

Sundials, 92
Sunnyside, 73
Sweet pea, 110

Terrariums. See Wardian cases
Thompson, Mary Clark, 104
Tiles, 60–61
Tools, garden, 16, 35, 36–38, 119
Topiary garden, 128–29
Trees, popular, 74
Tuberose, 3
Tweedie, Mr., 41

Urns, 12, 52, 91–92, 161, 163

Vegetable growing
  city garden, 158, 166
  kitchen garden, 141, 142–51
Veranda, 77, 84–85
Vick, James, 28–29, 32, 33
Victorian garden
  elements of, 5
  historic, 177–80
  restoring and re-creating, 5, 8–13, 15
  social history of, 18–45
  20th-century concept of, 15–16
  See also specific garden types and plants
Vines, 74, 75, 77, 81, 163
Violet, 106
Virginia creeper, 75

Walkways, 65, 77, 78, 147, 161
Walt Disney World, 61
Ward, Henry Chase, 44
Wardian cases, 2, 41, 42, 44–45, 97, 126, 158
Warmer, Anna, 16
Washburn & Company, 29
Washington, George, 28, 139
Weed killers, 33
Wheelbarrow garden, 163
White garden. See Moonlight garden
Wilde, Oscar, 16
Window box, 20, 157–58, 163, 166–67
Winter garden, 64
Women
  gardening attire, 25, 36
  gardening benefits and appeal, 27–28
  as gardening influence, 102
  garden-inspired handicrafts, 3
  garden writers, 16
  kitchen gardens, 138, 139–40
  lawn mowers for, 36, 37
World's Columbian Exposition, 41
Wycoff, Ellen Frizell, 162

Young Florist, The (Breck), 117